CREW

CREW

THE STORY OF THE MEN WHO FLEW
RAAF LANCASTER *J FOR JIG*

MIKE COLMAN

ALLEN&UNWIN
SYDNEY•MELBOURNE•AUCKLAND•LONDON

Allen & Unwin
83 Alexander Street
Crows Nest NSW 2065
Australia
Phone: (61 2) 8425 0100
Email: info@allenandunwin.com
Web: www.allenandunwin.com

 A catalogue record for this
book is available from the
National Library of Australia

ISBN 978 1 74237 911 1

Index by Puddingburn
Set in 12.5/17.5 pt Minion Pro by Midland Typesetters, Australia
Printed and bound in Australia by Griffin Press

10 9 8 7 6 5 4 3 2 1

 The paper in this book is FSC® certified.
FSC® promotes environmentally responsible,
socially beneficial and economically viable
management of the world's forests.

This book is dedicated to the men of RAF Bomber Command and those who loved them, and to my own ground crew—Linda, Matilda, Amelia, Isabelle and William.

You didn't make close friends because you didn't know how long you, or they, would be alive, but your crewmates were different. Your crew was everything. They were your life.

Laurie Woods, Bomb aimer, RAAF 460 Squadron

CONTENTS

1

FOUR HEADSTONES

Villers-sous-Prény is a small village in north-eastern France. Sitting about halfway between the cities of Metz and Nancy, it is fairly unremarkable except for two things: its location close to the border with Germany, and the graveyard behind its church.

In World War II, the historic garrison city of Metz, with its ancient forts and battlements, was the site of a bitter three-month battle between German occupation forces and General George S. Patton's advancing US Third Army—a battle that ended when the Americans captured the city in December 1944. Today, the 22-kilometre drive from bustling Metz to the all but deserted streets of Villers-sous-Prény is a journey of around 40 minutes—and 70 years. While Metz has boomed since the end of the war, the little village has hardly changed.

A narrow road, Rue de l'Église, takes you to a church surrounded by a stone wall with an iron gate. A plaque beside the gate reads:

Tombes de Guerre du Commonwealth
—COMMONWEALTH WAR GRAVES

Many generations of local families are buried here, their graves packed tightly around the church. But one plot sits apart. Its single grave has four identical headstones, all made of white granite, expertly carved in the uniform style of the Commonwealth War Graves Commission. The inscriptions are simple, but they tell a wrenching tale—of four young men in the prime of life shot down from the sky, their lives cut short, their futures snuffed out. When they were buried, thousands paid tribute, but few visit these headstones now. Few remember who the four men were or what they did, whom they loved or whom they left behind.

There were seven men in RAAF Lancaster bomber *J for Jig* that night in February 1944, heading for Germany—seven out of a total 125,000 who served as air crew for RAF Bomber Command between 1940 and 1945. Their backgrounds were not unusual. They weren't a special crew, a famous crew; they were as ordinary as can be. And that's what makes them important. Because their stories are also the stories of the 125,000—who they were, what they did, whom they loved, and whom they left behind.

Dave Baxter

2

THE PILOT

Dave Baxter would never forget his fourteenth birthday. It was the day his father died.

Born in 1896, Frank Baxter was a miner from eastern Scotland who had migrated to Australia in 1922 with his wife Jane—known as Jean—and their year-old son, also Frank. A gunner with the Royal Garrison Artillery in World War I, he had been mentioned in despatches for his service in the Middle East. Family members believe Frank may have been impressed with the Australians he met during the war and, with the Scottish coal-mining industry closing down as electricity overtook steam power, he saw Australia as the place for a new start.

The Baxters, together with both Frank's and Jean's parents, moved to Wonthaggi North, a coal-mining town 110 kilometres south-east of Melbourne. Over the next seventeen years, they built a life in the tight-knit community. With their parents living within a kilometre or two, they bought a comfortable three-bedroom weatherboard home and started enlarging their family. A year after they arrived, on 15 February 1923, David was born. He was followed by Margaret, Alan and, in 1935, Ronald.

David, known as Dave, and his older brother Frank became close mates. Just two years apart in age, they were inseparable. Dave followed Frank into the local state school and technical high school, where he was an outstanding student, a prefect and a star sprinter—and where he met his future wife, Irene 'Joyce' Gillman, the daughter of a local miner.

As Dave and the other Baxter children were becoming well known for their sporting prowess, their father was working his way up in the mines and gaining local recognition as a singer of light opera with local musical groups and a soloist with the Methodist church choir.

On 15 February 1937, miners working No. 20 shaft in Wonthaggi's State Coal Mine called a stop-work meeting and refused to go underground, claiming it was unsafe. Frank Baxter, now aged 41, had risen to the position of deputy manager, an underground role that provided a link between the miners and management. With talks at a stalemate, it was suggested that a group, including the mine deputies, go down to assess the situation for themselves. Frank and twelve others headed underground. Soon afterwards, the earth shook from a mighty blast. The strikers—including Joyce Gillman's father, Johnny—and management forgot their differences and rushed to the site to start a rescue operation, but it proved hazardous. Caged canaries lowered into the shaft died immediately, indicating that the area was full of noxious gas. Rescue workers required respirators, and extra masks had to be rushed from Sydney. There were no survivors. It took a week to recover all thirteen bodies; meanwhile, family members waited, desperately clinging to hope.

Melbourne's *Sun* newspaper of 17 February 1937 published a poignant photograph from the disaster site. It shows a group of men in overcoats and hats, heads bowed in serious discussion as an exhausted rescue worker walks past. To one side, a teenage boy leans against a wall with a look of shocked resignation on his face. The caption reads: 'Waiting in vain. The lad on the right of this picture, watching a volunteer leaving the mine shaft, is a son of Frank Baxter, one of 13 men entombed at Wonthaggi.' The 'lad' is David Baxter.

The death of her husband left Jean Baxter with six mouths to feed. As the miners were State government employees, the *Victorian Workers' Compensation Act* (1928) entitled their widows to a lump sum of around £750 each. This enabled Jean to pay off the family home. She also received a widow's pension of 8 shillings a week, and another weekly payment of 2 shillings 6 pence per child from the Miners' Accident Relief Fund. But even so, making ends meet and raising five children alone was not easy. The youngest child, Ron, who was two years old at the time, says he grew up unaware of his mother's struggles.

I have no memory at all of my father, and as a child I wasn't aware of what was happening around me. All I remember is growing up in the country and having a lot of fun climbing trees and playing down at the creek ... But I have seen photographs and read some reports [of the disaster] and I know how it affected people. Money was donated and some was put away for the children of those killed, to be granted to them when they turned 21. I think I received £100.

Dave received his final school report card in December 1939. The headmaster wrote: 'Excellent student and a lad of the finest type. Excellent physique. Capable and reliable. Excellent moral character. Should do well in any vocation.' Now seventeen, Dave was offered a scholarship to the University of Melbourne, but he turned it down and began looking for work. Australia had been involved in World War II for three months, and the workforce was starting to be affected by the loss of men, who were enlisting in their thousands.

Dave was offered a job with the Commonwealth Public Service, as a clerk in the finance branch of the Department of Air, in Melbourne. Working out of the Century Building in Swanston Street, he stayed with his aunt's family in Hampton, a beachside suburb 20 minutes by tram from the office. Even though he impressed his superiors, he had no intention of being a clerk for long. His brother Frank had already joined the air force and would eventually head to England, where he would serve at RAAF Overseas Headquarters in London. Dave harboured a secret desire to follow him into the service as soon as he reached the enlistment age of eighteen.

'He was a brilliant scholar, a great athlete,' says Ron. 'You'd describe him as a conservative sort of person. He was thoughtful and kind. I think he could have achieved so much, but you have to play the cards you're dealt and Dave played his. The story is that as soon as he was old enough to enlist, he came home one night, gave Mum a box of chocolates, and he said he wanted to join up. She said OK.'

One other woman was consulted on Dave's plans and would wait anxiously for news when he headed overseas. Joyce Gillman was born eleven months after David. 'We were in the same class at school,' she says. 'That's where we met, and we were together from then on. Dave was always quiet, he didn't talk a lot about the war, but when he went away we wrote to each other as much as we could.'

On 15 May 1941, the RAAF Recruiting Centre in Melbourne received an Application For Air Crew from David Wright Baxter of 17 Reid St, Wonthaggi. The form noted that 'Candidates who apply for selection as Air Crew may be selected for training as Pilots, Air Observers, and Air Gunners for service in the Royal Australian Air Force at home or abroad.' If successful, candidates would be trained under the Empire Air Training Scheme, a joint program established by the governments of the UK, Canada, Australia and New Zealand in December 1939 to provide air crew to supplement the Royal Air Force. Under the scheme, 50 elementary flying schools were established in Australia, New Zealand and Canada. Many graduates received advanced training in Canada before the majority headed to England.

While the aim of the scheme was for the three Commonwealth nations to provide air crew for the British war effort, the Australian government was determined that the RAAF should retain its identity within the combined force. On 15 November 1939, Prime Minister Robert Menzies told Parliament that the government would strive to ensure that Australian airmen being seconded to the RAF would wear RAAF uniforms, fly with Australian squadrons and be led by Australian officers.

If the RAAF had wanted a poster boy for their recruitment drive, they could have done a lot worse than use Dave Baxter. Flight crew required a high-school leaving certificate as well as good health, but the qualities recruitment officers were looking for were less easy to measure. Pilots needed to have a certain aura. They needed to be natural leaders, as they would often be put in charge of older men with more life experience and sometimes even higher rank. Recruitment officers liked pilots to have a sense of humour and to have played team sports, preferably as captains. As the US Air Force would later say of its elite pilots, they needed to be made of 'the right stuff'.

On his application, Dave listed his academic and sporting achievements and certified that he was a British subject 'of pure European descent'. He was eighteen years and four months old, 69 inches (1.75 metres) tall, and weighed 160 pounds (72.5 kilograms). As he was under 21, the application was also signed by his mother and two Wonthaggi neighbours who attested that they had known him for over six years.

It was the first step in a process that would eventually include a police check by the Hampton constabulary ('Not known personally but from inquiries he appears to be honest, sober and reliable') and attendance at an interview and medical examination at No. 1 Recruiting Centre, 104 Russell Street,

Melbourne, on 23 June 1941. Although the form letter Dave received noted that applicants were 'required to pay their own travelling and other expenses connected with the journey to and from places of interview', it included a warrant allowing him free train travel.

Throughout the day, Dave had three interviews with recruitment officers who variously rated his appearance and manners as 'neat' and 'good', and his intelligence as 'above average'; they noted he was 'a bright lad'. His personality struck them as 'strong', 'pleasing' and 'youthful'. On the subject of 'general promise of fitness for service', two of his examiners noted he was 'good material', but it was the third, and senior, officer, who had the crucial say. 'Should make grade as Pilot,' he wrote. On the section headed Board's Recommendation, which listed 'Pilot, Air Observer, Wireless Operator–Air Gunner—strike out two', he put a line through the last two.

Two days later, in the same building, Dave was given the choice of swearing an oath or making a non-religious affirmation. Having given his religion on the enrolment forms as Presbyterian, he took the oath: 'I, David Wright Baxter, swear that I will well and truly serve Our Sovereign Lord the King as a member of the Air Force Reserve of the Commonwealth of Australia, and I will resist His Majesty's enemies and cause His Majesty's Peace to be kept and maintained, and that I will in all matters appertaining to my service faithfully discharge my duty according to law. So help me God.'

On 5 July, after another medical examination, he was enrolled in the RAAF Reserve, subject to a chest X-ray. Five days later he received a letter from No. 1 Recruiting Centre:

CREW

Dear Sir,

With reference to your recent application to serve with the Royal Australian Air Force as a member of an Air Crew under the Empire Air Training Scheme, I have to inform you that at your examination you were successful in passing the necessary tests. In the first instance, therefore, you have been selected to enter an initial Training School as trainee air crew. Final assessment will be dependent upon the progress and ability displayed by you during the Initial Training Course. As the number of air crew applicants offering at present is in excess of the capacity of the existing training organisation, it will be necessary to place successful applicants on a waiting list from which they will be called up when additional training facilities are created. It is thought unlikely you will be called up before November 1941.

The call-up came on 8 November, when Dave was enlisted as an air-crew trainee in Group V with the rank and pay of Aircraftman Class 2. Enlistment was 'for the duration of the war, and for a period of up to twelve months thereafter'. Pay for all air-crew trainees was 5 shillings a day for the first period of initial training. After that, candidates would be selected for training as pilots, observers or wireless operators–air gunners. If Dave was chosen as a trainee pilot, his pay would jump to 11 shillings 9 pence a day; on graduation, it would increase again to 12 shillings a day, with an additional 4 shillings a day when he was on active service.

His first posting was to No. 1 Initial Training School at Somers, 72 kilometres south-east of Melbourne. The site had been purchased in 1940, and the buildings and facilities of the Lord Somers Camp, a holiday camp for boys, requisitioned for the training school. One of six such schools, No. 1 offered several weeks of introduction to military life and courses in such subjects as mathematics, navigation and aerodynamics. Dave's aptitude as a student shone through in his earliest on-the-ground training: he scored 100 per cent in signals, 95 per cent in maths and 94 per cent in armament. He was selected for pilot training, and on 28 February 1942 was promoted to Leading Aircraftman, but whether he received his pilot's wings would depend on his ability in the air.

Next stop was No. 8 Elementary Flying Training School at Narrandera, in southern New South Wales. Pilot trainees were introduced to flying in the DH-82 Tiger Moth, a two-seater biplane designed by the British company De Havilland and first flown in October 1931. Cheap to produce and relatively easy to fly, the Tiger Moth was the perfect initial trainer because, due to its slowness to respond, it required positive and assured control. Any prospective pilot who did not show the necessary confidence with the Tiger Moth would soon be weeded out—'scrubbed'— and pointed towards a different area of service.

Leading Aircraftman Baxter demonstrated no such uncertainty. From his first hour-long flight with an instructor on 2 April 1942, he proved to be a natural pilot. He took his solo test eight days later, and on 11 April flew solo for the first time. By the time he left Narrandera, on 28 May, he had satisfactorily completed all stages of the course and logged 60 hours' flight time. On the 10-point assessment of Distinctive Qualities, Dave was marked Below Average in Endurance, but Average in Persistence, Sense of Responsibility, Leadership, Deliberation, Enterprise, Dash and Self-Control. His instructor judged him Above Average in Method ('Does he work systematically to a plan?'). General Remarks were: 'Good average pupil. Should overcome the dangerous habit of watching instruments too much.' Under 'Assessment of Suitability for Further Training', the instructor ticked Average for Larger-type Aircraft and Below Average for Fighter Aircraft and Potential Flying Instructor. The form was stamped: 'Recommended for M/E Pilot'.

The M/E abbreviation stood for multi-engine rather than single-engine aircraft such as fighters. In most cases that meant deployment to Bomber Command, the RAF-controlled operation that carried out 389,000 individual sorties from 101 bases across the east of England throughout the war, primarily during the so-called Battle of Berlin between November 1943 and March 1944. There will always be arguments and differences of opinion over the role of Bomber Command and the destruction it wrought on German-held cities and citizens. Commander-in-chief of Bomber Command Arthur Harris was known as 'Bomber' by his supporters and 'Butcher' by those who felt he had orchestrated the wilful destruction of non-military targets and ordered his crews into suicidal situations for questionable tactical gain. As the British journalist Peter Hitchens wrote in *The Mail on Sunday* on the eve of the unveiling of the Bomber Command Memorial in London's Green Park on 28 June 2012, 'not since the futile carnage of the Somme in 1916 had any British military commander been so wasteful of young life, broken so many homes, destroyed so many futures, turned so many living, laughing human beings into corpses'.

THE PILOT

Moral and ethical arguments aside, there is no questioning the bravery and sense of duty displayed by the air crews of Bomber Command on a nightly basis. As Hitchens wrote: 'I am lost in admiration for those crews. I do not know how, night after night, they left all that was dear to them, climbed into a cramped and freezing death-trap and set off into the dark. Nearly half of them would die horribly, and they knew it.' Of the 125,000 air crew posted to Bomber Command during the war, 55,573 were killed—a death rate of 44 per cent—while 8403 were wounded and 9838 became prisoners of war. Of those killed, 72 per cent were British, 18 per cent Canadian, 7 per cent Australian and 3 per cent New Zealanders. The estimated life expectancy of a Bomber Command air crewman in action was six weeks.

On 23 June 1942, Dave Baxter became one of the more than 37,000 Australian men who left home shores under the Empire Air Training Scheme when he was kitted out at No. 3 Embarkation Depot at Sandgate, Queensland, and boarded a ship bound for Canada. Seven weeks later, on 15 August, he reported to No. 3 Service Flying Training School at Currie Field, Calgary. For the earnest 20-year-old from Wonthaggi, and others like him who had never been out of Australia, arriving in Canada was the first instalment of what many believed would be a great adventure. Dave Baxter no doubt was slightly more realistic. He had already felt the pain of death and loss first-hand.

Dave and his fellow students in Course 62 of Service Flying Training found themselves in a picturesque prairie city not far from the snow-capped Canadian Rocky Mountains. Ranching was the major industry, and they soon got used to the sight of cowboys in Stetsons and boots walking down the main street. Far from home and blissfully ignorant of what awaited them in Europe, the trainees of Course 62 enjoyed their new surroundings and built a strong camaraderie.

The main aircraft used for training at No. 3 SFTS Calgary was the twin-engine Cessna Crane, a military version of a five-seat commercial aircraft designed and built by the Cessna Aircraft Company of Wichita, Kansas. Around 1200 Cranes (known as Bobcats in the US) were used by the Empire Air Training Scheme throughout the war.

Dave continued to show solid competence as a pilot, logging 135 hours in the air and scoring 625 out of a possible 750 in his ground-training tests. On his final assessment, his commanding officer wrote: 'Pleasant personality, sincere, should develop into above average pilot.' Dave finished 24th in his class of 56.

Almost three months after arriving in Canada, on 4 December 1942, the class of Course 62 graduated. A photograph taken that day shows a group of young men in uniform crowded around an aircraft. Some squat on their haunches; three stand on the wing, leaning against the fuselage. Most are smiling broadly, but Dave Baxter stares straight-faced at the camera, a look of pride and satisfaction on his young face.

He has the same look in another photograph taken that day, as fellow Australian Air Vice Marshal Stanley James Goble, DSO, DSC—three times Chief of the Air Staff between 1922 and 1940—pins the pilot's wings onto his tunic. On the back of the photo, Dave later wrote, 'The big moment, 4.12.'42'. He wasn't the only one to feel a sense of pride at the achievement. Back home, the people of Wonthaggi and surrounding districts were being kept up to date on the progress of the former schoolboy sports star. A few weeks later a copy of the local newspaper, *The Powlett Express*, contained an article headlined 'Dave Baxter Receives Wings in Canada': 'Word has been received by Mrs Baxter, North Wonthaggi, that her second son, Sergeant-Pilot Dave Baxter, has received his "Wings" in Canada recently. Heartiest congratulations are extended to this young airman and may he return safely in the near future.'

If Wonthaggi hadn't forgotten Dave Baxter, it was equally obvious that Dave Baxter hadn't forgotten Wonthaggi. A member of the class put together a souvenir booklet to mark the graduation ceremony. On the cover, together with the words 'Course 62 Graduation, December 1942 Calgary' is a drawing of a Cessna Crane in flight. Sitting on the outside above the cabin, with a map under one arm and looking through a telescope, is a Canadian beaver. Behind it, holding reins that are steering the aircraft, is a smiling kangaroo. Inside, the anonymous author has written a few lines of verse on each member of the graduating class, poking light-hearted fun at their foibles, habits and shortcomings.

Of a snorer he writes: 'Bill Williscroft doth shake each night, the roof, the floors and walls. With joyous note—deep slumber's sigh—just like Niagara Falls.'

Of the ladies' man: 'If Howey were married, and who says he's not, he might spend more time in his own little cot.'

But there is one whose homesickness is no joking matter: 'Dave Baxter grew his shaggy coat 'mid coal and dust and smoke. If he can't see Wonthaggi soon, his heart I know'll be broke.'

But Wonthaggi—and the heart of the newly promoted Sergeant Baxter—would have to wait. Most students in Course 62 headed to England and whatever the future held. For Dave, that initially meant a posting to RAF Station Ramsbury, a newly opened airfield close to Marlborough in Wiltshire, 110 kilometres west of London. Here he would start attaining the competency required to fly a bomber in combat.

After a break during which he and some fellow graduate airmen visited New York for a few days, on 12 April 1943 Dave arrived at Ramsbury and joined No. 15 (Pilot) Advanced Flying Unit. It used the twin-engine Oxford, a military version of the eight-seater Envoy built by Airspeed Ltd. (The company was founded in 1931 by designer Hessell Tiltman and aeronautical engineer Nevil Shute Norway, who later won renown as the novelist Nevil Shute.) The Oxford was the preferred trainer of the Empire Air Training Scheme because of its adaptability. With a crew of three for standard military operations such as reconnaissance, it could be reconfigured to enable training of pilots, navigators, bomb aimers, gunners or radio operators on the same flight. As well as introducing novice pilots to the largest and heaviest aircraft they had flown, the Advanced Flying Unit was seen as an opportunity to acclimatise airmen from warmer countries such as Australia, New Zealand and South Africa to the heavy conditions they would encounter flying in and out of England. As part of the training unit, Dave completed six days of Beam Approach School at nearby RAF base Watchfield. The blind approach beacon system, or BABS, helped pilots land in severe weather using radio beams transmitted from a beacon at the end of the runway.

The training was becoming ever more complex and dangerous, and hundreds of novice air crewmen were killed. Just a week before Dave was due to move to his next posting, he narrowly missed joining the list of fatalities. On 27 May 1943, the Oxford he was flying was struck in the rear by a similar aircraft. Fortunately, both pilots managed to land safely. Dave pulled part of the tip of the other plane's propeller from the tail of his trainer. Keeping it as a reminder of the close call, he wrote on it: '27/5/43 15 (P) AFU Ramsbury Wiltshire. Portion of airscrew of Oxford A/C which struck tail section of Oxford A/C X6879 piloted by self. No injuries sustained.'

After two months at Ramsbury and 70 hours of flight time, including 10 hours of beam approach training, on 4 June 1943 Dave was promoted to Flight Sergeant and transferred to No. 27 Operational Training Unit. It was headquartered at RAF Lichfield, 26 kilometres north of Birmingham, but because the base was so busy—with around 115,000 movements between May 1942 and the end of the war—training was also conducted at 'satellite' airfields. Dave was sent to RAF Church Broughton, sixteen kilometres west of Derby, where he arrived on 6 June. No. 27 OTU used Vickers Wellington bombers converted to trainers. The only British bomber produced continuously throughout the war, the Wellington was a twin-engine long-range aircraft. It was used heavily as a night bomber early in the conflict before being replaced by the

RAF's four-engine bombers, the Short Stirling, Handley Page Halifax and Avro Lancaster.

For the fledgling airmen the Wellington was their first experience of flying in a bomber. It was also at this stage in the training program that the pilots formed their crews, most of which would stay intact when they were assigned to combat squadrons. It was here that they met, often for the first time, the comrades with whom they would live, fly and, in some cases, die. Dave reported to 27 OTU on 8 June. The other six men who would remain part of his and each other's lives until the end of their days would meet up at various times over the next few weeks. Bomb aimer-front gunner Anthony D'Arcey, 20, and mid-upper gunner Bill Martin, 31, were from Sydney, New South Wales; navigator Clifford Hopgood, 27, and wireless operator Ronald Ferguson, 25, were from Queensland; and the two RAF men, rear gunner John Dunlop, 19, and flight engineer Peter Mallon, 20—the last to join the crew—were both from Ayrshire, Scotland.

There was one final step before Dave got his hands on the controls of a Lancaster. On 5 September 1943 he reported to No. 1656 Heavy Conversion Unit at RAF Lindholme, near Doncaster, in South Yorkshire. As its name implies, the unit represented the final bridge between the twin-engine trainers and the 'heavies', the fully laden four-engine bombers the crews would fly over enemy territory. No. 1656 HCU provided training on Halifax and Lancaster aircraft.

Dave was initially trained on the Halifax. It was designed by Handley Page as a twin-engine bomber in 1937, but before it went into production the company was told to redesign it as a four-engine aircraft. As war approached, the prototype of the new Halifax had yet to make its first test flight. The RAF placed an order for 100 'off the plan', and Britain's newest heavy bomber took its maiden flight just days after war was declared. The Halifax repaid the faith shown in it by the RAF hierarchy. Over 2000 were built throughout the war. Dave completed fifteen hours' flying time on the Halifax before he moved to the final stage of his training at the No. 1 Lancaster Finishing School, also at Lindholme.

If, as Winston Churchill said—in words carved into the west end of the pavilion of the Bomber Command memorial in London—'the Fighters are our salvation but the Bombers alone provide the means of victory', then it was the Lancaster that shouldered most of the load. In fact, of the bombs despatched by Bomber Command during World War II, nearly 64 per cent (over 600,000 tons) were dropped by Lancasters on some 156,000 sorties. With more than 7000 built, the Lancaster was one of the most successful warplanes of all time. It was also one of the most unusual: from its first prototype flight in January 1941 to operational duty just 13 months later, it required virtually no corrections, alterations or fine tuning. Designer Roy Chadwick got the plans almost 100 per cent right from the start—although it was his second crack at them.

Chadwick had begun working as a draughtsman with the Avro company in 1911, at the age of 18. Within a few years he was designing aircraft, including the Avro Baby, in which Australian Bert Hinkler set a distance record in 1921, flying the 1400 kilometres from Sydney to his mother's home in Bundaberg, Queensland, in nine and a half hours. But Chadwick's design of the Manchester, a twin-engine medium bomber that Avro submitted in 1937 in response to the same Ministry of Air specification that led to the Handley Page Halifax, was less successful. In fact, it was a stunning failure. Chadwick chose to power the Manchester with two Rolls-Royce Vulture engines that proved to be dangerously unreliable. While the twin-engine Halifax was reconfigured as a four-engine heavy bomber and took to the air just weeks after the start of the war, Avro would produce only 200 Manchesters before the RAF cancelled future orders and transferred its support to Handley Page and the Halifax. It was a major disappointment for Avro, but from the ashes of the Manchester would come Chadwick's greatest achievement, the aircraft that Bomber Command chief Arthur Harris would describe as 'the greatest single factor in winning the war'.

Just as Handley Page engineers had done with the Halifax, Chadwick had started work on plans to change the Manchester to a four-engine heavy bomber even before it went into production. When the Manchester proved disappointing, he doubled his efforts, scrapped plans for a Manchester III, and named his new creation the Lancaster.

Lancaster expert Andrew Panton, curator of the Lincolnshire Aviation Heritage Centre in East Kirkby, says of the aircraft: 'It's the kind of thing where if it looks right, it is right. Take the Spitfire—it looks beautiful and perfect and it is a brilliant fighter. It's the same with the Lancaster—it looks good and it did the job it was designed to do perfectly.'

While Chadwick made structural changes to his Manchester design, such as increasing the wingspan to fit four engines, the critical decision with the design of the Lancaster was to scrap the Rolls-Royce Vulture engines in favour of the less powerful but more reliable Rolls-Royce Merlins, which were proving a huge success with the Spitfire. 'The Merlin was probably the best engine of the Second World War,' says Panton. 'The Lancaster had that in its favour, and if you speak to any of the pilots, they say it was a dream to fly; quite heavy but very manoeuvrable. In terms of what made it such an effective warplane, the main thing the Lancaster had was the bomb bay. There were no spars running through it, so it could carry a large assortment of bombs. That's why it was used for the Tallboy (12,000 lb), Grand Slam (22,000 lb) and Dambuster (9250 lb) bombs.' Chadwick was awarded a CBE in 1943 after the Dambusters raids, in which Upkeep bouncing bombs were dropped by low-flying Lancasters, breaching Germany's Möhne and Eder dams. He was killed just over four years later when a prototype of his Avro Tudor crashed on take-off.

The Lancaster was a phenomenal workhorse, often carrying far more load than it had been designed for—'Bomber' Harris called it 'the camel that never knew the last straw'. But for the crews that flew it, the aircraft had feminine qualities. To them, the Lancaster was always a 'she'. As former RAF wireless operator and gunner John 'Ginger' Stevens recalled in the documentary *Battle Stations*: 'It was love at first sight. There she was, standing up on these long legs, a black beauty. Funnily enough, I didn't feel there was any rivalry with the rest of the crew. I felt like she was my girlfriend, but we all felt she was our girlfriend.'

Dave Baxter and his crew were introduced to Chadwick's masterpiece on 31 October 1943. It was a familiarisation flight in a Lancaster III, with another pilot at the controls and Dave observing. His role, officially Second Pilot, was more commonly known as Second Dickey, a term long used to denote the second mate on a ship but appropriated by airmen in reference to the flight engineer's fold-down 'dickey seat', behind which the trainee pilot stood during flights. Four days later, on 3 November, Dave got behind the controls of Lancaster E44779, taxied down the runway and took off into the sky above South Yorkshire for a routine C&L—Circuit and Landing—flight. Almost two years to the day after he had enlisted, he was a Lancaster pilot.

Over the next week, the crew would acquaint themselves with the aircraft and their roles in it on daytime training flights that went as far as Scotland and Wales, and night flights to Exeter, in England's south-west. At 20 years of age, Dave was one of the youngest in the crew—gunner Bill Martin was eleven years his senior and navigator Cliff Hopgood had eight years on him—but from the moment they came together, there was no doubt about who was the captain. Dave's mature, serious manner and meticulous attention to detail made him a natural leader, and the rest of the crew fell easily into the routine of following his commands.

Unlike on US bombers, there was no co-pilot on the Lancaster. The pilot was seated on a raised portion of floor on the left-hand side of the aircraft, directly above the bomb bay. In front of him was an array of lights, switches and gauges that might seem archaic by the standards of today's computerised jet aircraft but were in fact quite complex and very effective. The Lancaster Pilot's and Flight Engineer's Notes, a 46-page booklet 'Promulgated by Order of the Air Council in May 1944', listed 82 different controls that a Lancaster pilot would need to operate, monitor and use if needed on any flight. From preliminary checks just before climbing into the aircraft to switching off the fuel-booster pumps after the initial climb following take-off, the pilot was required to perform 66 individual tasks. In addition to flying the aircraft, the pilot also had to command his crew. This included maintaining proficiency in emergency drills and calling crew checks on the intercom. Every man in the crew played an important role, but it was the captain's job to make life-or-death decisions in an emergency. He pulled the lever that opened the bomb bay doors; he made the call on whether to press on or abort a mission; and, in the event that he had to order the crew to bail out, he was often the last man to leave as he attempted to hold the aircraft steady to give his comrades the best chance of escape.

On 11 November 1943, the crew left Lindholme to begin operational duty with 625 Squadron RAF. It was time to go to war.

Cliff Hopgood

3

THE NAVIGATOR

In early 1940, Clifford Berger Hopgood made a promise to his pregnant wife Margaret. Their first child was due in September, a year after the outbreak of war.

'I won't join up,' Clifford said, 'until after the baby has turned one.'

Cliff and Margaret's son Robert James Hopgood was born in Brisbane, Queensland, on 27 September 1940 and, true to his word, Clifford was at Margaret's side when they celebrated the boy's first birthday with a family party. Just fifteen days after the celebration, on 12 October 1941, Cliff left his city office at lunchtime, walked the short distance to No. 3 RAAF Recruiting Centre in Creek Street, and enlisted.

Clifford Hopgood was born in Toowoomba, 125 kilometres

west of Brisbane, on 3 August 1915, the first child of Francis William Hopgood and his wife May, who had been married the previous year. It was the second marriage for Frank, who had fathered nine children with his first wife, Phoebe.

Frank, born in England in 1869, had arrived in Brisbane with his parents and six younger siblings in 1885. He was 23 years old and his bride Phoebe Stone just sixteen when they wed at Toowoomba in August 1892. Their first child, Cecil, was born nine months later. Cecil and three more of their children would die during childhood, but when Phoebe died, aged 35, in March 1912, Frank was left with six children ranging in age from six to eighteen.

On 31 January 1914, Frank Hopwood married 29-year-old May Lindgren. Now 45, he worked in the print room of the local newspaper and was well known in the district for his skill as a marksman. His new bride's father, Otto, had been born in Sweden, and her mother, Mary (née Berger), in England. The newlyweds wasted no time building on their already large family. Clifford was followed in close succession by brothers Colin, David and Spencer, and sister Joy.

In the mid-1920s the family moved from Toowoomba to Brisbane, settling at Kangaroo Point, close to Frank's new workplace, the print room of *The Brisbane Courier*. In September 1927, tragedy struck with the death of seven-year-old Spencer. The following year, at the age of thirteen, Clifford began his secondary education at Brisbane Church of England Grammar School in East Brisbane, today one of Queensland's most prestigious schools. The school's founder, Reverend—later Canon—William Morris, took a holistic view of education, believing the role of the school was 'the training of character on the foundation of Christian faith as taught by the Church of England'.

Cliff was enrolled as a 'choir scholar', meaning that on Sundays he sang in the St John's Cathedral Choir, earning a reduction in fees. A talented athlete, he competed in the school's annual Pocket Swim around Norman Creek and scored tries in intercollegiate rugby matches in the 1930 season. He left 'Churchie', as the school is now known, at the end of 1931 after sitting his Junior Examination and achieving good B Level results in English, Latin, arithmetic, algebra and geometry. Despite failing French and geography, he was awarded his Junior Certificate.

After a few months at Central Technical College, Cliff worked as a clerk for six months while studying bookkeeping. For the next year and a half he worked alongside his father as a newspaper compositor—one of the tradesmen who set the lead type in place prior to printing—at *The Brisbane Courier* and *The Courier-Mail*. He then found his true vocation, in sales, working in the Brisbane office of the British wholesale and distribution giant Gollin and Company. Cliff began as a junior salesman of Holeproof hosiery products and rose through the ranks to departmental manager.

Some four years after starting with Gollin and Company, Clifford met Margaret Emma Warren, who was working at the O'Brien paper-bag factory in the inner Brisbane suburb of Spring Hill and living nearby with her father, two sisters and baby brother. The family had moved to Brisbane from the North Queensland town of Charters Towers in 1917, when

Margaret was six, after her mother Ellen died in childbirth. Margaret's oldest sister Sarah, eleven at the time, left school to help raise the younger children. The family struggled during the Depression, to the point where Margaret refused to marry Clifford until they had built their own home.

'She'd been the one sent to tell the landlord that they couldn't pay the rent,' says Cliff and Margaret's son Robert. 'She never wanted to go through that again.'

The couple were engaged, and Margaret marked the occasion by giving her husband-to-be a watch engraved on the back with the words 'To Cliff from Margaret'. Saving every spare penny, they bought a block of land in Royal Parade, St Johns Wood, and for several years their outings involved picnicking on the site as they saved to build the home they named Glen Arran. They married on 27 May 1939, just over three months before Australia entered the war against Germany. Less than two and a half years later, Cliff was in uniform.

Early in the war, the role of Bomber Command had been to bomb specific military targets such as shipping ports, factories and rail yards in what is known as precision bombing. In 1941, a study of the effectiveness of the campaign showed that the bombers were much less accurate than anticipated, leading Prime Minister Churchill to approve a change to strategic bombing. From 14 February 1942, Bomber Command was ordered to significantly increase the number of raids and target German industrial areas in an attempt to slow production of armaments and lower the morale of factory workers and the general populace. The increase in bomber activity led to a corresponding increase in casualties among Allied airmen, and by the time Clifford Hopgood joined up in October the pressing need for replacements meant there was no need for him to spend time in the Reserve. He went straight to No. 3 Initial Training School at Sandgate, north of Brisbane. After twelve weeks of initial training, during which he was identified as a potential navigator/observer, he was sent to No. 1 Air Observers School at Cootamundra, in north-western New South Wales. He then spent two months at No. 1 Bombing and Gunnery School (BAGS) at Evans Head, a coastal town in northern New South Wales.

The aerodrome at Evans Head, built as an emergency airstrip in 1936, had been quickly upgraded when the war began. No. 1 BAGS was Australia's first bombing and gunnery school opened under the Empire Air Training Scheme, and at its peak it was considered the largest air-force training facility in the Southern Hemisphere. When the school closed in 1943, more than 5500 crew had been trained at Evans Head. Over 1000 of them were later killed in action.

Cliff's training in Australia ended with two months at No. 1 Air Navigation School at Parkes, in western New South Wales. It was here that he learnt the rudiments of navigation, both in the classroom and flying in Tiger Moths. Then, on 31 October 1921, just over a year after his enlistment, Cliff was sent by sea to England. After a stopover in Canada to offload a group of trainee pilots, he arrived at 3 Personnel Reception Centre in Bournemouth.

The Personnel Reception Centres located throughout the UK were the disembarkation points of thousands of

Commonwealth servicemen and -women throughout the war. It was here that they underwent initial processing and were based, often for several months, as they awaited posting to their next station. During this time they underwent courses to brush up on skills grown rusty during the weeks at sea, and were given leave to acclimatise to their new surroundings. Cliff was at Bournemouth for almost three months before being posted to No. 3 (Observer) Advanced Flying Unit at the quaintly named Halfpenny Green airfield in Staffordshire. Flying in Avro Anson aircraft, navigators who had previously trained in the broad expanses of Australia, Canada or Rhodesia familiarised themselves with the different conditions in the UK, mainly in regard to map reading.

The Anson was a twin-engine monoplane with a retractable undercarriage based on the six-seater Avro 652 airliner, and it was used for a variety of military roles such as coastal reconnaissance, search and rescue, and short-range bombing. Early in the war an Anson was credited with sinking a German U-boat, and in June 1940 a flight of three Ansons came out on top in a dogfight with nine Messerschmitt Bf 109s, destroying two enemy aircraft and damaging a third without loss. But such victories in battle were few and far between. Reliable, sturdy and easy to fly, the Anson earned the nickname 'Faithful Annie' from its crews, but its lack of speed, range and armament made it unsuited to the tasks for which it had been commissioned. Instead, it proved ideal as an air-crew trainer. Designed to take a crew of four—pilot, bomb aimer, radio operator and gunner—it could be used to train every member of a Bomber Command aircraft and became the mainstay of the Empire Air Training Scheme, with some 10,000 Ansons produced by the end of the war.

On 8 June 1943, Cliff—and future crewmates Tony D'Arcey and Ron Ferguson—arrived at 27 OTU at RAF Church Broughton, where David Baxter had been posted just two days earlier.

For Cliff and the other new arrivals, the move from the Ansons and Tiger Moths on which they had been trained to the Wellingtons at Church Broughton was a huge jump, but they soon got up to speed. Because they had been posted to the unit at the same time, Cliff, Tony, Ron and Dave found themselves in the same training groups. They stayed in the same barracks and ate at the same times. It was natural that they should get to know each other, and Dave thought enough of the other three to ask them to be the first members of his crew. By the time they took the next step on their journey together, to 1656 Conversion Unit at RAF Lindholme, they were already very much a team, looking out for each other, depending on each other.

As Laurie Woods, a Queenslander who was awarded the Distinguished Flying Cross when serving as a bomb aimer with 460 Squadron RAAF, put it: 'You didn't make close friends, because you didn't know how long you or they would be alive, but your crewmates were different. Your crew was everything. They were your life.'

Tony D'Arcey

4

THE BOMB AIMER

Tony D'Arcey was under no illusions about the horrors of war. He had only to look at the scar on his father's left leg, or listen to him talk of being forced to march, hungry and cold, through France at the point of a German bayonet, to know there was nothing glamorous about it.

Tony's father, also named Anthony, joined the Australian Imperial Force (AIF) in June 1916 at the age of 21, and less than a year later was with the 18th Battalion as it attacked German forces holding the French village of Bullecourt. Known as the Second Battle of Bullecourt, this ultimately successful but strategically questionable action lasted fourteen days and cost 7482 Australian casualties. Acting-Corporal Anthony D'Arcey was one of them, shot through the lower leg on 3 May 1917, the day of the initial attack. He was evacuated and admitted to Northampton War Hospital sixteen days later. After ten months of treatment and recuperation, he was back at the front. On 15 March 1918, as the 18th Battalion took part in an unsuccessful attempt to take the German stronghold of Hangard Wood, south of Villers-Bretonneux, Anthony D'Arcey was one of 26 Australians captured by the enemy. He remained a prisoner for eight months, until the end of the war, and arrived home to the inner Sydney suburb of Redfern on 8 April 1919.

'Dad was a lucky fella,' says Peter D'Arcey, Anthony's younger son. 'He came back from the war with a hole in his leg but he was alive. He didn't talk about what happened over there much but he did tell us about when he was a POW. It was towards the end of the war and the Germans were marching the prisoners back from the front. They didn't feed them. They were starving and being pushed along. Dad saw a lot of his friends drop, and they didn't get back up.'

Anthony had good fortune after the war. He returned to work as a wool clerk, married local girl Johanna Mary O'Brien, and bought a block of land on Sydney's North Shore. 'There were some bargains going,' says Peter. 'Dad bought some land in Artarmon and built a house.' Anthony (known as Tony) was born on 22 May 1923 and Peter four years later. The boys attended Marist Brothers High School in Mosman, founded in 1922 with the motto *Virtus Ubique Vincit*—Courage Conquers All.

'He was a good sportsman and student,' says Peter. 'He got good marks, unlike his younger brother.' In 1938 Tony passed his Intermediate Certificate with excellent results—four As, three Bs—and received a glowing reference from the school principal, Brother Augustine, who recommended him as 'a reliable, honest lad of upright character and pleasing disposition. He is a keen scholar, courteous in manner, an outstanding sport and I am sure he will be a credit to his home and to his School.' Tony began work as a junior clerk with Sydney County Council, studying at night for his Senior Certificate at North Sydney Technical High School, but would never sit the exams.

On 17 October 1941, Roger Vine-Hall, general manager of the Sydney County Council, signed a standard form stating that Anthony D'Arcey, clerk, had 'made application for the consent of the General Manager to his offering himself for enlistment in the Commonwealth Defence Forces and there does not appear to be any reason, in the National general interest, why any restriction should be placed upon his enlistment in the RAAF'.

Eleven days later Tony joined the RAAF Reserve at No. 2 Recruiting Centre, Woolloomooloo, and commenced a series of courses designed to help him make an easy transition to air-crew training when his call-up came. 'I'd say Dad might have tried to talk him out of it,' says Peter. 'But knowing my brother, nothing would have made him change his mind.'

Tony returned to Woolloomooloo to be sworn into the RAAF Permanent Forces as an Aircraftman Class 2 on 22 May 1942. It was a date he wouldn't easily forget: his nineteenth birthday. His first posting was to No. 2 Initial Training School at Bradfield Park, Lindfield, almost within walking distance of the D'Arceys' home. All recruits being trained in New South

Wales under the Empire Air Training Scheme went through RAAF Bradfield Park. Previously a racetrack on a clearing known as Cook's Flat, Bradfield Park was the site for an international gathering of Boy Scouts held from December 1938 to January 1939. When war was declared, the RAAF took over the facilities that had housed thousands of scouts and used them as a base for No. 2 and No. 6 ITS, as well as WAAAF—Women's Auxiliary Australian Air Force—training units. By the time it was decommissioned after the war for use as a migrant hostel, RAAF Bradfield Park had provided the first taste of military life for more than 20,000 trainees.

While Tony's initial posting could not have been much closer to home, his next was 16,000 kilometres and several weeks away by ship. After four months at Bradfield Park, Tony was reclassified as a Leading Aircraftman and kitted out for sea passage to Canada. Arriving in Edmonton on 21 October 1942, he spent two weeks at No. 3 M (for Manning) Depot, then headed east to the prairie town of Dafoe, in Saskatchewan, home to the Royal Canadian Air Force's No. 5 Bombing and Gunnery School. Like many of the 107 Canadian bases built specifically for the Empire Air Training Scheme, the Dafoe area was chosen for its flat terrain and sparse population, making it cheap to build on and reducing the risk to the public as thousands of trainee air crew from around the Commonwealth practised their bombing and shooting skills night and day in the skies above. When it opened in May 1941 with the motto 'We Aim To Teach And We Teach To Aim', the school accommodated 43 officers, 486 airmen and 69 trainees but soon reached maximum capacity of 1400 personnel, including 366 trainees at a time. By January 1945, when the airfield was disbanded, 131,553 air crew had been trained there.

Set amid rolling prairies and grain farms about 20 kilometres north of the township, the base functioned as its own community, with a station headquarters, military police station, hospital, dental clinic and post office. Buildings were devoted to armament and parachute training, photography and meteorology. Maintenance Wing was responsible for a fleet of Fairey Battles, Avro Ansons, Bristol Bolingbrokes and US-designed T-6 Texans, known in the UK as Harvard Trainers. Westland Lysanders were used to pull the air sock targets, known as drogues, for gunnery practice.

To keep the trainees occupied and out of trouble during their rare free time, the RCAF and local residents organised a steady program of activities and social events. The YMCA ran a Hostess House, and there were a station band and orchestra for on-base dances and concerts attended by the community. Local ranch families took the airmen horse riding, but while the trainees appreciated the hospitality shown by their hosts, they were never allowed to forget that they were in Canada for one purpose: to learn the art of war. They followed an extensive syllabus of lectures, demonstrations, day and night flying exercises, tests and assessments before being passed fit for the next step on the road to combat.

After passing the bombing and gunnery course, Tony and his fellow trainees took the 400-kilometre train trip east to No. 1 Central Navigation School, outside the town of Rivers in Manitoba. Opened in 1942, RCAF Rivers was a large base that is still in operation today. The main training aircraft was the

Avro Anson, and the trainees were in the air almost non-stop. There were so many of them that at peak periods, classroom training had to be broken into shifts, with some trainees having classes from 6 a.m. until 2 p.m. and others from 2 to 10 p.m. Since those on the later shift tended to sleep in and miss breakfast, an enterprising local opened a diner outside the main gate. It served a full breakfast for 75 cents, and did a roaring trade.

At Rivers, many hours were spent learning to navigate using a sextant, the idea being that airmen on night sorties would be able to map their location using the stars. A standard three-week course at Rivers included ten cross-country flights, half of them usually at night. By the time the trainees found their way to bomber squadrons, radio and radar technology had advanced to the point where the sextant was rarely used on operations, but many a shot-down airman would be thankful for the ability to navigate by the stars when making his way on foot through occupied territory.

Like Dafoe, Rivers was a prairie town with little in the way of night life or entertainment for the thousands of young men who passed through the base during the war years. The camp commander and locals did their best to keep the short-term visitors occupied, with dances, horse riding and home visits. RCAF Rivers also took part in one of the inter-service Canadian football tournaments held throughout the war, giving trainees from Australia, New Zealand and South Africa the opportunity to watch, and sometimes even play, an unfamiliar football code.

The flying segment of the course was held after written exams had been completed. There was no formal passing-out parade or pinning of badges. Trainees were simply told whether they had passed or failed, their logbooks were marked accordingly and, if all had gone well, they climbed back on the train for a 3700-kilometre trip to Halifax, where they would board a ship for England. Tony passed all his exams and exercises with top marks. The qualities that had seen him stand out at school both in and out of the classroom five years earlier were just as evident to his RAAF superiors. After a series of interviews, he was granted a commission. In an example of Air Force bureaucracy, he was promoted to the rank of Pilot Officer, but as regulations prevented a trainee from becoming a commissioned officer immediately, on 19 October 1943 he was first promoted to Sergeant. His promotion to Pilot Officer was approved the next day.

On 10 April, Tony landed at Bournemouth, England, and reported to No. 11 Personnel Despatch and Receiving Centre. After a month there, he was posted to RAF Llandwrog, near Caernarfon in Wales, home of No. 9 (Observers) Advanced Flying Unit RAF.

At first sight, Llandwrog must have seemed an idyllic posting. The airbase—the largest in Wales—was in one of Britain's most picturesque areas, between the coast and the mountains of Snowdonia. But the natural features that made its landscape so stunning also made it a challenging, and sometimes deadly, training site. The combination of offshore winds and mountain updrafts brought many a pilot and crew undone. Throughout the war years, 34 aircraft crashed in the area. Four were Anson trainers from No. 9 (O) ATU.

At the time, the RAF policy was that any air-crash rescue operations should be handled by the medical officer from the nearest base. RAF Llandwrog was hopelessly under-equipped for such a task, and during the early days of the war, airmen crash landing in Snowdonia often survived the initial impact but died of their wounds or exposure before help could reach them. Soon after being posted to RAF Llandwrog as medical officer in 1942, Flight Lieutenant George Graham established an informal mountain rescue team manned by RAF volunteers that saved many lives by administering first aid at crash sites. Graham and fellow medical officer Flight Lieutenant David Crichton lobbied furiously for the creation of specialised units to perform this role, leading to the establishment of the RAF Mountain Rescue Service, which is still active today.

After successfully completing the observers' course, Tony headed back to England. He arrived at No. 27 Operational Training Unit RAF Church Broughton on 8 June 1943, the same day as Cliff Hopgood and Ron Ferguson. From that day on, their lives would be linked forever.

Ron Ferguson

5

THE WIRELESS OPERATOR

Ronald Cedric Ferguson loved the outdoors. As one of his relatives described him in the language of the day, 'he had the country in him'. Born in Bundaberg, North Queensland, on 27 October 1917, Ron was the third son of Charles Ferguson, a schoolteacher, and his wife Ruby, whose father, Hermann Lassig, was a wealthy cattle farmer and entrepreneur. Charles Ferguson's father Henry was also a schoolteacher, and by acquiring property through marriage and canny investment he was able to provide a comfortable lifestyle for his wife Fanny and their six children. When Charles wed Ruby in August 1912, he intended to follow his father's example. 'I believe in the acquisition of wealth' was one of his favourite sayings.

The newlyweds set about building a family on solid financial foundations. Their first son, Charles Jr, was born in January 1913, Reginald followed in 1915 and Ron two years later. A daughter, Merle, was born in 1921. Charles and Ruby continued to live in the Bundaberg district, where Charles worked as a teacher, but they bought an investment property, Lagoondale, a 1500-acre cattle station about 25 kilometres west of the town. They were well known and popular in the area, their main social activities revolving around the tennis club, where Charles was a champion player. Another of his passions was cars—in 1912, he purchased one of only two Cadillacs in Queensland. But the good times didn't last. Soon after Merle was born, Ruby began to feel unwell. She pushed on, thinking it was the after-effects of childbirth and the physical strain of chasing three active young sons, but eventually there was no escaping the fact that she was seriously ill. Charles took her to a doctor in Bundaberg, who diagnosed breast cancer. There was little that could be done. Ruby died, aged 31, on 3 January 1922, leaving Charles with four children aged nine, seven, five and not yet one year.

It soon became obvious that Charles was not going to be able to cope with teaching, running the property and raising the children, especially when, a year after Ruby's death, eight-year-old Reg contracted infantile paralysis or, as it is now known, polio. With Reg requiring lengthy hospitalisation and ongoing treatment, it was decided that two-year-old Merle should live with Ruby's parents, Hermann and Mary, on their property Yarral, outside Bundaberg, while the boys stayed with their father Charles. In 1927, when Ron was ten years old, Charles married Isabella Thomson.

The three boys and Merle would grow up 25 kilometres apart in geographic distance, but much further in regard to home environment and upbringing. Their grandfather Hermann, who had migrated to Australia from Germany, had done well in his new country. As well as Yarral, a large cattle station, he had interests in sugar-cane farms, was part owner of a gold mine, and owned Bundaberg's Queen Cinema and a string of racehorses. However, a number of poor business decisions, including financing his six sons in unsuccessful farming ventures, being cheated by his partner in the gold mine and backing too many slow horses, eroded Hermann's fortune. By the time of his death in 1957, 'he didn't have two bob to rub together', as Merle's son Michael McBride put it. Even so, Merle grew up at Yarral almost as if she were an only child, wanting for nothing in terms of love or material possessions.

Her brothers were living in a very different environment. In and out of the classroom, their father Charles was a tough taskmaster. He expected high standards of his three oldest children and worked them hard both in their studies and on the property, where they were regarded as his main work-force. Complicating matters for the boys was the arrival of their father's new wife. Charles and Isabella started a family of their own, and Isabella soon had five young children of her own to care for. It was hardly surprising that Ron and his brothers grew up feeling distanced from their stepmother and, to a lesser degree, their half-siblings. It is a division that has continued through the generations. At a family funeral in 2012, Charles Jr's daughter Diane and son-in-law Gordon

Ellem met a descendent of one of Isabella's children who said to them, 'Oh, you're part of the other mob.'

In October 1931, Charles was appointed head teacher at Kolan South State School, not far from Lagoondale, a position he would occupy for the next 25 years. The two older boys had already left school by then. Charles Jr had qualified as a teacher after being apprenticed to his father. Reg had doggedly refused to let the calipers he wore on his legs as a permanent reminder of polio stop him from playing sport, riding horses, or living a full life. He studied bookkeeping and worked in a series of clerical jobs. Ron started at Kolan South school on the same day as his father.

The boys often visited their sister Merle, and as teenagers Charles and Ron would take her to local dances. Ruby's four children formed a close bond that would last as long as they lived. When Reg was killed in 1953 at the age of 38, hit by a car when he stepped off a tram in Brisbane's Queen Street, it was his brother Charles who went to the police station to collect his personal effects. Charles took his younger brother's calipers home and put them on a hook in his garage, where he saw them every day for the next 30 years, not having the heart to throw them out.

Of all Ruby's children, it was Ron who most took to life on the land. While Charles Jr and Reg provided unpaid labour for their father at Lagoondale under sufferance, Ron relished the experience. When he announced that he intended to make farming his living, his father insisted he do it with academic qualifications. After two years at the Queensland Agricultural College at Gatton, west of Brisbane—a school that represented the cutting edge of agricultural science at the time—he returned to Lagoondale and his first love, working on the land. His brothers had already moved south to Brisbane.

For six years after leaving Gatton, Ron split his time between Lagoondale and other properties in the district. By 1941 he was working as a jackaroo at Toraran, a large cattle station 80 kilometres north of Bundaberg, but his mind had moved further afield.

The war in Europe had been raging for two years and, like most young men in the district, Ron decided it was time he did his bit. On 12 July 1941, aged 23 years and 8 months, he presented himself to No. 3 RAAF Recruiting Centre in Creek Street, Brisbane, and enrolled in the Royal Australian Air Force Reserve. His enrolment form lists him as a jackaroo, a British subject and a member of the Church of England. He was 5 feet 8½ inches tall and weighed 137 lb. His hair was light brown and he had grey-green eyes and a fair complexion. His vision was excellent and he was classified A1B and A3B, fit for all flying duties.

It would be five months before Ron was called up from the reserve to begin his active service, and a lot happened to him—and the country—in that time. The date of his call-up was 7 December 1941, the day Japan attacked Pearl Harbor, bringing the US into the war and opening another front for Australia. By then Ron was firmly set on a course of action. He decided that he wanted to be a radio operator and, perhaps influenced by his schoolteacher father's example, left nothing to chance. Unlike many other young men who entered the armed forces unprepared and unconcerned about where they ended up, Ron set himself a goal and worked towards it. He borrowed a Morse-code transmission key from a friend and practised until he exceeded the required level of expertise. He also got hold of some old school textbooks and studied trigonometry.

But while Ron returned to No. 3 RAAF Recruiting Centre far more qualified for duty as air crew than on his previous visit, it was his personal life that had undergone the greatest change. On his original RAAF Reserve enrolment form, the question 'Are you Married or Single?' had been answered 'Single'. By the time he returned to fill out his certificate of active service, signing up for the duration of the war and 'up to 12 months thereafter', the answer had changed to 'Married'. While that was not entirely correct—he and his fiancée wouldn't walk down the aisle for almost four months, alongside Next of Kin he wrote, 'Doris Marjorie Ferguson, Wife.'

Doris 'Fae' Norman was born in Maryborough but grew up in Cairns, in Far North Queensland. Her father, Robert Carleton Norman, had served with the Australian Infantry Forces in France during World War I. He fought at the First Battle of Bullecourt, where the Australians suffered over 3300 casualties with 1170 taken prisoner. He was one of only nineteen men of his battalion to get through Bullecourt in one piece, but he would suffer from the effects of mustard gas for the rest of his life.

With her husband ill, depressed and seeking solace in drink, the 1920s and early '30s were hard both financially and emotionally for Robert's wife Muriel and their children Bob, Doris, Bill and Ron. When Robert died, in 1933, Muriel took the family to Cairns, her home town, to build a new life. It was difficult at first but Bob, the oldest child, then nineteen, proved a good provider. He began selling apples door to door, then rented a shop. The family lived out the back, Muriel and Doris served behind the counter, and Bob drove a horse-drawn fruit cart.

Like his future brother-in-law Ron Ferguson, when war came Bob was keen to join the RAAF. A childhood memory of seeing the great Australian pilot Bert Hinkler landing his Avro Avian on Maryborough Showground had given Bob a lifelong passion for flying, but he knew his lack of education would prevent his being accepted as a pilot. Instead, he applied for enlistment as an RAAF truck driver. Even then, Bob's lack of a leaving certificate went against him. He was turned down. Undeterred, he studied at night school, gained his certificate and re-applied. By then the air force had plenty of truck drivers. It was air crew they needed, and Bob was accepted into pilot training. While training in Canada, he saw the local air service known as Bush Pilots, which serviced remote areas and transported doctors and medical supplies.

After gaining his wings, Bob was posted to the Middle East with 459 Squadron RAAF, flying light-attack bombers. After the war, he returned to Cairns, where he and his wife started a dry-cleaning business. He also gained his commercial-pilot's licence and flew regular mercy missions, getting supplies to properties stranded by floods, and flying sick and injured people from remote areas to hospital in Cairns.

In 1951, inspired by what he had seen in Canada, Bob started Bush Pilots Airways with one Tiger Moth aircraft. By

1988, when the airline was sold and renamed, it had 33 aircraft and had flown thousands of medical missions and regular commercial services. Bob Norman was also the driving force behind the establishment of a Cairns campus of James Cook University. Knighted in 1989, Sir Robert Norman died in 2007 at the age of 93.

While her oldest brother was providing for the family and working towards gaining his pilot wings, Doris Norman was training to become a nurse. When Bob joined the RAAF, she and her mother moved to Brisbane. Ron Ferguson had joined the air force reserve and was renting a room not far from their home as he waited to be called up. He and Doris met and fell in love. They were married in Brisbane on 28 March 1942. At the time, Ron was between postings, having just completed four months at No. 3 Initial Training School at Kingaroy, roughly halfway between Brisbane and Bundaberg. Four days after the wedding he was sent to No. 3 Wireless Air Gunnery School, Maryborough.

Training as a wireless operator–air gunner (wireless air gunner for short) was the most diverse undertaken by Bomber Command air crew because it involved two distinct and unrelated skills. Although 'wireless air gunner' was a single designation, its holder could not perform both duties on the same Lancaster flight. Once he joined a crew, he was either a wireless operator, sending and receiving Morse-code messages, or a gunner. The training was therefore split into two parts at two locations. Wireless training started in the classroom and progressed to the air in Australian-designed and -built CAC Wackett trainers. Two hundred of these two-seat tandem aircraft were built during the war and used primarily at the wireless schools at Parkes, Tamworth and Tocumwal in New South Wales; Ballarat in Victoria and Maryborough.

A journalist's report of an inspection of No. 1 WAGS at RAAF Ballarat in the 22 January 1942 edition of the Melbourne *Argus* gave a good account of what the trainees went through:

> The party saw hundreds of men at work at all stages of training: automatic Morse Instruments, direction finders, aircraft installations in use on the ground, Morse tapes sending out messages to several classes simultaneously, and instructors taking big classes and correcting messages. Trainees included clerks, managers, miners, musicians, graziers, barmen, commercial travellers, chemists, builders, orchardists, and apiarists. A remarkably high standard of efficiency is demanded. It is the proud boast of the school, however, that less than 8 per cent of trainees fail to make the grade, and that some fail only because they cannot overcome air sickness.
>
> After they graduate to the school after a period of preliminary training at an Initial Training School the wireless air gunners spend a period at Morse and electrical science, a second at Morse and radio theory, a third and fourth at Morse and practical radio, a fifth at practical operating of aircraft wireless equipment on the ground, and a sixth in radio sending and receiving from Wackett trainers. They must then be capable of sending at least 18 words a minute in Morse, either in plain language or code, though the goal

aimed at is much higher. They receive their wireless badge and move off for a course at a bomb and gunnery school. An instructor said that under the present scheme every wireless air gunner should be competent enough when he passes out of the school to take on operational flights immediately. In normal times two and a half years were spent on this job, which is now being done much more speedily.

Having already put himself through a course of Morse code and trigonometry, Ron breezed through the four months he spent at No. 3 WAGS. For the second part of his course, he was posted to No. 1 Bombing and Gunnery School at Evans Head, where his future crewmate Cliff Hopgood had trained two months earlier. On 15 October 1942, Ron was awarded his Wireless Air Gunner badge, a half wing coming off a crowned circular wreath with the letters WAG centred above RAAF. He was also promoted to the rank of sergeant. From Evans Head, he went to No. 1 Air Observers School at Cootamundra, in southern New South Wales. The AOS course was a combination of classroom sessions, in which students learnt to identify varieties of aircraft by sight, and airborne exercises designed to sharpen their skills of observation. On 9 January 1943, just over two years after he had been called up, Sergeant Ronald Ferguson was posted to England.

On 3 May, six weeks after landing at Brighton, he was posted to No. 2 (O) AFU, an Observer Advanced Flying Unit at RAF Millom in Cumbria, in north-western England. After completing a four-week course there, the newly promoted Flight Sergeant Ferguson made the move that would bring him into the orbit of Dave Baxter. On 8 June 1943, the same day as Cliff Hopgood and two days after Dave, Ron arrived at No. 27 OTU at RAF Church Broughton. He would stay there for the next three months, flying in Wellington bombers, furthering his skills as an observer and wireless operator, and impressing Dave Baxter so much that he asked Ron to join his crew. On 5 September, they moved to No. 1656 Heavy Conversion Unit at RAF Lindholme to be introduced to the 'heavies', first the Halifax and then the aircraft in which they would go to war, the Lancaster.

The Lancaster wireless operator sat in semi-darkness on the port side of the aircraft, directly behind the navigator's position, with his code book and the air log in which he recorded all messages. His T1154/R1155 wireless was known as a Marconi and also as a 'rainbow' set because of its multi-coloured knobs. Most communication with the outside world was by Morse code and, except for regular wind speed and direction reports, this was minimal. The wireless operator was also kept busy assisting the navigator by establishing the bomber's position from base-radio transmissions, and it was his task to drop bundles of 'window'—foil strips intended to confuse German radar.

By early November, when Ron and his new crewmates arrived at 625 Squadron RAF to begin active duty, Doris was working as a nurse at the Community Hospital in Canberra, wondering every day if she would ever see her husband of less than two years again. It was a question Ron also asked himself as he and his crewmates settled uneasily into a hellish routine of dropping bombs and dodging death.

Bill Martin

6

THE MID-UPPER GUNNER

Bill Martin never drank heavily or gambled. It wasn't that he was a wowser; it was more that he blamed those vices for the deprivations he had endured as a child. Bill knew very little about the circumstances surrounding his birth. There was no notice placed in the newspaper by the proud parents or even a birth certificate that he knew of. When he went to enlist in the air force in 1942, he had to fill out and sign a statutory declaration affirming that: 'To the best of my knowledge and belief I was born at North Sydney in the state of New South Wales on the 16th day of March 1912.' He also filled in a standard form that was then checked against records in the Registrar General's Department. Included were: Name: William James Martin. Place of Birth: North Sydney. Mother's Maiden Name in Full:

Quinn. Father's Name: George. Surname: Martin. When the document was returned, the government official had marked corrections in pencil. North Sydney was amended to 'Sydney'; Quinn was ticked as correct and 'Anastasia' written underneath, but the name George was crossed out and the 'Father's Name' section left blank. Under Surname, the officer put a line through Martin and wrote, 'Robinson, known as Todd'. By then Bill was days away from turning 30, and any interest he had in his father had long since evaporated. All he knew was that the man was a drinker and gambler who had walked out on him and his mother soon after his birth.

Life was tough for Bill and his mother as they moved around Sydney's inner eastern suburbs. One of the places they rented was a semi-detached cottage in Darlinghurst, where their neighbours were tram driver Robert Freeman, his wife Margaret and their four children. The oldest, Jim, who was five years older than Bill, was ordained as a priest at the age of 22, served as the Catholic archbishop of Sydney from 1971 to 1983, and eventually became Cardinal Sir James Darcy Freeman.

As Larry Writer describes it in his book *Razor*, East Sydney in the 1920s and 1930s, when Bill was growing up, 'was one of the most dangerous places on earth. Paddington, Darlinghurst, Kings Cross, Surry Hills and Woolloomooloo were sprawling slums of ramshackle rat- and roach-infested terraces and shacks where lived criminals, violent alcoholics and drug addicts and those too poor to escape to more salubrious suburbs.' Darlinghurst—or 'Darlo', as the locals knew it—was a hotbed of prostitution, drug dealing and sly-grog shops. Standover men and thugs intimidated their prey and fought turf wars with their rivals using pistols and, after a handgun licensing law was introduced, cut-throat razors. It was hardly an ideal environment for a fatherless boy whose mother's life was a daily struggle.

Born to Ellen and Jeremiah Quinn in Wagga Wagga, in south-western New South Wales, in 1875, Anastasia became a mother at the age of 37 and was abandoned soon afterwards. A single mother in the Depression received little sympathy and no government assistance, and Bill never mentioned having any contact with grandparents or extended family. He did, however, speak of his mother taking in washing to help make ends meet, and of her determination that he should be raised as a good Catholic. For a youngster growing up in Darlo, the temptation to follow a life on the wrong side of the law must have been almost overwhelming. To many in the district, crime seemed the only way out of poverty. Author Larry Writer says Bill would have had a choice to make: 'Go straight or . . . follow a life of crime, it was that clear cut.' Brothel owners and gangsters were rich, powerful and 'seen as the real figures of authority. It was definitely tempting to go their way, and most people did'.

Not Bill Martin. Whether it was because of the influence of his mother, his strong Catholic faith or even the example of the Freeman boys next door—whom he followed into Christian Brothers High School at St Mary's Cathedral—Bill chose to stay on the straight and narrow. The Christian Brothers gave preference to local boys and made special allowance for those in financial hardship. Bill stayed at 'the Cathedral school' for four years. He took part in athletics, swimming and rugby league, and proved himself to be a diligent student.

On 25 November 1928 he sat for the Intermediate Certificate. He passed English, history, geography, shorthand, maths I, maths II and business principles—the latter three subjects at First-Class level—and failed only technical drawing.

For a young man of Bill's background and means, the idea of tertiary study was inconceivable. The most attainable options were to enter the Church, apply for a job in the public service or seek work that would lead to a trade. Bill followed the last path, and found a job at Lustre Hosiery, which had a factory on the border between Darlinghurst and Paddington. It was one of the country's larger manufacturers of hosiery, lingerie and menswear. Bill was taken on as a trainee machinist and rose to the position of textile knitter. Australia at that time was said to 'ride on the sheep's back', and with an estimated 300 knitting mills operating in the country, his new trade was respected and sought after.

Around this time, he took the ferry from Sydney's Circular Quay to Manly to attend the Corpus Christi mass and procession, held at St Patrick's Seminary at the end of May each year. This was a huge event on the Sydney Catholic calendar, attracting upwards of 12,000 people. Travelling across the harbour, Bill found himself in conversation with a young woman who was headed to the same destination. Anne Patricia Carroll, who lived in Kensington, a short bus ride from Darlinghurst, was a member of the young Catholic women's group Children of Mary.

When Anne was a teenager, her mother had died suddenly, leaving her husband Thomas, who laboured on the roads, to care for three children. As the oldest, with two younger brothers, Anne took on the duties of running the home. Also living in the house was Anne's aunt Eileen, her mother's sister, who was intellectually impaired. An unusual extended family it might have been, but a family it was, and to Bill the Carroll home was a world away from 'Darlo'. As he and Anne grew closer, he spent more and more time in Kensington. Eventually, he moved in. While he continued to support his mother, he was warmly welcomed by the Carrolls. His first contribution to the household was a tiny white kitten, which he brought in his pocket. It was to remain part of the household for the next eighteen years.

When Australia went to war, Bill was in a quandary. For the first time in his life he felt part of an extended family unit. He and Anne were in love and planned to marry. And he was already seen to be doing his part for the war effort. At the start of the conflict, England had committed to buy Australia's entire yield of wool for the duration. Shearers were refused permission to join up. Australia's knitting mills were working furiously to meet the demand for woollen products such as uniforms and socks needed for the troops. In April 1941, the chairman of Lustre Hosiery would announce to shareholders that the company's sales had exceeded those of the previous year, largely because of a 'considerable amount of work for the Defence Department'. As an experienced textile knitter working for a 'required industry', Bill could have qualified for an exemption from active service, and even though he and Anne were married at Our Lady of the Rosary Church, Kensington, on 25 January 1941, the call of duty proved too great. On 17 December 1941 he went to the RAAF Recruiting

Centre in Woolloomooloo and filled in an Application for Air Crew.

Just over a year later he received a letter summoning him to No. 2 Recruiting Centre. On 2 March 1942, he quit his job and headed back to Woolloomooloo to join up.

The RAAF Medical Officer who examined Bill that day recorded that he stood 5 feet 8½ inches tall and was heavy set. His complexion was fair, and he had blue eyes and fair hair. Certified medically suitable for service with a classification of A1B A3B—fit for full flying duties—he went straight from the doctor to the Enrolling Officer and took the oath. Now officially a member of the RAAF Reserve, he waited to be called up. In the meantime he was assigned to 112 Independent Brigade General Purpose Ordnance Workshop, where his machinist skills were put to use in the manufacture of much-needed military equipment. After just over five months the call came, and on 17 August 1942 he was discharged from the workshop and returned to No. 2 Recruiting Centre to enlist in the permanent forces of the RAAF. By now aged 30 years and four months, he again took the oath, swearing that he would 'resist His Majesty's enemies and cause His Majesty's Peace to be kept and maintained'. The night before he left for war, Bill and Anne prayed together and agreed that they would each say the same prayer every day they were apart.

Aircraftman Class 2 William Martin reported to No. 2 Initial Training School, at Bradfield Park, Lindfield, on 27 August 1942 and stayed there for nearly two months before being selected for training as a wireless operator–air gunner. Promoted to Leading Aircraftman, he was posted in October to No. 2 Wireless Air Gunnery School at RAAF Parkes. After he had been there for a month, Bill spotted a familiar face. Jim O'Riordan had been behind Bill at the Cathedral School. 'He was about ten years older than me, but we'd met each other at an Old Boys' function,' Jim says. 'We were in Parkes for about four or five months, so I saw a lot of him. I didn't take to the wireless training and became a gunner. Bill ended up a gunner too, so I suppose he didn't go too well in Parkes either for some reason.'

For Bill and Jim, the gunnery part of the course was at No. 2 Bombing and Gunnery School in Port Pirie, South Australia. For young men preparing for war, the experience of shooting Vickers machine guns from the open cockpit of a Fairey Battle three-seat bomber was a lot more exciting than tapping out Morse code in a classroom, but it was also a lot more dangerous. The Port Pirie War Cemetery has 29 graves; 22 of them hold the remains of airmen killed in World War II training mishaps.

The Fairey Battle was a British single-engine light bomber that proved hopelessly inadequate in combat. Withdrawn from active service, the planes were recommissioned as training aircraft. At Port Pirie one of the aircraft would pull a cloth target drogue—basically a large air sock secured by long cables. Two or three gunnery trainees following in a second Battle would attempt to shoot the target.

'We were firing gas-operated Vickers guns with drums holding a hundred rounds of .303 ammo,' recalls Jim O'Riordan.

They'd dip the tips of the rounds in different coloured paint so they could tell who was hitting the target. If you got 4, 5 or 6 per cent of hits, you were doing pretty well. The pilot of the gunnery plane would tell the pilot of the other plane what move he wanted him to do. They'd simulate various types of attacks. It might be slightly elevated on the port side or below from the starboard side. Sometimes they'd bring it right past and you could take a shot. You had to be careful not to shoot your own tail off; it wasn't easy.

One time this bloke, Sid Kelly, was struggling so he asked the pilot, 'Do you mind flying a bit closer?' He offered him a quid. The pilot went right up close and Sid got behind the gun and really shot the damn thing. He must have hit the cables because it just fluttered down to earth and landed in this mud flat. Sid knew he had a good score so when he got back down he said to the officer, 'Those things cost a lot of money. I think we should go and get it.' They sent him out in a truck and when they got as close as they could Sid got on his pushbike and found it. They brought it back, and Sid got his score.

After three weeks at Port Pirie, Bill qualified as an air gunner. On 29 April 1943 he was promoted to Flight Sergeant and issued with his badge, a half wing alongside a circular wreath with the letters AG in the centre. The next day he was on his way back to RAAF Bradfield Park, this time to prepare for the sea voyage to England. After arriving in Bournemouth, he was posted to No. 27 Operational Training Unit. By the time Bill arrived at 27 OTU, in mid-July, Dave Baxter had been there for a month and a half, honing his skills on the Wellington and looking around for the right people to make up his crew.

'It was pretty much a case of them letting you sort it out for yourself,' says Jim O'Riordan of the crew selection process.

> They'd let you mix around in the mess. You might be lining up for your food in the sergeants' mess and you'd chat with someone or you might be doing a training flight with them. You'd just mill around to get crewed up and you'd talk to different people, and if the pilot thought you were all right he'd ask you to join his crew. The pilot had to be pretty astute to look at people and know what he wanted and how someone would fit in with someone else.

During the five weeks he spent training at RAF Church Broughton, Bill impressed Dave Baxter enough to be invited to join his crew. From that moment on he was no longer an Aussie alone in a strange and dangerous world. He was part of a team. The former Darlo boy who had grown up alone with his mother suddenly had six brothers. When Dave packed up his kit and headed to No. 1656 Heavy Conversion Unit at RAF Lindholme on 5 September 1943, Bill went with him.

As Dave's crew made the progression from Halifax to Lancaster bombers at Lindholme, it was Bill's turn to make a choice. The Lancaster had three sets of guns: in the nose, where they were operated by the bomb aimer; in the mid-upper turret; and in the tail turret. The two forward positions were armed with two .303 Browning machine guns; the tail gunner operated four. It was up to the two air gunners in each crew to decide which position they would man. The rear gunner was the most vulnerable member of the crew, since attacks by

German night fighters almost invariably came from below and behind. The mid-upper gunner was marginally safer, but his position was the most uncomfortable on the aircraft. While the rear gunner was in a cramped and cold space, at least he was seated. The mid-upper gunner spent the flight perched on a triangular strip of canvas slung beneath the domed turret like a hammock. For Bill the decision of which position to take was simple. A large man, he would have found it difficult to fit into the rear turret, let alone go through the involved process of getting out in an emergency. Mid-upper gun it was.

John Dunlop

7

THE REAR GUNNER

John McClymont Dunlop knew what he was getting into. For most of his young life his father William had been in uniform. He saw him re-enlist at the outbreak of World War II and head to France with the Royal Engineers, and just over a year later, a month before his sixteenth birthday, he stood beside his mother as a bugler played 'The Last Post' beside his father's grave. Two and a half years later, he enlisted in the RAF.

John Dunlop was born on 14 June 1924 in his parents' home in Ayrshire, Scotland. John's father, William Cuthbert Dunlop, was a private in the Royal Scots Fusiliers when he married; his bride, Mary Alexander Heptinstall, was a domestic servant. John was later joined by brothers Thomas, born in 1923, and Billy (who died in 1929 at the age of two), and four sisters—Wilhelmina, Moria, Janet (known as Jenny) and Mabil.

William, who was born and raised in Ayr, had joined the Fusiliers at the age of eighteen a year after the end of World War I. When his term in the regular army ended, he made a living as best he could as a bookmaker, fielding bets among drinkers in local pubs. He remained in the Reserves until he was honourably discharged in July 1939, just two months before the outbreak of war. Five months later, as German forces began to advance through Europe, William re-enlisted and was posted to the 697 General Construction Company of the Royal Engineers. It was as untried as a combat unit could be. Raised complete in just fourteen days, the company had less than a month's training before it was sent to Grévillers, in the north of France.

On 10 May 1940, as German armoured divisions moved into the Ardennes Forest region, 697 General Construction Company at Grévillers came under fire for the first time. It would not be the last. A week later, with Allied forces in France trapped between the advancing enemy and the Channel, the surviving members of the unit were ordered to abandon their gear and proceed to Calais for evacuation to England. Their three months in France had been a baptism of fire from which the company had emerged with distinction. The same was true of William Dunlop. Not only did he survive, he shone. In quick succession he was promoted from lance corporal to corporal to sergeant. Back home in Ayr, his family were proud and relieved that he had returned from the war zone in good health. Their joy was to prove short-lived. With the company split up among RAF stations around the country, in late June William suffered a minor injury. To aid his recovery, he was advised to swim in the hospital pool. One day, diving in at the shallow end, he struck his head on the bottom. At the age of 39, he was dead.

Two and a half years later, on 8 February 1943, William's son John Dunlop, aged eighteen, enlisted in the Royal Air Force Volunteer Reserve. By that time he had been out of school for four years and working as a heavy-machinery operator for a large construction and contracting firm. An average student with a love of sport, especially football, he had always had an interest in aircraft and an ambition to be a pilot. Though the opportunity to fly had never come his way, as soon as John could afford it he bought a motorcycle. He would disappear for days at a time, exploring the country-side with his cocker spaniel Charm tucked up in his leather coat. He joined up as soon as the opportunity arose, but his limited education meant he was still unable to fulfil his dream of becoming a pilot. Instead he was assigned the rank of Aircraftman Class 2. This was the lowliest position on the RAF totem pole, more commonly known as AC2 or, to older hands, AC Plonk, or simply Plonk. John was told to make his way immediately to the RAF's No. 1 Air Crew Reception Centre in Regents Park, London.

The haste with which John was ordered to London was not typical for all recruits. Those with the aptitude and education to be trained as pilots were sent back home and placed on reserve for up to a year before they were called up. Engineers, navigators and radio operators would often have to wait for several months, but in February 1943 there was one kind of air crewman the RAF needed in large numbers and without delay: rear gunners.

Known in the RAF as Tail-End Charlie, the rear gunner was the most exposed, isolated and unprotected of the seven crew members of a Lancaster bomber. He sat at the back of the aircraft in a cramped, freezing pod, with only a sheet of Perspex between him and the German night fighters who at any moment could come roaring into range, below and astern, with cannons blazing. If forced to bail out, the process by which he exited the stricken aircraft was complicated and fraught with possible glitches. Once the pilot gave the command to abandon the aircraft, the rear gunner would have to disconnect the intercom and any other wires, such as those to his electrically heated suit. Worn underneath their flying suits by both gunners on a Lancaster, these were vests lined with thin heating elements and plugged straight into the aircraft's electrical system. He would then have to push open the turret doors behind him and reach back for his parachute, which was hanging on a hook. Clipping it on, he would get back into position and slant his gun barrels vertically so that they did not hit the side of the aircraft as he spun the turret around. Praying that the hydraulics had not been damaged in the action, he would then spin the turret 180 degrees so that he was facing into the fuselage with his back to the open air. He would then 'simply' fall backwards out of the aircraft—or he would if the many layers of clothing he was wearing made movement within the turret in any sense 'simple'.

With so many parts of the procedure dependent on each other, more often than not, if the aircraft went down, the rear gunner would go down with it. As the military historian Richard Holmes put it, his was 'the coldest, loneliest, most dangerous job of all'. And in the Lancaster, the odds of survival were worse than on any other aircraft. A quarter of the air crew of Halifax bombers shot down in the war managed to bail out successfully. In US Air Force daylight bombing raids, the success rate was closer to 50 per cent, but due to factors such as the small size of the escape hatches and, in the case of the rear gunners, the complicated procedure of extricating themselves from the tail turret, only 15 per cent of the crew of downed Lancasters survived. Which raises the question, why do it? Of all the positions on an RAF bomber—of all the roles within the RAF as a whole, in fact—why volunteer for the one that could be viewed as little more than a nightly airborne version of Russian roulette?

According to Andrew Panton, curator of the Lincolnshire Aviation Heritage Centre at East Kirkby, it came down to two things: limited choices and personal pride.

They thought they couldn't do anything else. They hadn't gone to grammar school, so they couldn't become a pilot, and of course the air-gunner's training course was six months. The pilot's training course was two years, so if you wanted to get in and get fighting you went in as a gunner. Plus there was a certain amount of kudos to be a rear gunner. If you could say you were a rear gunner on a Lancaster, you were the bee's knees.

Rear gunner Jim O'Riordan—Bill Martin's former school-mate—flew 30 missions as a rear gunner with 550 Squadron RAF out of North Killingholme, in Lincolnshire. He says the Tail-End Charlies—like all of Bomber Command air crew—went in with their eyes open. 'When we first arrived at North Killingholme, the Intelligence Officer told us, "Your life expectancy is six weeks, now go back to your huts and make out your wills." It didn't matter what category you were, pilot, radio operator, gunner . . . everyone aspired to do two tours. That was 30 missions. The average was thirteen, so you had to be lucky. You had to beat the average by more than twice to survive.'

O'Riordan says he chose to be a rear gunner 'because the night fighters would fly up from behind, and I reckoned if we were going to get hit I'd be the first bloke to know about it. I'd be there with my guns. At least that way I'd have some say in my fate. If I had to do the whole thing again, I'd still go in the rear.'

For the young Scotsman John Dunlop, the first steps towards the rear gunner's seat started in a ragged-looking parade of 30 recruits, still dressed in their civilian clothes, at Lord's Cricket Ground. Living in nearby flats requisitioned by the Ministry of Defence for the duration of the war, and fed daily in the café of the London Zoo, the young men were first subjected to inoculations and medical examinations—including the genital inspection known as 'Free From Infection', or FFI—and issued with kit. Then followed three weeks of drill, physical exercise (including swimming) and lectures on RAF procedures. At the end of the initial training, the recruits had a passing-out parade at Lord's, and, with a white flash on their hats to mark their status as Recruits Under Training, moved on to their next posting—in Dunlop's case No. 14 Initial Training Wing (ITW) at RAF Bridlington, in Yorkshire. A popular seaside resort in peacetime, Bridlington was very much a town prepared for war when John Dunlop and his fellow trainees arrived there in late February 1943. The beach and shoreline were lined with barbed wire and pillboxes in readiness for invasion, and the shops, cafés and amusement arcades were closed and boarded up. Homes closest to the sea had been taken over by the RAF to house air-force personnel and recruits, who did their drills on the Promenade, now deserted of holiday-makers. A large hotel was pressed into service as a makeshift school, its dining room and lounge areas transformed into classrooms. One institution that retained its peacetime identity was the Spa Pavilion, a large entertainment venue, which presented free Sunday-night variety shows for the troops.

To wide-eyed young recruits such as eighteen-year-old John Dunlop, who had never set foot outside Scotland before enlisting, there were worse places to do their two-month training course. That process was about far more than teaching them to slow march and fire a shotgun at clay pigeons in the hotel grounds. It was also the chance for superiors to assess their capabilities and channel them into the most suitable field of operation. In the case of AC2 Dunlop, that proved to be as an air gunner. Following two weeks' introductory training at Bridlington's No. 1 Elementary Gunnery School, he was posted to No. 2 Air Gunnery School (AGS) at Dalcross, near Inverness in the Scottish Highlands. It may have been a return to his homeland, but there was little chance of a family reunion. The training was becoming serious. Opened in August 1941, RAF Dalcross was equipped with Defiant, Lysander and, by the time John Dunlop arrived, Anson aircraft.

First produced by the Boulton Paul company in 1935, the Defiant was a two-man aircraft that resembled the Hawker Hurricane in appearance, except for the addition of a dorsal rear-facing turret equipped with four .303 Browning machine guns, similar to those used by rear gunners in the Lancaster. At Dalcross, trainee gunners would shoot from Defiants or Ansons at the sock-like drogues dragged by Westland Lysanders, old-fashioned looking but surprisingly advanced and adaptable aircraft originally commissioned by the Air Ministry in 1936 to be used for army reconnaissance and photographic support. While the Lysander was not favoured by the army for those roles, its ability to land and take off from unprepared airstrips made it far more suited to clandestine operations such as working with Resistance fighters behind enemy lines. It also proved to be a reliable and safe workhorse in training applications.

In truth, for rear gunners like John Dunlop, such training was all but useless. By the time Dunlop arrived at Dalcross, the Germans had developed the tactic that would make the Lancaster's Browning .303 machine guns virtually obsolete. Prior to 1943, German night fighters had been equipped with standard front-facing machine guns and cannons. The Luftwaffe pilots' usual tactic was to fly in a straight line towards the rear of the enemy aircraft while getting into a firing position. There were two disadvantages: the target area was small, and the fighters came into the firing zone of the RAF heavy bombers' rear gunners. From 1941, Oberleutnant Rudolf Schönert, an officer in a night-fighting squadron, began experimenting with the use of upward-firing cannons in his Dornier Do 17. He wanted to fly underneath the British bombers and attack unseen by their crew and away from their guns, which were mounted only on the front, top and rear of the aircraft. Despite early scepticism, his results were good enough to gain official support, and German night fighters began to be fitted with guns slanted at around 65 degrees. The first RAF bomber was shot down using the new system in May 1943, and hundreds were to follow. Since the German word for slanted, *schräge,* was also used to describe 'funky' jazz music, Schoenert's tactic was called *Schräge Musik.* It was a deadly tune that air crew of Bomber Command came to fear.

The new German approach meant that gunners in Bomber Command became as much look-outs as marksmen. With no ventral gun turret on the undercarriage of their aircraft, bomber pilots developed their own tactic—the corkscrew manoeuvre—to combat the night fighters. Rather than relying on their gunners to shoot down the enemy before they suffered the same fate, the pilots now needed them to spot the fighters in time for them to perform the corkscrew, a series of steep diving and climbing turns they believed made it hard for the Germans to use their fixed guns. The bombers were virtually stationary, and therefore at great risk, when the controls were reversed at the top and bottom of the manoeuvre, but there was precious little else the pilots could do once an enemy night fighter had moved into position.

For this reason, as well as giving trainee gunners the opportunity to shoot at drogues in the air, RAF Dalcross set up three gunnery turrets on the ground from which they could practise spotting aircraft approaching at various speeds and angles. Whether shooting or observing, AC2 Dunlop proved an apt student, passing all his tests and moving steadily through the two-month course. At the halfway mark he was promoted to Leading Aircraftman, or LAC. A month later, at the end of his training, he was given time off to visit his family. As he left Scotland for a second time to take up his posting at No. 27 Operational Training Unit at RAF Church Broughton, it was as a Temporary Sergeant. His ten-year-old sister Jenny proudly sewed the stripes and the woven Air Gunner badge of single wing and AG insignia on his sleeves and cap.

John arrived at RAF Church Broughton on 15 June 1943, the day after his nineteenth birthday. Four of his future crewmates—Dave Baxter, Cliff Hopgood, Ron Ferguson and Tony D'Arcey—had already been at the base for just over a week. The teenaged Scot had little in common with the Australians, who were naturally drawn to each other, but as they all trained on the Wellingtons, something about him caught Dave's attention when it came time to choose a crew.

The process of 'crewing up' was purposely left casual and unregulated. It was felt that the camaraderie required to create a smooth-running team could not be forced or defined in any book of regulations. In an organisation still being run along English public-school lines, with prowess on the rugby field or cricket pitch seen as a key qualification in the selection of pilot officers, it was felt—and probably rightly so—that no one was better placed to choose the right mix of men to go to war with than the team captain. The choosing would be done in the mess or pub; some OTUs had the pilots wait in a room and sent in the navigators, radio operators and gunners in groups for informal interviews; others brought everyone together in an empty hangar, like a meet-and-greet function. For some, the process proved relatively easy and even enjoyable. For others, it could be torture, with airmen feeling like wall-flowers at a dance, left without a crew as others joined up. The newly promoted Sergeant Dunlop had no such problems. He was welcomed into the fold, becoming the youngest member of Dave Baxter's team. On 9 September 1943, he accompanied five of his crewmates on the next leg of their journey, to No. 1656 Conversion Unit at RAF Lindholme in North York-shire, where they would be joined by the last member of the crew, Peter Mallon, and introduced to the 'heavies'.

Their first flight together in a four-engine bomber was on a Halifax. It would be six weeks before they finally climbed aboard a Lancaster and then moved on to service with 625 Squadron RAF. Before that could happen, Dave had to complete a course at Lindholme's No. 1 Lancaster Finishing School. With their skipper occupied elsewhere, the rest of the crew also underwent more training, with John—or Jock, as he was now known by his crewmates—ordered to a gunnery-training unit, 1481 Bomber Gunnery Flight (9). The training flights were squadrons of combat-ready aircraft used to provide final instruction under the tutelage of hardened veterans, many of whom had already completed their thirty-mission tours. On occasion, training flights were called into action to make up the numbers for large operations, as was the case with 1481 on 30 May 1942, when Bomber Command launched the first of its 'thousand bomber' raids, on the city of Cologne.

When he arrived to begin his short training course on 29 September 1943, Jock would have been too focused on his work to pay much attention to his surroundings or to the other squadrons operating from the airfield, but they were to have enormous significance to him and his crewmates in the months to come.

The base was RAF Binbrook, at Grimsby, in Lincolnshire. Five months before Jock Dunlop began his brief stay there, it had become home to what the official base history would describe as a 'foreign contingent': Squadron 460 of the Royal Australian Air Force.

Peter Mallon

8

THE FLIGHT ENGINEER

Given his family history, it might have been expected that Peter Mallon would join the navy rather than the air force. Perhaps, coming from a shipbuilding family, he had seen and heard enough about boats throughout his life and wanted a change. Or maybe, experiencing first-hand what had happened to the ship industry in his home town of Irvine, Scotland, he saw that the future lay elsewhere. Regardless of his reasons, nineteen-year-old Peter Mallon enlisted in the Royal Air Force Volunteer Reserve at Edinburgh on 26 January 1942.

Like his future crewmate John Dunlop, Peter was an Ayrshire lad, born in Irvine, on the coast of the Firth of Clyde, on 21 September 1922. His father Edward had worked as a riveter in shipyards all his life. His first job was at the Govan shipyard in Glasgow, which turned out naval vessels that saw action in World War I. They included the light cruiser HMAS *Sydney*, which was responsible for the Royal Australian Navy's first, and arguably greatest, military victory when it sank the German cruiser SMS *Emden* in 1914. By the time Peter was born, Edward had moved to the smaller shipyards at Irvine, some 50 kilometres south of Govan. After the war, the local council had sponsored a housing program to attract workers to Irvine, giving the town the appearance of having a bright future. In 1922, Edward married a local shop assistant, Helen McCormick—known as Nellie—and they started a family. Peter was soon followed by siblings Annie, Bernard and Margaret, known as Greta. The Mallon children attended St Mary's Catholic Primary School and St Michael's College Secondary School.

Peter left St Michael's at the age of fifteen to begin learning a trade. By then it had become obvious that following his father into shipbuilding was not an option. The yards at Govan and Irvine were now a shadow of the once-thriving enterprises that had employed tens of thousands of workers. In 1920, soon after Edward had arrived in Irvine, two ships of 7600 tons each—the largest ever built there—were completed for the giant shipping company Clan Line. By 1936, a year before Peter left school, the last two vessels ever built at Irvine were finally sold after sitting unwanted in the stocks for five years. From then on, the Irvine shipyards were used only for repairs and servicing, including some military work on landing craft during World War II, until all maritime work was phased out in 1959.

With the prospects of making a living in the shipyards less than meagre, Peter chose joinery—the trade of making items such as doors, windows, stairs and furniture by joining pieces of wood without nails or glue. At the time it was a five-year apprenticeship, but like many young men of his age, Peter couldn't wait to get involved in the war. He left one year early to join up, making the 125-kilometre trip to Edinburgh to fill out his forms. On 27 January 1942, he took an oath of allegiance and was inducted into the Royal Air Force Volunteer Reserve. Formed in 1936 as a way of boosting the ranks of the regular air force—then called the Royal Auxiliary Air Force—the RAFVR was initially made up of members of Reserve Flying Schools. The schools, run by civilian contractors, taught members the rudiments of flying and navigation with the understanding that they would be called into service in the event of war. By the time Peter Mallon joined up, the need for air crew had long since exhausted the ranks of the original reservists. The RAFVR was still the conduit into the RAF, but recruits were accepted virtually straight off the street and placed into the system according to demand for their speciality.

Although he had not quite finished his apprenticeship, Peter's bright personality and experience working with tools made an impression on the recruiters. He was sent home to Irvine to await call-up for training as a flight engineer.

In terms of the team effort required for the crew of a Lancaster to do its job, the role of the flight engineer was crucial, but no more so than any other. If the navigator failed, the crew would not reach the target; if the bomb aimer fell short in his duties, the target would not be hit. The gunners had to watch out for enemy aircraft and try to shoot them down. If they dozed off, they were all dead. And so it went on: the radio operator, the pilot—every man had an equally important task to perform in the nightly game of life and death that was Bomber Command. The role of the flight engineer was basically to keep the aircraft flying.

The flight engineer sat on the 'dickey' seat that folded down beside the pilot for take-off and landing, then spent the flight standing or kneeling, always ready to take over the controls in an emergency. On the starboard wall behind the dickey seat was a bank of levers, dials and gauges that the flight engineer needed to monitor constantly, updating the pilot with any relevant information and taking action, such as shutting down damaged engines, when required. The official Lancaster Pilot's and Engineer's Notes lists these instruments as: ammeter, oil-pressure gauges, pressure-head heater switch, oil-temperature gauges, coolant-temperature gauges, fuel-content gauges, inspection-lamp socket, fuel-contents gauge switch, fuel-tanks selector cocks, electric fuel-booster pump switches, fuel-pressure warning lights, emergency-air control and oil-dilution buttons.

The flight engineer's role included starting the engines and going through the pre-flight checks with the pilot, monitoring engine performance and fuel consumption throughout the flight, transferring fuel between tanks, checking the crew's oxygen supply and acting as an observer. Occasionally he would drop 'window'—the silver foil strips used to disrupt enemy radar.

The flight engineer was also trained in the rudiments of flying the aircraft in case the pilot was killed or incapacitated. In fact this knowledge was rarely utilised in an emergency because getting a stricken pilot, in full flying gear, out of his seat and taking over the controls was extremely difficult and time-consuming. There were, however, cases of flight engineers coming to the aid of a wounded pilot and assisting him in flying the aircraft. The most famous of these was the action for which 21-year-old Flight Lieutenant William Reid was awarded the Victoria Cross. Reid was captain of a 61 Squadron RAF Lancaster on a bombing raid over Düsseldorf on 3 November 1943. Shortly after crossing the Dutch coast, the aircraft was attacked by a Messerschmitt Bf 110. The pilot's windscreen was shattered, and Reid was wounded in the head, shoulders and hand. The aircraft's elevator trimming tabs were damaged and it became difficult to control. The rear turret was also damaged and the compass and communications system put out of action. The Victoria Cross citation noted: 'Flight Lieutenant Reid ascertained that his crew were unscathed and, saying nothing about his own injuries, he continued his mission.' In an interview for the 1973 TV series *The World at War*, Reid said: 'I didn't see any sense in saying "I'm wounded" in case they all thought, "He's going to pop off at any minute now."'

Shortly afterwards, the Lancaster was again attacked, this time by a Fokker-Wulf Fw 190. Reid was hit by shrapnel in the head and hand, and his flight engineer, Flight Sergeant James W. 'Jim' Norris, who was standing beside him, was shot in the forearm. Norris also did not let on that he had been wounded—his arm was later found to be broken. The wireless operator was fatally wounded and the navigator killed instantly. Despite the damage to the aircraft and the injuries sustained by the crew, Reid pressed on. As he recalled:

> It wasn't a case of a 'press on regardless' feeling. It was just a fact that the four engines were still flying. If an engine cut, I'd have thought, 'Well, we can't get any further,' but another factor here was [that] if I started back we'd have another 600 or 700 planes that were more or less on the same track and spread something like 8 or 10 miles and maybe 4000 to 6000 feet deep. And you're turning back right into them and going through this lot to get back. Then again, if I'd turned off say 90 degrees to avoid them, you're still turning across quite a number of them.

With the pilot weakened by loss of blood and the plane hard to control, it became a team effort by Reid, Norris and bomb aimer Les Rolton to keep the Lancaster in the air.

> The port elevator had been shot off the plane. That's the elevator that keeps the plane straight on either side, and this meant you had to hold the stick right back as if you're going to climb to keep the plane straight and level. So the bomb aimer helped push this back as well, because my shoulder was weak and my hand was weak and it was a case of keeping the stick back with the hands in front. The engineer held it with his other arm, his good arm. So we held it combined back in order to keep it straight and level.

With the oxygen system shot out, Flight Sergeant Norris held a face mask up to Reid and fed him oxygen from a portable cylinder. The VC citation continues:

> Flight Lieutenant Reid refused to be turned from his objective and Düsseldorf was reached some 50 minutes later. He had memorised his course to the target and photographs show that, when the bombs were released, the aircraft was right over the centre of the target. Steering by the pole star and the moon, Flight Lieutenant Reid then set course for home. He was growing weak from loss of blood. The emergency oxygen supply had given out. With the windscreen shattered, the cold was intense. He lapsed into semi-consciousness.

Norris then managed to keep the aircraft straight and level until Reid regained full consciousness, close to the coast of England. 'We were shot at a few times on the way back,' Reid recalled. 'We weren't hit again. Eventually we did come over England when I saw these beacons flashing. At touchdown, the legs of the undercarriage collapsed and we went along on our belly for about 50 yards or so and came to a stop, and I switched off the engines to keep the fire hazard down. It was only then I knew the navigator was killed because he slid forward beside me.' For his part in the operation, Flight Engineer James Norris was awarded the Conspicuous Gallantry Medal.

Another flight engineer who was recognised for his efforts in trying to keep his aircraft in the air and save the lives of his fellow crew members was 23-year-old Flight Sergeant Norman

Jackson. On 26 April 1944, Jackson was wounded when his 106 Squadron RAF Lancaster was attacked by a German night fighter while returning from a raid over Schweinfurt. With fire breaking out near a petrol tank on the wing, and despite freezing temperatures and the aircraft still being under attack, Jackson strapped on his parachute, grabbed a fire extinguisher and climbed out onto the wing. His efforts to extinguish the flames proved unsuccessful. The fire spread and he was badly burned. With his parachute only half inflating, Jackson survived a heavy landing and was captured. The plane crashed to earth, killing the pilot and rear gunner. The remaining crew members joined Jackson as prisoners of war. His attempt to save the crew, knowing that he could not return to the cabin, was described by *The London Gazette* as 'an act of outstanding gallantry'. Flight Sergeant Jackson was awarded the Victoria Cross for valour.

While such instances of individual gallantry were rare, the more standard routines followed by the flight engineer in an emergency were those listed in the official manual. The most common of these was 'feathering', used when an engine had failed or, as often happened when a plane was under attack, burst into flame. First fuel to the engine was shut off, then the propellers were feathered—that is, their pitch was reduced so they were parallel to the airflow, thus reducing drag. This had a two-pronged effect, cutting off fuel from the fire and making the aircraft easier to fly.

For 20-year-old Peter Mallon, whose technical experience before joining the RAF had been four years as an apprentice joiner, earning his wings as a flight engineer was a giant leap, but one he achieved with relative ease. His time in reserve lasted six months. He was called up on 30 July 1942 and sent to No. 9 Recruit Centre in Blackpool, Lancashire, a week later. At the Centre, headquartered at the Brighton Hydro Hotel on Blackpool's south shore, recruits were kitted out and received inoculations. They were then billeted in surrounding boarding houses and private homes, and underwent basic training, including marching up and down the Esplanade and exercising on the beach. After six weeks of training, Peter was posted to No. 3 School of Technical Training (S of TT), also at Blackpool, housed near Stanley Park aerodrome in a factory where Wellington bombers were assembled. Each morning, recruits would be collected from their billets and transported to the school in double-decker buses. Lessons were held in classrooms, with the recruits sitting at long tables on one of which someone had inscribed, 'Abandon Hope All Ye Who Enter Here'. After morning lessons, the recruits would be taken back to their lodgings for lunch and returned for afternoon lectures before climbing back on the buses around 5 p.m.

Although there was no camp, Blackpool was very much a military town throughout the war, with the recruitment centre, technical school and parachute-training centre bringing thousands of young servicemen and -women into the area. They would visit the public baths once a week and, although many of the regular holiday attractions were closed down for the duration, there was still plenty of entertainment for them, including dances, concerts and sports.

Peter spent nine months in Blackpool, attending classes, viewing instructional films, working on engines and recording his progress daily in a hard-covered log book. At the end of his time at No. 3 S of TT, he was fully adept at stripping down and reassembling a Rolls-Royce Merlin engine and well versed in the purpose and usage of every button, gauge and dial on a Lancaster control panel. The only problem was that he had yet to even leave the ground in an aircraft. This was not altogether rare. By mid-1943, with Bomber Command nearing peak activity in its nightly war against German cities, there were precious few aircraft available for training purposes and it was becoming common for flight engineers to qualify for their flying badges without ever having flown. In fact, during his initial training, the closest Peter got to a Lancaster was when he spent a week seeing how they were made.

On 9 June 1943, he was posted to No. 4 School of Technical Training at RAF St Athan, near Cardiff. At one stage in the war the largest RAF base in the UK, St Athan became the main training centre for Bomber Command flight engineers in June 1942. The course included a one-week familiarisation at the Lancaster assembly plant in Woodford, near Manchester, which Peter completed before returning to Wales and joining the No. 1 Air Gunnery School at Pembrey for another three months' training. On 17 September 1943, he graduated as a flight engineer and, promoted to temporary sergeant, was posted to 1656 Heavy Conversion Unit at RAF Lindholme.

By the time Peter arrived in North Yorkshire two days later, Dave Baxter and the rest of his crew had been at the base for over a week. Together for about a month, they were already getting to know each other well and develop into a close-knit team. As they prepared to acquaint themselves with the Lancaster, all they needed was a flight engineer to complete the crew. As a fellow Ayrshire lad only one year his senior, it was inevitable that Jock Dunlop would be drawn to the newly arrived Flight Sergeant Mallon, and just as natural that he should introduce him to Dave and the others. Dave was impressed and asked Peter to join the crew. The last piece in the puzzle was in place. On 11 November 1943, the seven men—five Australians, two Scots—left for 625 Squadron RAF, and their fates, together.

9

REAPING THE WHIRLWIND

The new crewmates were about to become participants in the most concentrated part of what would become known as the Battle of Berlin, a period of sustained bombardment that Commander-in-chief of Bomber Command Arthur Harris was certain would bring an end to the war. In May 1942, after the RAF's bombing operations on German cities had begun, Harris had said in a newsreel address: 'The Nazis entered this war under the rather childish delusion that they were going to bomb everyone else, and nobody was going to bomb them. At Rotterdam, London, Warsaw and half a hundred other places, they put their rather naïve theory into operation. They sowed the wind, and now they are going to reap the whirlwind.'

The first targets were cities such as Cologne, Dortmund, Essen and Düsseldorf, but after eighteen months of concentrated bombing with little military result, Harris decided to up the ante and strike at the very heart of the enemy. In November 1943, he wrote to Churchill, 'We can wreck Berlin from end to end if the U.S.A.A.F. will come in on it. It will cost us between 400 and 500 aircraft. It will cost Germany the war.' The Americans did not 'come in on it', believing the casualties would be too high, but Harris would not be deterred from his plan. A month later he advised Air Chief Marshal Sir Charles Portal, the RAF Chief of the Air Staff, 'It appears that the Lancaster force alone should be sufficient, but only just sufficient, to produce in Germany by April 1st, 1944, a state of devastation in which surrender is inevitable.'

Harris's objective for the Battle of Berlin was clear and obvious—level the city from the air, destroy public morale and force Germany into surrender. Easily said, not so easily done. The air war was a technological game of chess, each side developing new tactics for attack and defence; each advance in technique and technology giving its innovator the upper hand until it could be countered and the situation reversed. Bomber Command's assault on Germany began with daylight raids on specific military targets. This proved unsuccessful for two reasons: the inaccuracy of the bombers, and the quality of the three-pronged German defences of radar, anti-aircraft guns and fighters. In late 1939, Bomber Command changed to night-time bombing on moonless nights. Even so, the percentage of direct hits remained low, forcing Harris to change his strategy. In 1942, Bomber Command moved away from military-only targets to 'area bombing', in which the built-up areas of entire cities would be attacked by huge numbers of bombers.

Night bombing created its own problems, mainly the difficulty for navigators and bomb aimers in finding the target areas. This led to the introduction of the Pathfinders: Mosquito, and then Lancaster, units that flew at the head of the main force and dropped colourfully lit target indicators— TIs—which the following pilots and bomb aimers could use as reference points, and flares and incendiary bombs, which illuminated the area to enable visual identification from the air. To help the Pathfinders find their way to the target zone, usually under heavy attack over unfamiliar surroundings in pitch darkness, the RAF developed two radar systems. The first, code-named Oboe, sent signals from bases in England to a small number of aircraft, guiding them to the destination. Fitted to Mosquitos, Oboe was accurate but had a short range that made it unsuitable when Bomber Command began concentrating on Berlin. The next system developed by RAF boffins was called H2S and worked by bouncing sound waves off the ground's topographical features. It was initially fitted to Lancaster Pathfinders.

Finding the target was one thing. Staying in the air long enough to drop bombs on it was another. The Germans occupied enough of Europe to build a highly effective chain of spotlight and anti-aircraft 'flak' emplacements that spread from Paris to Denmark. More deadly for the Allies was the combination of radar and night fighters. The first system employed by the Germans was to take a map and divide their occupied territories and the sky above them into cubes. Each 'box' would be patrolled by a small number of night fighters fitted with on-board radar units that picked up signals from specific beacons. The beacons in turn would be activated by radar emplacements set up along the coast or even on ships. In the early stages of the war, when the RAF sent small numbers of aircraft to bomb individual targets, the German radar operators would pick out a bomber as it entered a patrolled box and direct the fighter to it, at which point the pilot could use his own on-board radar to stalk his quarry. The RAF countered this measure in two ways: by concentrating their attacks—sending huge numbers of bombers out together in the so-called 'thousand-bomber raids'—and by using 'window'. Window was remarkably simple and incredibly effective. Thin metal strips similar to tin foil were dropped from bombers and floated slowly to earth, spreading over a wide area and disrupting the German radar. The strips would give the impression of thousands of aircraft in flight and, caught in the wind currents, would drift in a different direction to the path of the bombers. Confused radar operators would then pull night fighters away from the main targets.

The German solution was to scrap the box system and introduce a tactic known as *Wilde Sau*—Wild Boar—in which night fighters would be concentrated over the main target area in large numbers and simply pick out and attack RAF aircraft illuminated by the glow of the burning city below. This brought its own problems. The night-fighter pilots preferred a more structured approach than that provided by the new system: a furious melée of aircraft shooting at each other in the darkness while flak batteries continued firing into the night sky. A combination of improved radar, the Bomber Command practice of sending huge numbers of bombers to targets in one 'stream', and the slanted-cannon *Schräge Musik* tactic turned the odds back in the Germans' favour. *Wilde Sau* was replaced with *Zahme Sau*—Tame Boar—under which the night-fighter pilots would be brought to the stream by radar installations and then, using their on-board radar, single out a target and fly behind it. Coming from behind and below, in the rear gunner's blind spot, the German slanted cannons would shoot upwards, often with destructive effect. Although Berlin was protected by unequalled radar, spotlight and flak defences, it was estimated that by war's end 70 per cent of Bomber Command losses were due to the night fighters.

Not that the enemy guns and night fighters were the only dangers facing the Allied airmen. Even if they were hit in the air but managed to crash-land or parachute to the ground in one piece, they were at great risk from the local civilians. While Air Command continued to promote the tactical advantages of area bombing, there was no denying it caused widespread damage to residential areas and major loss of civilian lives. To the German population, the Bomber Command airmen became known as *Terrorflieger*, or Terror Flyers, and it became common practice for civilians to execute them upon capture. There were reports that Adolf Hitler had actually made a specific order in early 1944 that any downed Terror Flyers should be shot on sight, but this was later denied by Luftwaffe Commander-in-Chief Hermann Göring, who said Hitler had simply voiced an opinion, not made a decree.

Asked at his 1946 trial for war crimes whether he had

issued an order to shoot the so-called Terror Flyers in accordance with Hitler's decree, Göring testified:

> The concept 'terror flyers' was very confused. A part of the population and also of the press, called everything which attacked cities 'terror flyers', more or less. Tremendous excitement had arisen among the German population because of the very heavy and continued attacks on German cities, in the course of which the population saw in part that the really important industrial targets were less frequently hit than houses and non-military targets. Some German cities had thus already been hit most severely in their residential districts, even though the industry in these cities remained on the whole untouched.
>
> Then with the further flights of enemy forces to Germany there came so-called low-flying aircraft which attacked both military and non-military targets. Reports came repeatedly to the Führer, and I too heard of these reports, that the civilian population was being attacked with machine guns and cannons, that single vehicles which could be recognised as civilian vehicles, and also ambulances which were marked with a red cross, had been attacked. One report came in—I remember it distinctly because the Führer became especially excited about it— said that a group of children had been shot at. Men and women who stood in line in front of stores had also been shot at. And these activities were now called those of terror flyers.
>
> The Führer was extremely excited. The populace, in its excitement, resorted, at first, to lynching, and we

tried at first to take measures against this. I heard then that instructions had been given through the police and [Hitler's deputy Martin] Bormann not to take measures against this. These reports multiplied, and the Führer then decreed that these terror flyers should be shot—or rather he made such a statement on the spot.

Little wonder, then, that pilots in trouble would do their best to get their aircraft outside German borders before ditching or ordering the crew to bail out.

To Harris, such issues were little more than a distraction. He would not be diverted from his belief that the only way to achieve peace was through sending more and more Lancasters over Germany. As he said in his 1942 newsreel address: 'There are a lot of people who say that bombing cannot win a war. Well, my answer to that is that it has never been tried yet, and we shall see.'

10

TAKING FLIGHT

When Dave Baxter and his crew arrived at RAF Kelstern in Lincolnshire on 11 November 1943 to begin operations with 625 Squadron RAF, they were about as green as could be—but so was the squadron itself. Formed just over a month earlier, 625 Squadron had flown its first mission on 18 October, with nine Lancasters taking part in a raid on Hanover. The unit's origins, however, were in a squadron that had already seen meritorious action and suffered horrendous losses on the other side of the world. The core of the new 625 Squadron came from the C flight of RAF 100 Squadron, which had been formed in 1917 as the then Royal Flying Corps' first-ever special-ised night-bombing unit. At the outbreak of World War II, 100 Squadron was based in Singapore, equipped with ageing

Vickers Vildebeest torpedo bombers. Despite assurances that their obsolete aircraft would be replaced by Australian-built Bristol Beauforts, then the fastest medium-sized bombers in the world, the upgrade never took place.

When the Japanese entered the war in December 1941 and began their advance southwards, 100 Squadron fought a brave but ultimately futile rearguard action during the Malayan Campaign against a far better equipped enemy. Hopelessly outnumbered and under-supplied, throughout January 1942 the squadron lost nearly all its Vildebeests, and those pilots and crew who were not killed in dogfights with Japanese Zero fighters or shot down by naval gunners were captured and subjected to horrific deprivation as prisoners of war. Although its major force had been all but wiped out in Malaya, some of 100 Squadron's personnel had earlier been posted back to Australia. They formed the basis of the RAAF's 100 Squadron, and on 15 December 1942 the RAF re-formed the squadron proper at RAF Grimsby, in Lincolnshire.

Within twelve months, 100 Squadron—now equipped with Lancasters—had completed the second largest number of successful operations by a unit of No. 1 Group of Bomber Command, and with the lowest rate of aircraft lost. With such a pedigree, it is little wonder that 625 Squadron was soon to build a strong reputation of its own. Equipped with Lancaster I and III aircraft—the main difference being the Lancaster III had larger Merlin engines and fuel-injection rather than suction carburettors—the squadron would fly 3385 sorties over 191 targets during the war, with the loss of 66 aircraft.

Dave and the crew arrived at RAF Kelstern during a time of great activity in Bomber Command, and their superiors wasted no time in getting them into the air. Dave's RAAF Flying Log notes that on the night of their arrival they were in a Lancaster III flying to Scotland and back, reaching a height of 20,000 feet. They would make six more flights over the next week, going to Wales and over the cities of Manchester, Leeds and Stratford-upon-Avon as they practised bombing drills and flying with fighter escorts. On the morning of 18 November, Dave was given a new destination for that night's flight: Berlin.

In the history of World War II, that date is significant. Some historians consider it a turning point. Berliners remember it as the start of a nightmare. The eighteenth of November 1943 is recognised as the start of the Battle of Berlin, Bomber Command's unrelenting bombardment of the city, which continued until 31 March 1944. In that time Bomber Command would lose nearly 500 aircraft, with 2690 crewmen killed in action and nearly 1000 taken prisoner.

Like all Bomber Command pilots, Dave would be given his first taste of operational flying as an observer, or Second Dickey, alongside a more experienced officer. In Dave's case, he was in good hands. Piloting Lancaster III ZW5009 that night was Flight Lieutenant John Clifford Day, one of the most experienced pilots at Kelstern. Five months earlier, while on a mission over Turin, Italy, one of his engines had failed but he managed to bring his crew back to base safely after a twelve-hour flight. He received the Distinguished Flying Cross in February 1944.

Dave would not have his own crew with him for his first flight over enemy territory. Day commanded his regular crew, with Dave standing behind him in the cockpit, observing. The Lancaster was loaded with one 4000-pound high-capacity bomb, fourteen Small Bomb Containers (SBCs), each holding 236 four-pound incendiary bomblets, and four SBCs, each containing 24 30-pound incendiary bombs. It is impossible to imagine the combination of excitement, fear, trepidation and exhilaration that Dave would have felt as Day opened up the throttle and brought the flying control towards his chest and the aircraft lifted off the runway to join 439 other Lancasters and four Mosquito Pathfinders en route to Germany. It proved to be an anticlimax. With the Lancaster unpressurised, crews relied on oxygen masks above 8000 feet. The note beside 18 November in Dave's Flying Log says simply: 'Berlin. DNCO (Did Not Complete Operation). Oxygen trouble.'

Four nights later, they tried again in the same aircraft, with the same bomb load and the same target but a different crew. This time, Day had only his regular navigator and rear gunner on the operation. The rest of the crew comprised Dave Baxter as second pilot, Tony D'Arcey as bomb aimer, Peter Mallon as flight engineer, Ron Ferguson as wireless operator and Jock Dunlop as mid-upper gunner.

This was the second raid of the Battle of Berlin, and it proved more successful for both the crew of Lancaster ZW5009 and Bomber Command. The night of 18 November had been cloudy. Visibility was poor, and damage to the city not extensive. Conditions for the operation of 22 November were predicted to be close to perfect. The skies of England were dull but clear, while over much of the route across Holland and western Germany to Berlin there was low cloud and fog, minimising the effectiveness of Luftwaffe night fighters. Cloud over Berlin itself was expected to be lighter and broken up, making it possible for the pilots and bomb aimers to see the Target Indicators dropped by the Pathfinders.

With all those factors in the bombers' favour, the 22 November raid was the most effective on Berlin of the entire war, with major damage inflicted on residential areas to the west of the city centre, such as Tiergarten, Charlottenburg, Schöneberg and Spandau.

The fact that an operation resulting in major loss of civilian life and residential property could be classed as 'successful' is a sobering reflection of the attitudes of the times. In his 1982 study *Die Luftangriffe auf Berlin: Ein dokumentarischer Bericht* (*The Air Raids on Berlin: A documentary report*), the German author and historian Laurenz Demps estimates that during the Battle of Berlin 7480 civilians were killed, 2194 left missing, 17,092 injured and 817,730 made homeless.

The carnage was repeated in other German cities. In the most notorious Bomber Command operations of the war, the bombing of Dresden, in which 722 RAF and 527 USAAF bombers conducted four raids between 13 and 15 February 1945, a firestorm destroyed the city and an estimated 22,700 to 25,000 people were killed.

While the civilian deaths caused by Bomber Command would create collective guilt and controversy after the war, at the time they were seen by most as a legitimate, if unfortunate, tactic. To some, the Battle of Berlin was merely a form of payback. Thousands of British people had endured similar aerial bombardment three years earlier when the Luftwaffe was given the task of destroying infrastructure and public morale in advance of a planned German invasion. From September 1940 until May 1941, when the success of RAF fighters in the Battle of Britain saw Hitler shelve plans to invade England and concentrate his efforts on the Soviet Union, cities across Britain were targeted by enemy bombers. Ports such as Liverpool, Bristol, Portsmouth, Plymouth, Southampton, Hull, Cardiff and Swansea were hit, as were the industrial cities of Coventry, Birmingham, Manchester, Sheffield, Glasgow and Belfast, but the majority of German bombs fell on London.

From 7 September 1940, the city was bombed for 56 of the next 57 days and nights. By the time what became known as The Blitz finally ended, more than one million London homes had been damaged or destroyed and 40,000 civilians—almost half of them in London—had been killed.

Soon after the start of the Blitz, Bomber Command had begun its own raids on German cities such as Hamburg, Mannheim, Bremen and Hanover. When the concentrated bombing of British cities ended, the raids on Germany continued. On 14 July 1941, Prime Minister Winston Churchill delivered what became known as the 'Do Your Worst and We'll Do Our Best' speech to Cabinet. In it he said: 'We ask no favours of the enemy. We seek from them no compunction. On the contrary, if tonight the people of London were asked to cast their vote whether a convention should be entered into to stop the bombing of all cities, the overwhelming majority would cry, "No, we will mete out to the Germans the measure, and more than the measure, that they have meted out to us.'"

The men of Bomber Command followed their flight orders without question. Any doubts or self-recrimination would have to wait until after the war—if ever. In his 1985 book *Tales from The Bombers*, the aviation historian Chaz Bowyer quotes Flight Sergeant 'Buck' Rogers, a former RAF Lancaster bomb aimer who survived seventeen missions before being shot down over The Netherlands early in 1945 and spending the rest of the war in a prisoner-of-war camp. Asked shortly before his death in 1983 about critics of Harris and Bomber Command, Rogers answered:

> Too many of them harp on about how many German civilians, especially women and children, we killed with our bombs and set out to condemn people like Bomber Harris and other top brass for the so-called area bombing policies. These so-called experts all forget—or don't understand— that this country was engaged in a total war against Hitler and his regime. And total war meant every man, woman and even child being part of their country's war effort. We didn't start the war but we had to fight to survive. Nobody living in Britain now who is younger than 50 has had any experience of a total war, so they have no real idea of what life was like then. All the talk about morals etcetera is pure hindsight moralising. We can all be bloody experts afterwards.
>
> I, for one, will never offer any sort of apology for having bombed and killed Germans during the war. Hitler's Nazis were a cancer which had to be eliminated. Bear in mind too

that how we killed that cancer was not of our choosing on bomber squadrons. The brass worked out the strategies but we crews carried them out willingly. We were all volunteers, not conscripted thugs. So I can see no earthly reason why I or the other bomber crews should have to justify our actions to any latter-day moralists. If it hadn't been for our generation of servicemen, those moralists might now be part of Hitler's dream world.

As Flight Lieutenant Day landed his aircraft that morning, 20-year-old Dave Baxter had no time to question the morals or otherwise of what he and his crewmates had achieved on their first operation together. He was too relieved to be back on the ground safely, and exhilarated to have finally experienced the taste of aerial warfare first-hand. In his log book, alongside the underlined words 'Ops. Berlin' is the numeral '1'.

11

STRIKE AND RETURN

It would prove to be the crew's first and only operation for 625 Squadron. On 23 November they received a new posting, to 460 Squadron RAAF, one of the most renowned Australian units of the war.

Formed as part of No. 8 group at RAF Molesworth, Huntingdonshire, in November 1941, 460 Squadron was originally equipped with Wellington bombers. In January 1942, it joined No. 1 Group and moved to Breighton, Yorkshire. After being re-equipped with Lancasters, the squadron moved to its permanent home at Binbrook, Lincolnshire, in May 1943. With its squadron badge featuring a kangaroo and boomerang and the motto 'Strike and Return', 460 might have operated under the umbrella of the RAF, but its heart and soul were very much Australian. The squadron had crewmen of other nationalities, such as Peter Mallon and John Dunlop, but the majority were Australian, creating a typically laid-back, irreverent Aussie atmosphere, coupled with a reputation for enormous bravery and devotion to duty.

Laurie Woods DFC, who has written several books about his time with 460 Squadron and recorded much of its operational history on his meticulously maintained website, has collected a storehouse of tall tales and legends about the antics of the 'wild colonial boys' who wore the squadron insignia with pride and distinction. One concerns a time when the squadron was still based at Breighton, before the move to Binbrook. While the local inhabitants enjoyed having the Aussies around, they were becoming tired of their regular practice of 'borrowing' bicycles to ride back to base after a night out at the two nearby pubs, the Black Swan—known to the Australians as the Dirty Duck—and the Seven Sisters, which they christened the Fourteen Titties. The bicycles were always left at the gates of the base so the locals could easily retrieve them the next morning, but even so the local constabulary were alerted and two policemen rode out to discuss the matter with 460 Squadron's then commanding officer, Wing Commander Chad Martin. After a long and civil conversation in which a compromise was reached—all squadron bicycles would be painted white so that any airman seen on a differently coloured vehicle was obviously breaking the law—the policemen left the office, only to find their own bikes had been pinched.

According to Laurie Woods, who flew 35 missions with 460 Squadron, the parties held around the Binbrook base are still spoken about by those who lived there during the war. He recalls one after-party prank in which 'one of the crew was sleeping off a heavy night in the mess when it was decided to give him a surprise. His bed was carried gently out of the house the crew shared—the sleeping airman blissfully unaware of what was happening—and left at the end of the runway where Lancasters were thundering over every few minutes. He only woke up when it started to rain.'

But while some of its members might let their hair down on rare occasions, 460 Squadron would earn a reputation as one of the most committed and daring of all Bomber Command squadrons, flying 6262 sorties—more than any other Australian bomber squadron—and dropping 24,856 tons of bombs, more than any other squadron in Bomber Command. For those records it paid a terrible price, with 1018 men killed in combat, 586 of whom were Australian—the greatest loss of life in any RAAF squadron during the war.

With such an attrition rate, it was hardly surprising that morale in the squadron was not always high. There was a feeling that 460 Squadron, along with other Australian units, was being stretched to the limit while much needed reinforcements, often from Australia, were sent to bolster RAF units. Australian ground crew at Binbrook were also upset at the length of time they were required to serve overseas: the Australian War Cabinet's quota of only 50 repatriations a month meant it could take over three years to get home. Both concerns were raised directly with Australian Prime Minister John Curtin during a visit to the base in May 1944, with satisfactory results.

The fact that 460 Squadron could continue to function at such a high level of efficiency, despite the immense pressure under which the men operated, can be attributed in no small measure to the character, personality and empathy of Binbrook's remarkable station commander, Group Captain Hughie Edwards VC. Later to become governor of Western Australia, Sir Hughie Idwal Edwards was born on 1 August 1914 at Fremantle. He enlisted in the permanent army in March 1934 and served with an artillery unit for just over a year until he was accepted as a cadet in the RAAF. Tall and well built, he was a top-grade Australian Football player and cricketer, and a natural leader. After completing his flight training, in August 1936 he was one of seven new RAAF pilots chosen to go to the UK under secondment to the RAF. In May 1938 he was at the controls of a Blenheim bomber when it iced up in cloud and went into an uncontrollable spin. After getting his crew safely out of the aircraft, Edwards followed, but his parachute caught on the radio aerial and he was pulled with the aircraft to the ground. Critically injured, he spent the next two years in and out of hospital and recuperating. He would walk with a distinct limp for the rest of his life. After badgering medical authorities, he convinced his superiors to allow him back into active service and in February 1941 was again flying Blenheims. Five months later, he earned the Distinguished Flying Cross for his actions during an attack on an enemy merchant convoy off the Dutch coast.

Less than a month after that, Edwards led twelve Blenheims in a daylight raid on the German city of Bremen from which he returned with a wounded gunner, a shot-up radio and a large part of the port wing missing. It was for this action that he was awarded the Victoria Cross. The citation read:

Wing Commander Edwards, although handicapped by a physical disability resulting from a flying accident, has repeatedly displayed gallantry of the highest order in pressing home bombing attacks from very low heights against strongly defended objectives. On 4th July, 1941, he led an important attack on the Port of Bremen, one of the most heavily defended towns in Germany. This attack had to be made in daylight and there were no clouds to afford concealment. During the approach to the German coast several enemy ships were sighted and Wing Commander Edwards knew that his aircraft would be reported and that the defences would be in a state of readiness. Undaunted by this misfortune he brought his formation 50 miles overland to the target, flying at a height of little more than 50 feet, passing under high-tension cables, carrying away telegraph wires and finally passing through a formidable balloon barrage. On reaching Bremen he was met with a hail of fire, all his aircraft being hit and four of them being destroyed. Nevertheless he made a most successful attack, and then with the greatest skill and coolness withdrew the surviving aircraft without further loss. Throughout the execution of this operation which he had planned personally with full knowledge of the risks entailed, Wing Commander Edwards displayed the highest possible standard of gallantry and determination.

In February 1943, by which time he had also been awarded the Distinguished Service Order for his part in a Mosquito raid on the Philips factory at Eindhoven in the Netherlands, acting Group Captain Edwards arrived at Binbrook. By then an almost legendary figure to the men he had commanded, Edwards soon set about earning similar respect from 460 Squadron and others based at Binbrook. The squadron's Warrant Officer, Ken Baker, went so far as to say the men regarded Edwards as 'a god'. There was nothing they wouldn't do for him. Soon after the Australians left Binbrook at the end of the war, a journalist from the local *Wickenby Register* newspaper wrote a poignant report of walking through the now eerily vacant airbase, 'deserted and empty except for an enormous amount of junk left behind by No. 460 Squadron: bikes by the dozen, old cars on every corner. Dustbins full of uniforms and silent radios on every shelf and window ledge.' Behind the mess, the reporter found a well-constructed bar. 'In pride of place in the corner stood a splendid oak chair into the back of which was carved the name of Group Captain Hughie Edwards, VC.'

Edwards was supported by a good team, notably the base commander, Air Commodore Arthur Wray, who, like Edwards, walked with a limp courtesy of a crash and used a cane. Also like Edwards, Wray led by example, often flying with new crews on their first missions and being awarded the Distinguished Flying Order for his actions during a 460 Squadron raid over Hamburg. Directly under Edwards' command came the squadron's commanding officers, seven in all, beginning in February 1943 with Wing Commander Chad

Martin, the first graduate of the Empire Air Training Scheme to command a heavy bomber unit, and ending with Wing Commander 'Mick' Cowan at the end of the war. When Dave and his crew joined 460 Squadron, the officer commanding was Wing Commander Frank Arthur, who was replaced four months later by Wing Commander Horton 'Spike' Marsh, who took over the squadron at the age of 23.

All were excellent leaders and courageous pilots, and all received the Distinguished Flying Cross. Yet perhaps the most important member of Edwards' immediate command was a man who never once sat behind the controls of an aircraft, picked up a spanner or loaded a bomb. Sergeant Perc Rodda, a 25-year-old accountant, had been rejected from air-crew training because of colour blindness, so he enlisted as a paymaster. But his contribution to 460 Squadron was far greater than making sure the men received their monthly wages. The first time they met, Hughie Edwards realised that Rodda was a masterful organiser and recruited him to be his right-hand man in raising the morale of the base. It was Rodda who took the men's grievances directly to Prime Minister Curtin during his 1944 visit. Just as importantly, he organised a base cricket team that played in the local competition—with Edwards hobbling in to bowl his off-spin and always fielding at first slip to avoid chasing the ball. He also arranged dances with local girls and WAAFs, and acted as a surrogate father, relationship counsellor and confessor in matters of the heart. As Edwards remarked to Rodda soon after he arrived at Binbrook, while the station commander knew everything there was to know about flying and very little about administration, the new paymaster was exactly the opposite. Together they made an outstanding team.

It was this environment of camaraderie, companionship and the constant threat of death that Dave and the crew soon came to think of as routine. Attached to 460's C Flight, they were given their own rooms within the two-storey housing blocks that were located just inside the main gate of the base, not far from the separate officers' and sergeants' mess halls. When off duty, they would go with others from the base to the nearby town of Grimsby, and the local pub, The Marquis of Granby. On his website, Laurie Woods described the pub and its operator, Rene Trevor, who took over when her husband went to serve in the Middle East, as the heartbeat of the squadron.

> Grimsby and Market Rasen were places to visit but none so popular as The Marquis of Granby pub in Binbrook village. Rene Trevor ran the Marquis of Granby throughout the war. She was the licensee but found herself thrust into the role of 'mother' to hundreds of young Australian airmen. She sewed on buttons and new decorations, mended jackets and cooked meals for the young men who flew the bombers. The youngsters who flew those aircraft never forgot Rene Trevor.

Rene played the piano and led the singing. The men loved 'Cowboy Joe' and 'Goodnight Sweetheart'—and Rene's breakfast of sausage, two eggs and toast for 1 shilling 6 pence. The Marquis of Granby became a home away from home for the Australians, who made an immediate impression on

Rene's three-year-old daughter, Anne. Told a few weeks earlier that England was at war with Germany, Anne heard the alien-sounding Australian accents and ran away screaming, 'Mummy, Mummy, Germans!'

Whenever an airman finished his tour and was to be sent home, the occasion would be marked with a party at the Marquis of Granby, culminating in his being held aloft while he wrote his name on the ceiling. On one wall was written the ditty, 'If Hitler wants more babies/From his frauleins fair/ Just remember the old motto boys/Australia will be there.'

And if the boys from 460 Squadron would never forget Rene Trevor, neither would she forget them. When the pub was sold after the war and she retired to an apartment by the sea, she took with her the squadron's kangaroo and boomerang crest, which had once hung at the Marquis of Granby, and placed it above her fireplace.

But nights at the pub, cricket matches or dances could never entirely distract the men from the job they were in England to do, or from the real possibility that they might never get home alive. They would feign nonchalance, saying those who were killed in the war had 'bought it' or 'Gone for a Burton', but the odds were very much against them. 460 Squadron consisted of three 'flights' of twelve Lancasters each—at full strength a total of 200 flying personnel. With 188 aircraft destroyed and over 1000 men killed, the squadron was effectively wiped out five times during the war.

It was hardly surprising, then, that the crews grew as close as the tightest of families. As former RAF bomb aimer Stamper Metcalfe put it in the historic documentary *Battle*

Stations, 'You live and sleep and eat together. You go out together. They rely on you and you rely on them. You weren't just a crew of seven. You had the ground crew as well. They were the boys that would get that aircraft so that it would get you back. We'd do anything for them, and they'd do anything for us.'

Dave and the air crew wasted no time getting to know the ground crews at Binbrook well, and continued to hone their skills in the air. While all but Bill Martin and Cliff Hopgood had experienced the operation over Berlin with John Day in the pilot's seat, they had yet to fly in combat as a complete crew, or prove themselves to the veterans of 460 Squadron.

As it turned out, the first member of the crew to fly with the squadron was the youngest—eighteen-year-old Jock Dunlop. On 2 December, he was called in to Flight Sergeant J.R. Howell's crew for that night's operation over Berlin. Although Dave and the rest of his crew fretted like mother hens until their junior member returned to base safe and sound, in fact he was in the best of hands. Howell and his crew of Jewitt, Lukies, Moorhouse, Field, Hill and Shaw survived 26 operations together and, with four replacements, including Jock Dunlop, completed their two tours of 30 missions unscathed. They even found their way into Australian folklore as one of the crews who flew 460 Squadron's *G for George*, the country's most famous Lancaster.

A replacement used by crews whose regular aircraft was not operational, *G for George* took part in 96 sorties over enemy territory and brought home every crewman alive. In 1944, the aircraft was presented to Prime Minister John Curtin during his visit to 460 Squadron at Binbrook. It was flown back to Australia by an RAAF crew of Bomber Command veterans and then barnstormed around the country to help sell war bonds. At the end of hostilities, it was parked beside a hangar at RAAF Fairbairn in Canberra and left to decay until the early 1950s, when it was moved to the Australian War Memorial. In 1998 a project began to restore *G for George* to its wartime state, and in 2003 it returned to the War Memorial, where it is now on permanent display.

Jock Dunlop did not get to fly in *G for George*. Flight Sergeant Howell was at the controls of aircraft JA687 that night, but it proved just as reliable. Others were not so lucky. Of 458 aircraft on the operation, 40 were shot down, with the loss of 228 lives. The raid was not a success, with few targets hit, but Howell could still tell debriefers that it had been a 'satisfactory route and a good attack on a well marked target'. Dave and the others were just relieved to have Jock back in one piece.

The next night they would have their own chance to dodge the German flak and night fighters—or so they thought. In accordance with standard procedure, they were informed around 10 a.m. that an operation was scheduled for that night. Pilots, navigators and bomb aimers were briefed separately in three Nissen huts. They would then pass on relevant information to the rest of the crew. There would be a late meal, and the navigators would make up their maps while the others checked and loaded ammunition and guns before dressing in their heavy flying outfits and catching a lift in a truck to the aircraft.

The target was Leipzig. Dave climbed into the pilot's seat and, with his full crew in place for the first time, he taxied down the runway, gained speed, pulled back the controls and lifted the aircraft into the air. Within minutes, the port outer engine cut out. Peter tried to restart it, but it would not fire up. Dave had no alternative but to abort the mission and return to land.

It is impossible to imagine what thoughts passed through Dave's mind as he went through the pre-take-off check list and taxied across the field at Binbrook in preparation for take-off that afternoon. He never spoke of his feelings with the rest of the crew or with family or friends, but another pilot who flew with 460 Squadron put down on paper thoughts that might have been shared by any pilot in Bomber Command.

Bill Brill was a former Riverina farmer. Ending the war as a wing commander, Brill flew 58 operations, including the first ever carried out by 460 Squadron, in March 1942. He was Second Pilot in a Wellington that night, but was soon leading his own crew and earning a reputation as a laconic but fearless pilot. Even so, after completing his first tour unscathed, he wrote of the anxiety he had experienced in the hours before piloting his first operation. 'I wandered around with a feeling of having a half pound of lead in the pit of my stomach,' he recalled. 'Perhaps it was fear. How could I get back from this when others who are better than I'll ever be, have fallen on such targets? Will I funk if I'm in a tight spot? Will I let the rest of the boys down? Who am I to hold the lives of five other men in my hands?'

12

DESTINATION BERLIN

Dave and the crew were left stewing over the disappointment of the aborted Leipzig operation for four days. They had watched from the sidelines as other crews returned safely to Binbrook and headed to the mess relieved and happy at their good fortune. By now, all but Cliff Hopgood and Bill Martin had seen combat—Jock had been over Berlin twice—but Dave had yet to pilot an operation, and they had never been in action together as a crew. Until that happened, they couldn't feel part of the squadron or, for that matter, part of the war.

That was about to change.

Their long-awaited baptism of fire began with a quick look at the battle orders in the mess as they trooped in for breakfast on the morning of 22 December. Seeing their names listed for that evening's operation, they tried to feign noncha-lance, then spent the rest of the morning in a state of nervous excitement. Surely this time they would have success, but how would they react to what would be thrown at them over Europe? Would they be able to put their training into practice in the heat of battle? Would they let their mates down? Would they survive?

Tony, Bill and Jock went straight from breakfast to the armoury, where they cleaned, checked and rechecked their guns before catching a ride with a WAAF driver out to the plane. The rest of the crew were already there. Dave was walking around the outside of the aircraft doing his checks as ground-crew finished their final inspection. Peter was inside the cockpit checking his switches, having already sat in as the ground crew sergeant fired up the engines. Ron checked his Morse-code set as Tony, Bill and Jock climbed aboard, put their guns in place and loaded the ammunition belts. After Tony had checked his bombsight and the bomb load had arrived—one 4000-pound, two 30-pound bombs and eleven containers each holding 236 four-pound incendiary bomblets—they rode back to the Flight Centre together. For the next few hours they tried to stay occupied and calm.

At 2.30 p.m., it was time for the first briefing, attended by pilots, navigators and bomb aimers. It was here that they would learn the night's destination. As new boys, Dave, Cliff and Tony found a table towards the front of the room. Just like at school or on the rugby-team bus, the experienced crews sat at the back with a confident, almost disinterested air. At the front of the hut was a raised platform and, on the wall behind it, two large maps covered by curtains and guarded by an MP. All talking stopped when the navigation and bombing leaders walked up to the dais with maps and notes under their arms. They were followed by Group Captain Hughie Edwards and Wing Commander Frank Arthur. The crews stood until Edwards told them to sit. There was a roll call of pilots, who confirmed that their crews were complete, fit and ready for action.

By now any disinterest, feigned or otherwise, was gone. The crews were all business, totally focused on what lay behind the curtains at the front of the room. At a signal, the MP left and the curtains were lifted.

'Your target tonight,' said Arthur, 'is Berlin.'

There were murmurs, whispered asides between crewmates, and a few whistles.

Using a pointer, Arthur indicated the route, which was marked out on the map with lengths of dark twine. Part of a force of 390 aircraft, made up of 375 Lancaster and seven Halifax bombers and eight Mosquito fighter-bombers, they would head south-east across the Channel, then roughly follow the Netherlands–Belgian border into Germany. They would then fly due east before heading north, close to Leipzig, where a separate force of nine Mosquitos would peel off and carry out a diversionary raid to confuse the German defences. The main force would continue to Berlin, then return directly across Germany and the Netherlands to England.

The flying control officer announced the line-up procedure, start times and runway in use. After receiving more logistical information, the pilots and bomb aimers went to another hut to learn the bomb load, weight distribution, fuse types, and the panel switches to select. The importance of staying over the target long enough to bomb effectively and then take accurate photographs was stressed, and any questions were answered. While this was happening, the navigators stayed in the main briefing room to rule up the route on their maps and mark in known areas of searchlights, flak placements and night-fighter zones. The pilots and bomb aimers then returned, and the pilots marked up their small-scale Captains of Aircraft maps, to be used in an emergency if the navigator was incapacitated.

It was then time for the doors to be opened to the engineers and gunners. As with every other crew, Peter, Bill and Jock went straight up to their mates and asked the question that had been torturing them all day.

'Where are we going?'

When they heard the news, they felt a combination of excitement and trepidation. It didn't get any bigger than this.

Before the start of the Battle of Berlin, rookie Bomber Command crews might be fortunate enough to be blooded on softer targets, such as shipping lanes or leaflet drops. The chances of mishap on these flights were also high: aircraft could still collide or malfunction, and flak and fighters were lethal no matter where they operated. But nowhere was better defended or more terrifying than 'the Big City', as the men called Berlin.

As Flight Lieutenant R.B. Leigh, a bomb aimer with 156 Squadron RAF, told author Martin Middlebrook in an interview for *The Berlin Raids*: 'Lying in the nose of a Lancaster on a visual bomb run over Berlin was probably the most frightening experience of my lifetime. Approaching the target the city appeared to be surrounded by searchlights and the flak was always intense. The run-up seemed endless, the minutes of flying "straight and level" seemed like hours and every second I expected to be blown to pieces. I sweated with fear, and the perspiration seemed to freeze on my body.'

Half an hour after the briefing, the men sat down for a meal of bacon and eggs, a treat not available to many in war-rationed England. Even so, as they tried to look as calm and professional as the more experienced airmen seated around them, all shared the same thought: 'Is this the last meal I'll ever eat?'

The answer wasn't long in coming. The operation was scheduled to begin at 5 p.m., but with poor weather threatening to get even worse at bases around the country, it was postponed by seven hours. The frustrated crews headed back to their quarters or played cards or snooker until a late dinner.

Following a final briefing at 10 p.m., during which they were given the latest weather forecasts and the wireless operators were handed their codes—printed on rice paper so they could be swallowed if the men were captured—they went to the locker room to get into their flying gear. For those in the main part of the aircraft, including Tony, who would descend into the nose only when required, this was a relatively simple affair: long underwear, a flying suit and a sheepskin Irvin jacket put on over their uniform. For the two gunners whose positions were not heated, it was a case of pulling on every piece of warm clothing they could get their hands on.

As RAF gunner Greg Gregson recalled in his memoirs: 'If I could get a pair of silk stockings I'd wear those. Then woollen socks and then flying boots, which were fur-lined, then an inner jacket with a canvas coating, then a leather jacket with fur, three pairs of gloves—a silk pair, wool and then leather gauntlets.'

Even weighed down with all those extra layers and possibly a notoriously unreliable heated suit, the gunners would be subjected to hours of freezing temperatures, with little respite.

'You had to sit there and try to think warm,' said Gregson. Usually that wasn't enough, especially for the rear gunners. On particularly cold trips it was not unusual for their oxygen mask to freeze against their faces and tear the skin as it was removed.

When Bill and Jock were finally dressed, the seven crew-mates milled outside the building along with the other crews, waiting for transport out to the aircraft. When their turn came, they climbed into the back of a small lorry driven by a WAAF. Unable to use their lights, the trucks were directed by blinking torches held by ground crew. Once back at the aircraft, the crew climbed aboard and took their places, Dave and Peter going through their pre-flight routine and intercom check, the others settling into their positions and concentrating on their jobs. Cliff pulled the blackout curtain across behind him, turned on the lamp and laid his maps out on the desk. Behind him, Ron began coded communication with flight command as the two gunners squeezed into their cramped, uncomfortable posts and prepared for a long, cold night.

It was close to midnight when Dave finally warmed up the engines and taxied to the runway. When he got the green light, he gave the crew a 'Ready for take-off. All crew strapped in.

Here we go' over the intercom and opened the throttles against the brakes to check that the engines were responding evenly. He then throttled back, released the brakes and opened the throttles gently, reaching a speed of over 150 kilometres per hour before easing Lancaster JA687 off the ground and into the ominous black sky.

From the moment they headed to the runway until the moment they touched down back at RAF Binbrook, the men were at great risk. The most obvious threats were the Luftwaffe night fighters and flak. The German ack-ack (anti-aircraft) gunners' job was made easier when a bomber was caught in the beams of two or more searchlights—a potentially deadly experience known by the airmen as being 'coned'.

But enemy action wasn't the only peril facing the crew throughout the operation. Aircraft regularly collided soon after take-off—sometimes even during taxiing. As the operation proceeded, the chances of flying into another of the hundreds of bombers following the same route were multiplied. Then there was the possibility of being struck by friendly fire as bombs fell from aircraft above. Even after they had dropped their bombs, stayed level and steady long enough to take photographs, and turned for home, the crews could not relax. All the dangers they had faced on the way to the target remained just as real on the way back.

All aircraft from 460 Squadron got off well that night, but the same wasn't true elsewhere around the country. Two Lancasters from 12 Squadron RAF at Wickenby never got off the ground—they collided while taxiing, though there were no injuries. Two other crews from 550 Squadron RAF weren't as fortunate. Their aircraft collided soon after take-off from RAF Grimsby, and all on board were killed. Another 30 of the original force of 390 aircraft turned back with equipment failure, but JA687 powered on through the night.

Because the operation had started so late, the crew could see nothing but blackness as they cleared Beachy Head and crossed the Channel before heading over Belgium and then making the long run across Germany. Thanks to bad weather over the German airfields, the response of the Luftwaffe night fighters was not as strong as on some nights, but it was deadly all the same: six bombers were shot down. It was not all one-way traffic, though. In *The Berlin Raids*, Martin Middlebrook noted that six night fighters were also destroyed that night, including a Junkers JU-88C shot down by Warrant Officer Fidge, tail gunner of a 514 Squadron RAF Lancaster. The Lancaster's forward crew had seen the Junkers flying towards them and about to pass overhead and alerted Fidge, who was ready when it entered his sights. He hit the oil tank in the German's port wing. It burst into flame, and attempts by the pilot to extinguish the fire by going into a dive failed. The three-man crew bailed out and came down near Frankfurt on Oder, 80 kilometres south-west of Berlin.

As they flew further into enemy territory, Dave warned the crew to cut intercom use and be on the lookout for fighters. Bill, Jock and Tony primed their guns and tightened their grips. Peter, Tony and Bill spotted a flash in the distance on the port side as a bomber was hit, but no fighters came near them. Luck, one of the main elements of Bomber Command survival, was on their side.

Kiwi bomb aimer Ron Mayhill DFC, who flew 27 operations with No. 75 (NZ) Squadron, went so far as to rate it the most important element. 'Luck came in number one,' he said in the 2015 video series *Memories of Service*, made by David Blyth in conjunction with the New Zealand Returned and Services' Association. 'If a fighter came up below you, you had no chance. If the fighters picked on someone, that was just bad luck.'

On they flew, hour after hour in the darkness. When Hoppy announced that they were approaching the target, Tony set up the bombing panel, flicking the switches according to the plan they had been given at the briefing. It was vital that the bombs be dropped in a certain sequence to ensure that the aircraft remained balanced as the heavy load was released. He checked that the bombsight was functioning and tested the camera. With everything in working order, he went onto the intercom.

'Hoppy, what's your latest wind speed and direction?'

The answer given, he set the information on the bombsight and stared out through the Perspex nose cover, straining his eyes for the first glimpse of the pinprick of light that would grow to a golden glow as they flew closer: Berlin under fire.

'There it is!' he called. 'Straight ahead.'

Many people have described the sensation of flying into the maelstrom of a bombing raid in progress, but few can match the matter-of-fact yet powerful recollection of Ron Mayhill in *Memories of Service*.

It was fearsome to look at for the first time. So many searchlights, so many explosions in the sky, so many guns from the ground. All the flashes. I thought, 'How can we get through this stuff?' The German defences were very strong. We respected them. There was no hatred there. We all felt, these Luftwaffe boys are pretty good. They went through the same experiences as us. We had professional respect for what they were doing; their gunners on the ground too. Our losses were huge and theirs were too, but it was war. Total war.

Long before we got to the target we could see it. The Pathfinders had dropped flares so we had a yellow channel to fly along. We couldn't deviate. We could see all the other bombers keeping station. All keeping the same speed, at slightly different heights. You could see shapes all around you. The darting ones were Luftwaffe fighters. You could see duels, tracer from the gunners on the planes, explosions when a plane was hit. The sky was all lit up, like a kaleidoscope that was moving. It took three or four minutes to get into the target area. The searchlights below were waving. There was a forest of them. As we got closer there was the flak. The blacky-browny swirling moving ones were dangerous, full of shrapnel. The white ones were dispersing, much larger but not so dangerous. We flew through this stuff. On the ground you could see flashes of ack-ack guns and sticks of bombs landing. They were straight-line flashes. The guns were scattered all over the place. I saw planes coned, saw them wriggling and trying to get out, perhaps explode, perhaps spiral down on fire. Gradually the individual fires around the target would join together to form one huge conflagration, the smoke and dust half erasing the sight on the ground. I saw collisions, planes exploding for no reason—not sure whether hit by a fighter or bombs from above knocking it down. It was quite hectic and chaotic above the target. After we dropped the bombs we had to fly straight and level as the camera took a picture of the damage they had done, and how close to the target we had managed to get.

With the glow of the burning city getting ever closer, Hoppy called down to Tony, 'Two minutes to target, winds unchanged!'

At Tony's signal over the intercom, Dave reached down to his left and pushed the bomb door control from SHUT to OPEN. As soon as the doors opened, Tony was struck with the pungent smell of boiling, oily smoke. He looked through his bombsight, picking out the markers through the gloom.

'Right, right, steady!' he called to Dave, who responded with a subtle turn to the left of the control yoke.

'That's it, steady, steady . . . left, left, steady . . .'

Again Dave made a slight readjustment, made more difficult by the buffeting slipstream of the other bombers flying close by, all headed to the same destination.

'Right, steady . . .'

The target appeared in Tony's sight, then disappeared as the aircraft's nose lifted. Then it was back again, as Dave adjusted.

Tony hoped for the best and pressed his thumb down hard on the bomb release, known as the tit.

'Bombs going . . .'

With each release, the plane jolted up as the heavy load fell and the selector arm unwound. When the jolts ended, Tony activated the jettison bars, which cleared the bomb bay of any 'hang-ups'. He turned and double-checked by looking through the bomb-bay window behind his position.

'All gone, skipper!' he reported. 'Close bomb doors.'

They then had to endure the 20 seconds of flying straight and level along the bombing course as the camera did its work, the red tracer bullets dotting the sky and flak bursting all around them. Ahead there was a blinding yellow fireball as a bomber exploded and fell to earth. Dave banked to port and they headed for home.

Again their luck held. Three more Lancasters were shot down on the return journey in the early morning light, bringing the total destroyed on the operation to fifteen, with the loss of 104 crew. By Bomber Command standards, it was not a particularly bad night in terms of casualties. In fact, it could be considered better than average. Statistics compiled at the end of the war showed that for every 100 men serving in Bomber Command, 55 could expect to be killed, three injured, twelve taken prisoner, and two shot down before evading capture, with 27 surviving a full tour of operations. Given that 2730 men had started off on the operation and 2610 had made it back to their bases, it might have been regarded a good result, if only the raid had been more successful strategically. But the Pathfinders were unable to drop all their markers, and the majority of bomb aimers could not find the targets. Many bombs fell harmlessly in open countryside, although German authorities still reported 178 citizens killed and around 600 losing their homes. An unexpected military bonus for the RAF was that four loads of bombs were mistakenly dropped on a ball-bearing factory in the town of Erkner, causing major damage.

At the debriefing, Dave was able to report 'quite a promising attack without any difficulties', but in truth the real success of the operation was that they had completed it. They had survived, but more than that, they had done their job as a crew. They hadn't messed up or cracked under pressure. They had put their countless hours of training into practice, just as they had been instructed. They were part of the game.

Soon *The Powlett Express*, the local newspaper near Dave's home town, was reporting under the headline 'Dave Baxter Over Berlin':

Sergeant-Pilot Dave Baxter, second son of Mrs Baxter and the late Mr Baxter of North Wonthaggi, has been over Berlin. In a letter to his mother recently he said that he had been away from home for three Christmases and resolved he would be home for next Christmas if he had to swim. Congratulations are extended to this young airman for the wonderful work he is doing for the Allied cause. All his friends will wish him the best of luck and a safe return.

13

PART OF THE FAMILY

When they landed after their first operation and trooped to the Flight Centre to give their report, the crew could barely keep the smiles from their faces. As they entered the room, they came to a long table where WAAFs were serving mugs of tea.

'Would you like some rum with that?' one asked.

Even Bill nodded 'yes', and they quietly toasted the success of the mission. It had been frightening and thrilling in equal measure, and the adrenaline would flow for hours. They couldn't wait to do it again.

Bomber Command flew an operation over Berlin on 29 December, but Dave and his crew were not part of it, as they were carrying out tests on their aircraft. With no operation

'Your crew was everything . . .' Pictured at Binbrook, standing from left: Dave Baxter, Ron Ferguson, John Dunlop. In front: Tony D'Arcey. (Dunlop family collection)

'They were your life . . .' From left: Ron Ferguson, John Dunlop, Cliff Hopgood, Dave Baxter, Bill Martin. (Dunlop family collection)

Dave flies an Anson trainer in formation, with the Canadian Rockies in the background. Inscription reads, 'To Joyce with love Dave'. (Alan Baxter collection)

A last taste of peace. Dave (far right) and members of his graduating class visit Billy Rose's Diamond Horseshoe nightclub in New York before joining the war in the UK. (Alan Baxter collection)

'The camel that never knew the last straw . . .' Bomber Command chief Arthur Harris described the Lancaster as 'the greatest single factor in winning the war'. (Brian Hewitt/Alamy Stock Photo)

The Lancaster as seen through the sights of the Luftwaffe night-fighters. With no ventral guns the bomber was vulnerable to the *Schräge Musik* played by the Germans' slanted cannons. (Philip Bird/123RF)

The only photograph of the full crew in existence. Top from left: John Dunlop, Ron Ferguson, Peter Mallon, Tony D'Arcey. Bottom from left: Cliff Hopgood, Dave Baxter, Bill Martin. (Armand Casalini collection)

Villagers from Villers-sous-Prény inspect the wreckage the morning after *J for Jig* was shot down. A small girl, on left, carries flowers to place at the site.
(Armand Casalini collection)

Coffins, flowers and crosses, paid for by a public collection held in contravention of German orders, outside the home of Mayor Sophron on the morning of the funeral. (Armand Casalini collection)

'The paths were black with people . . .' Villagers from near and far cram into the church-yard to pay their respects—and defy the Germans—on 27 February, 1944. (Armand Casalini collection)

The original crosses are replaced by Commonwealth War Graves Commission head-stones, bearing inscriptions from the families. (Armand Casalini collection)

Graves dating back to 1765 are tightly packed around the church, but the plot of the four airmen sits apart in a place of honour. (D'Arcey family collection)

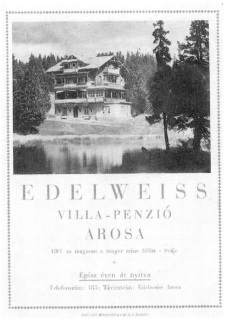

Tony's emergency certificate 'valid for the journey to the United Kingdom and residence in Switzerland'. (D'Arcey family collection)

Edelweiss Villa promotional brochure, written in Hungarian, souvenired by Dave Baxter. (Alan Baxter collection)

Australian and Canadian evaders pictured after lunch at Arosa's Hotel Beaurivage. Tony D'Arcey standing front row, third from left. (D'Arcey family collection)

Robert Hopgood at the memorial tree in St John's Wood, Brisbane after having just received his father's bag from Ron Baxter. (Photo by David Kelly)

scheduled for the night of New Year's Eve, the men of Binbrook celebrated hard. They awoke the next morning, many the worse for wear, to the news that they would be flying that night. Ironically, given that he wasn't a drinker, Bill Martin was unwell and unable to take part in the operation. His place in the mid-upper gun turret was taken by Flight Sergeant D.T. Baldwin. It was the start of a nightmarish few days.

Once again the destination was Berlin, with 421 Lancasters despatched to the main target while fifteen Mosquitos launched a diversionary raid on Hamburg in the hope of pulling away German defenders. The night fighters were not fooled. As with their last raid, Dave and the crew had to endure a tense few hours as concerns about the weather pushed the take-off time from mid-evening to midnight. The original route had been a wide arc over Denmark, but because of the late take-off, it was changed to a more direct course over the Netherlands. It was a route the night fighters knew well, and when the Lancasters flew into range they were waiting. Sixteen were shot down, including eight Pathfinders. As the remaining force neared the target, the marker aircraft were hampered by low cloud and strong winds. Another Pathfinder was shot down as it attempted to drop its markers. Again results were poor: bombs fell in open areas and the few buildings damaged were not of tactical importance. Around 80 Germans were killed by the bombing and some 1200 lost their homes. On the Allied side of the ledger, just about the only thing on target was Harris's initial estimate of losses, with 28 Lancasters shot down, 168 airmen killed and 34 taken prisoner. Back at base, Dave's only comment to the debriefers concerned the lack of markers.

The reason for his report's brevity might not have been disappointment at the performance of the Pathfinders on the operation. It was common for crews to fine-tune their reports before they prepared to land after a raid so the debrief would be quicker. The last thing they needed after up to ten hours of flying time, usually under attack, was to be unnecessarily delayed by red tape. They wanted to get in, say a few words, then have a meal, shower and sleep. That was even more the case after a big New Year's Eve celebration. But if they expected any respite that morning as they trudged wearily to their quarters through the snow, they were mistaken. Harris, disappointed with the results of the 1 January raid, scheduled another one straight away. Racked with fatigue, the men dragged themselves to the briefings and were shocked to learn they were going straight back to Berlin, along the same course that had proved so dangerous the previous night. There were grumblings and muttered expletives, but theirs was not to reason why. Snow was cleared from the runways and, with the men in poor spirits, the operation got underway at midnight.

This time the Mosquitos were back to lead the raid, twelve of them fronting a main force of 362 Lancasters and nine Halifaxes. It was hoped the Mosquitos' return would solve the problem of the markers from the previous night's raid, but their presence in that role meant they were unavailable for diversionary raids: the Germans could devote all their defences to protecting Berlin.

The mood was not improved when a Lancaster from 460 Squadron crashed on take-off with the loss of all crew. Conditions were poor as they neared the Netherlands, with thick cloud and ice. Even before they had cleared the North Sea, 60 aircraft aborted the mission and returned to base. Of these, fifteen went back because of a communications mix-up—another, unrelated operation was inadvertently using the same radio code signals as the Berlin mission. When aircraft from that operation were ordered to return to base, the pilots of the fifteen Lancasters thought they had been recalled, ditched their bombs in the sea and headed home. The other 45 aircraft turned back because of mechanical or weather-related difficulties.

The German defenders were having their own problems with the weather. Some of their airfields were closed, and the night fighters were unable to catch up with the Lancasters until they were already over Berlin. Even so, the bombers were unable to take advantage. Eight of the Pathfinders had turned back before reaching the Netherlands coast, six more were shot down as they approached the target area, and the rest could not drop their markers effectively because of cloud cover. The raid was even more disappointing than that of the previous night. The Lancasters that did make it to Berlin could not hit any significant targets. Broken up as a force by the weather and silhouetted against the low cloud by spotlights, they were easy pickings for the German fighters, which had arrived in large numbers. The German casualty reports for the night listed fewer than 80 people killed and a handful of buildings damaged. In comparison, the Allied toll was high: 28 Lancasters lost, 168 men killed and 31 captured.

Because of the poor weather, Dave's aircraft was diverted on its return flight to RAF Thornaby, in North Yorkshire, and the men did not return to Binbrook until the next day. When Dave was finally debriefed, it appeared that his crew might have been one of the few on the operation to make an impression. He reported attacking Berlin from 20,000 feet and identifying a target thanks to two groups of red and green markers. Bombs were dropped and an 'indistinct glow of fires' seen through the cloud.

Three nights later, Dave and his men were back in the air, but this time over Poland, not Germany. The target was Stettin, a river port close to the Baltic Sea and only 150 kilometres north-east of Berlin. Using large numbers of slave labourers, the area's German occupiers produced a wide range of armament parts and supplies, including silk for parachutes, synthetic oil, and light armoured vehicles. The raid of 5 January 1944—the first on Stettin since September 1941—was the start of a relentless barrage that would all but destroy the city by the end of the war.

By now Dave's crew had flown four operations together and were very much part of the 460 Squadron family. While keeping largely to themselves, as all crews did, they were accepted as a competent, trustworthy team of professionals. They had developed a routine and knew each other's strengths, weaknesses and foibles. Like every other crew, they had their own habits and superstitions. Bill never flew without his rosary beads, and Hoppy always wore the engraved watch that Margaret had given him. They were a unit now, and those around them knew it. Gaining the respect of the other crews was a very important part of squadron life. Everyone knew who they wanted flying alongside them and who could be a danger. In *The Lancaster Men*, author Peter Rees quotes an Australian airman attached to an RAF squadron. The airman recalls an operation in which another crew carelessly left their radio open while discussing details of the raid, including destination, target and bombing height. With German defenders listening in, flak was soon concentrated on the right area and altitude, leading to heavy losses. The furious surviving pilots made their feelings known in a formal complaint on their return.

To a group of young men, many still in their late teens or early 20s, the experience of being part of a squadron was not all that different to that of being on a school sports team. Now, however, the team's ranking was determined not by points scored or games played but by operations flown. In fighter squadrons, miniature swastikas were painted on the noses of Spitfires or Hurricanes to signify enemy aircraft shot down. Lancasters would often be adorned with a small bomb for each mission. Just returning from a flight over enemy territory was an achievement in itself, and those who survived the longest were afforded more respect than any sports star.

Bill Martin's fellow Christian Brothers old boy and mate from Gunnery School, Jim O'Riordan, had been posted to 550 Squadron RAF at nearby Waltham. During a spell when operations were grounded due to weather, he headed over to Binbrook to pay Bill a visit.

We went to the Sergeants' Mess and were sitting there having a chat. There were quite a few blokes around, playing table tennis or having a cuppa. Bill was pointing them out and telling me how many ops their crew had done. He was like, 'See those fellas there, they've done eight; those four blokes there have done thirteen.' That's what it was all about. You had to do 30 to get out of it, and everyone knew how many everyone else had done. You kept score, and the ones who'd done the most were something special.

At 460 Squadron, the pilot held in the highest esteem under that criterion was Flight Lieutenant Alex Wales, from Hawthorn, Victoria. Originally posted to the squadron in August 1942, Wales completed his first operational tour of 22 missions in six months, including flights over Mainz, Kassel and Bremen. Awarded the Distinguished Flying Medal, he was assigned to training and testing duties but returned to 460 Squadron for a second tour in November 1943, the same time as Dave's crew. He was appointed flight leader of C Flight— to which Dave and his crew were posted—and would go on to complete a second tour, earn the Distinguished Flying Cross and take part in sixteen operations over Berlin.

Wales's Lancaster was one of 348, along with ten Halifaxes, that bombed Stettin on the 5 January operation. So far, Dave and his crew had come through four missions unscathed, but apart from the first—flown for 625 Squadron with Flight Lieutenant John Day at the controls and without Bill and Cliff—none of them could be termed a success. In fact, all had failed to achieve any great strategic objectives but had resulted in major loss of lives and aircraft. The Stettin raid was different. For once, the operation worked as planned. A diversionary force of thirteen Mosquitos despatched to Berlin fooled the German defences and pulled the night fighters away from the main force. Able to approach the target along a relatively unused route, the Pathfinders managed to lay down markers and give the Lancasters a clear indication of where to drop their bombs.

As the Lancasters arrived back at Binbrook, the pilots were debriefed in order of landing. Alex Wales came in 34 minutes ahead of Dave and reported a copybook operation. 'Stettin was attacked at 03.52 hours, from 20,000 ft. Target identified by green and red Target Identifiers, red/green flares and visually. Bombed centre of several green T.I.'s. Built up area easily identified by green/red T.I.'s. Incendiaries outlined street and squares. Explosion at 04.06 hours. A very good raid, extremely well concentrated.'

Dave had flown over the target just one minute behind flight leader Wales and attacked from 21,000 feet. He reported 'a mass of fires all over built up area' and noted: 'raid appeared a great success'. But that success too came at a high price, with fourteen Lancasters, two of the Halifaxes and all their crews lost.

With the full moon making operations too dangerous, the crew now had a nine-day respite. It was a chance to go on bonding as a unit and become further acquainted with their surroundings. Despite their disparate ages and backgrounds, the seven men got along very well. Inevitably, they adopted nicknames, though not overly imaginative ones. Dave became Skipper, Tony was Darce, Cliff Hopgood was Hoppy, and Ron was Fergy. The oldest crew member, Bill Martin, was dubbed 'Pop', and the youngest, John Dunlop, was of course Jock. Only Peter Mallon, the last to join, kept his real name, remaining simply Pete. The men formed the closest of friendships, but none was closer than that of Fergy, the hard-working married man from the land, and Jock, the nineteen-year-old Scotsman. Hoppy, the only father in the crew, would put aside time to study and hone his skills in the hope of gaining promotion so he could send more money back to his wife and child.

The locals often opened their homes to the young men who had travelled from the other side of the world to help them fight the enemy. Tony became close to a local family and would join them for meals when he could. When on leave, he went further afield. Having struck up a friendship with an RAF pilot, Flight Lieutenant Herbert Perkins, he would stay with him and his wife Agatha at their home near Birmingham during extended breaks. The two young Scots met girls who lived and worked near the base. Pete starting seeing a lass named Nora Dobbs, while Jock became serious with Maria Sylvia Valente, known as Silvy. A shorthand typist who lived with her mother in nearby Grimsby, Silvy was eighteen, a year younger than Jock. Her late father, a confectioner, had run a small general store that her mother took over after his death. It was there, helping behind the counter, that Silvy met Jock. The two teenagers began to spend every spare moment together. As they grew closer, Silvy's mother became concerned. She tried to warn her daughter against getting too serious about the young Scot who risked his life night after night, but eventually softened and gave the couple her blessing.

On 14 January, with the weather improving, the crews were back in the air, this time headed for Brunswick, a town in central Germany that housed two Messerschmitt factories. Located 160 kilometres closer to England than Berlin but reachable along the same route, Brunswick had never been targeted before. The plan was that the main force of 496 Lancasters and two Halifax bombers would head to the Big City, but turn off to Brunswick while a smaller force of seventeen Mosquitos would continue to Berlin and Magdeburg to confuse the defences. It didn't work. The Germans' recently introduced *Zahme Sau*, or Tame Boar, system relied on ground radar combined with newly designed radar sets fitted in the night fighters. With their improved radar set-up, the Germans could detect whether the aircraft they were tracking were using the RAF H2S system. As the H2S units were in short supply, they were fitted only to Pathfinders headed to the major targets. It was therefore a simple matter of deduction to determine which aircraft were leading the main force and which were a diversion. As the Mosquitos headed on to Berlin and Magdeburg untouched, the night fighters caught up with the stream of Lancasters en route to Brunswick and wrought havoc. Thirty-eight Lancasters were shot down, eleven of them Pathfinders. With so many of the early force destroyed, the marking of the target areas was poor to non-existent. German records note ten houses destroyed and fourteen people killed. The next day, Dave was notified that he had been promoted to Warrant Officer.

With Harris unhappy at the lack of success over Brunswick, a raid was planned for Frankfurt the next night, but again the weather turned sour and the bombers were grounded for another week. It was a respite that Jock and Silvy made the most of, spending as much time as possible together, while the rest of the crew entertained themselves as best they could.

It was at this time that Jim O'Riordan paid his visit to Bill. While Bill was pleased to see him, O'Riordan could tell he was being worn down by the unimaginable physical and emotional strain:

> He'd made a friend in another crew. They'd got pretty close, which was something you probably shouldn't do, and one night this bloke didn't come back. Bill was upset by it, and on top of that he was having problems with his eyes. He told me they were going, but he wouldn't tell anyone. I told him, 'Mate, you've got to get it checked out. They might send you home.' He wouldn't do it. He said he wouldn't be able to face anyone at home knowing that he'd got out early, and he didn't want to let down the rest of the crew.

Bill might have been hoping for a rest to ease his eye trouble, but it wasn't to be. Rocked by the increased efficiency of the night fighters since the introduction of Tame Boar, Bomber Command ordered navigators to steer away from the predictable straight routes and plot much longer flights. These were deemed harder for the Germans to track, but they also meant smaller bomb loads and more fatigue for the crews.

In the late afternoon of 20 January, Dave and his men took off from Binbrook as part of a 769-aircraft force headed to Berlin. Once again, the German defences proved up to the task. The bombers were detected by a radar ship when they were still over the sea, 160 kilometres from the Dutch coast, but bad weather delayed the arrival of the night fighters until the stream was almost at the target area. Thirty-five Allied aircraft were lost—thirteen Lancasters and 22 Halifaxes—with 172 men killed, 75 taken prisoner, and ten evading capture. Given the large number of aeroplanes taking part in the raid, that toll was seen as acceptable, particularly in light of the success of the bombing. Collateral damage was severe, with 243 citizens killed and 10,000 made homeless. Five industrial buildings were destroyed, the most important being the Roland Brandt factory, which manufactured radar parts for the Luftwaffe. Another 41 industrial sites were damaged and the Lichtenberg Power Station put out of action, leaving much of the eastern part of the city without electricity and cutting the main rail line to Hamburg. Dave was happy with the route and, though he found it hard to estimate the amount of damage his bombs had caused, he reported a good glow of fires under the cloud.

With the weather remaining favourable and Harris not wanting to risk another delay, they were back in the air the next night, headed for Magdeburg, 155 kilometres south-west of Berlin. It was to prove a terrible night for both sides. Although this was the first attack on Magdeburg, the city was a major supplier of synthetic fuel products, and Bomber Command planned a diversionary attack on Berlin to give its main force a clear run. The Germans weren't fooled. Crews flying to Berlin encountered almost no resistance, and some even reported seeing night fighters taking off from local airfields, ignoring them, and heading to Magdeburg. Under heavy attack from the fighters, Bomber Command lost 55 aircraft and failed to hit any significant targets. But any satisfaction the Germans may have felt was tempered by the loss that night of two of their most revered pilots, Major Heinrich Prinz zu Sayn-Wittgenstein and Hauptmann (Captain) Manfred Meurer. According to Martin Middlebrook in *The Berlin Raids*, Prinz zu Sayn-Wittgenstein—at the time the Luftwaffe's top night fighter, with 83 claimed victories—was shot down by rear gunner Flight Lieutenant T.R. Thomson of 156 Squadron RAF. As the German ace moved into position and began firing on Thomson's Lancaster—inflicting damage that would eventually cause it to explode—Thomson managed to return fire until the last possible moment and inflict terminal damage on the German. Meurer, the third-ranked night-fighter ace, with 65 victories, was killed when the Lancaster he was attacking near Magdeburg exploded above him, destroying his aircraft.

Bomber Command had been relentlessly bombarding Berlin and other key targets for months, with enormous losses of men and equipment. After the Magdeburg raid, Harris informed his base commanders that there would be a two-week break so Bomber Command could lick its wounds and resupply in preparation for another major onslaught. The 1 April deadline for Berlin's capitulation that Harris had given to Air Chief Marshal Portal just over a year earlier was fast approaching, and he knew that once the D-Day invasion began—which would be very soon—his aircraft would be required elsewhere. Much-needed new crews and aircraft began arriving at bases. Some crews were given leave and others, like Dave's, were allotted training. After just over a week's rest, they began nine days of intensive training with the on-board H2S radar equipment. Between 3 and 12 February, they were in the air for almost nineteen hours, including two night flights. These would be their first flights in the new

Lancaster Mk III that was to be their operational aircraft. Carrying the serial number ND394, it was designated J2 by Squadron Operations. The aircraft's radio call sign, using the RAF alphabet, was *J for Jig*—the initials of Dave's sweetheart, Joyce Irene Gillman. He was chuffed, seeing it as a lucky omen.

On 15 February, all leave was cancelled and every available man and aircraft called into service for what would be the biggest raid on Berlin of the war. *J for Jig* was one of 561 Lancasters that joined with 314 Halifaxes and sixteen Mosquitos. The 891-strong force took off in the early evening and headed north-west towards the Danish coast. The German night fighters were waiting for the Allies as they crossed Denmark, and they were under fire all the way to Berlin and back over the Netherlands. Forty-three aircraft were shot down and 265 crewmen killed, but given the scale of the operation, the casualty rate was considered low. Surprisingly, only three bombers were shot down over the target itself. This was a result of the concentrated nature of the attack: with 40 bombers dropping their loads each minute, the actual bombing took only 20 minutes. It was all over so quickly that some bombers at the end of the stream failed to arrive in time.

For Dave it was very much a routine operation, except for one thing. It was his 21st birthday. Upon landing, his report was even briefer and more succinct than usual: 'Route quite good. T.I. reds and red/green flares well concentrated.' On that particular day, perhaps he had other things on his mind. Two of his crewmen certainly did. Earlier, Jock had approached Fergy with some news. He had asked Silvy to marry him.

'Will you be my best man?'

'Sure, mate. Of course.'

On 22 February 1943, Flight Sergeant John McClymont Dunlop, aged nineteen, from 460 Squadron RAAF, Binbrook, and Maria Silvia Valente, aged eighteen, of 140 Cart Lane, Grimsby, were married by licence at Grimsby Registry Office.

The honeymoon was brief. The newlyweds spent two nights in town, then Jock farewelled his bride and headed back to base. Word was that there would be a raid that night.

14

24 FEBRUARY 1944

It was a Thursday morning, cold and dreary. Tony D'Arcey woke at 7 a.m., looked out the window, saw the low grey cloud and falling rain, rolled over and went straight back to sleep. By the time he got on his bike and headed for the Bombing Section, picking up Bill Martin on the way, it was around 9.30. They went in and began cleaning their guns, as they did every morning, and were joined by Jock, who had just arrived back from town. The three were chatting—Darce and Pop looking forward to spending the night in a warm corner of their favourite pub and Jock keen to get back to his wife of less than 48 hours—when someone burst out of the Gunnery office, shouting: 'The game's on!'

Within seconds, the quiet scene of relaxed conviviality

was transformed. Air crew ran in and out of the room delivering and grabbing guns or looking for crew members. All had their own routine; all knew exactly what they had to do. Dave Baxter came in and joined his three crewmen. He and Tony went to the locker room to collect the crew's parachutes, harnesses and PFDs—Personal Flotation Devices, better known as Mae Wests—while Jock and Bill took the guns outside and looked for transport. When Dave and Tony came out with the gear, the other two were waiting in a crew bus, the engine running and ready to go. As they pulled up alongside *J for Jig*, on the far side of the airfield, the ground crew were fussing around it like mechanics at a car race. Pete Mallon and Ron Ferguson were there. The ground-crew sergeant had already run up the engines as Pete looked on. Fergy was aboard, tapping out messages to check that his Morse-code set was working properly. Bill, Jock and Tony climbed up, put their guns into place and fed in the ammunition belts, every five rounds made up of three armour-piercing, one tracer and one incendiary. Dave had a talk to the ground-crew sergeant while Tony checked his bombsight. With everything checked and re-checked, it was time to head back to the Flight Centre to receive their instructions. They climbed down and flagged a truck driven by a WAAF. They piled in the back and were pulling away as the bomb train arrived and unloaded one 4000-pound, six 1000-pound and two 500-pound bombs for the armourers to hoist aboard.

Back at the Flight Centre, Dave and Pete went off to sign for the fuel load. Jock and Fergy headed to the mess to finish a snooker competition with Bill as umpire. Tony walked over to the Navigation Centre and found Cliff Hopgood working on his maps. The target was still unknown, but Tony helped Hoppy rule up the maps and mark in the areas that intelligence had reported as heavily defended.

By now it was noon on the last day they would spend together as a crew—the last day some of them would ever see. The destination would be announced at the navigators' briefing at 2.30 p.m. There would be a meal for all those going on the operation at 3.15, before the main briefing at 4 p.m. After helping with the maps, Tony went to his room to put on his long woollen underwear, then headed back and met Hoppy for the navigation briefing. When they were all seated, the Navigation Leader announced, 'Your target tonight is Schweinfurt.' When the target was a known hot spot, such an announcement might be met with groans. On this occasion the reaction was more like, 'Where?'

While the majority of 460 Squadron had not heard of Schweinfurt, it was indeed a hot spot. In fact, the Americans had lost so many bombers on raids over the region the previous year that it became necessary to rethink tactics. About 160 kilometres east of Frankfurt, Schweinfurt's factories produced nearly all of Germany's ball bearings, needed for aircraft and tank manufacture. As such, it was a key target of Operation Pointblank, the first joint action undertaken by Bomber Command and the US Eighth Air Force. A US initiative that lasted from June 1943 until April 1944, the plan was to knock out Germany's capacity to build aircraft, leaving the skies over Europe free for Allied aircraft to focus on troop support. Although closer to Britain than Berlin, Schweinfurt was still well out of range of any Allied fighters that could provide support, so Bomber Command continued with its usual routine of bombing at night. The Americans believed that by flying their heavily armed B-17 and B-24 bombers in close formation, they had the firepower to counter the German fighters in daytime raids. It proved a disastrous miscalculation.

On 17 August 1943, 230 US bombers launched a daytime mission on the ball-bearing factories in Schweinfurt while another 146 targeted aircraft plants in Regensburg, 230 kilometres to the south-east. Of this combined force, 60 aircraft were shot down and another 87 so badly damaged that they had to be scrapped. Two months later, on 14 October, which became known as 'Black Thursday', the Americans tried again—and lost 77 aircraft and more than 600 men on a 291-bomber mission over Schweinfurt. The unsustainable losses forced a halt in daytime raids over Germany.

By February 1944, the battle lines had changed for the US Army Air Forces (USAAF, which became the US Air Force after the war). Three years earlier, the Americans had designed and built a long-range aircraft called the P-51. Powered by the Allison V-1710 engine, it had limited high-altitude performance and was used mainly for reconnaissance. In late 1943, it was transformed by fitting it with Rolls-Royce Merlin engines similar to those used in the Lancaster and Spitfire. Now known as the Mustang and armed with six .50-calibre M2 Browning machine guns, the P-51 gave the Americans a fighter that could support their bombers deep into enemy territory and match or outperform Luftwaffe fighters above 15,000 feet. Daytime bombing resumed with a vengeance. Between 20 and

25 February, the USAAF and Bomber Command launched a series of coordinated day and night raids on strategic targets all over Germany. Officially called Operation Argument, it became known as Big Week. On Thursday, 24 February, it was Schweinfurt's turn.

Tony and Hoppy drew up the route, identified the targets, and noted where the Pathfinders would drop their flares. As the crews sat down in the mess hall for a meal of bacon and eggs, Hoppy estimated that they could get to Schweinfurt and back in around six hours, compared to nine or ten for the Berlin run. At the general briefing, the Squadron Commander went over the tactics for the night, which came as a surprise to the crews. For the first time, Bomber Command had decided to split its force of 734 aircraft in half. The initial wave would be made up of 291 Lancasters from 1, 2, 3 and 6 Groups, trailing five Mosquitos and 46 Lancasters from 8 Pathfinder Group. The second force, of 331 Lancaster bombers guided by five Mosquito and 46 Lancaster Pathfinders, would follow two hours later. The reasoning was that after dealing with the first attack, the German defenders would not be expecting another and would be caught unprepared. In terms of aircraft lost, the plan would prove a success, with 22 shot down in the first phase and eleven in the second. But as the crew of *J for Jig* prepared for the operation, the new tactic was of no comfort whatsoever. Not only were they detailed to be part of the first wave, but they were also to back up the Pathfinders. That necessitated taking off at 5.45 p.m., eight minutes before the main force, meaning they would be almost 30 kilometres ahead of the rest as they passed over enemy territory.

The weather report told them they would be flying into a headwind and that the temperature at 20,000 feet would be below freezing. The five men sitting at the front of the aircraft would have the luxury of the Lancaster's heating system, but for the two gunners the cold would be torturous, no matter how many clothes they wore.

The meeting over, Pete went to the locker room with Jock and Bill to help them pull on layer after layer of additional clothing. It could take over half an hour for a gunner to get dressed. While Pete was assisting the two gunners, the rest of the crew were at the Flight Office, Dave signing for the aircraft and Tony for the bombs, Ron getting the night's secret wireless signals and Hoppy the latest wind speeds and directions.

Eventually, Jock and Bill were swaddled in all the warm clothing they could find. As always, Bill placed his rosary safely in his uniform pocket. The others wore their usual operational outfit: thermal underwear, white woollen sweater, electrically heated vest and fur-lined flying boots, as well as their regular uniforms. The only thing out of the ordinary for Hoppy was that he couldn't wear the engraved watch Margaret had given him. The strap was broken and he hadn't had time to have it repaired.

They collected their usual rations for a mission: two packets of chewing gum each, two bars of chocolate, a tin of Florida orange juice, a thermos flask of coffee and two ounces of barley sugar, which the crews would start sucking after a few hours to counteract the taste of rubber from the oxygen masks. Dave and Pete went out to the aircraft first and did a run-through of the engines. As they finished, they were joined by Tony, Ron, Jock and Bill. Hoppy stayed behind, furiously making calculations and writing figures into his flight plan.

At 5.20 p.m., 25 minutes before the scheduled take-off, Hoppy had still not arrived. The rest of the crew sat around and talked to the ground crew, but Dave was agitated, standing under the wing and looking out for the bus that would deliver his navigator. Ten minutes later, he told the others to get into their parachute harnesses and Mae Wests. Finally, a small van driven by a WAAF pulled up and, struggling with a large bombardier's bag that he had been given by a USAAF acquaintance, and with an armful of maps and charts, out climbed Hoppy.

'Come on, mate, hurry up,' snapped Dave.

'Don't worry,' said Hoppy. 'It's been put back fifteen minutes. Take-off's six o'clock.'

The others started taking off their awkward Mae Wests, but Dave was having none of it.

'Leave those on and get into the plane,' he said. 'We'll taxi over slowly.'

There were a few smiles as they climbed aboard and took their positions. Dave didn't know how to taxi slowly—his usual speed on the ground was around 50 miles an hour. This afternoon was no exception. Dave started up the engines at 5.40 p.m., bounced *J for Jig* over the grass, and arrived at the take-off point ten minutes before the official start time. They took off immediately and were first into the air.

Orders were to head to Reading, west of London, where the aircraft from Binbrook would meet up with hundreds of bombers and Pathfinders from other bases all over England.

The sun was just setting as *J for Jig* lifted off, and Dave stayed below 4000 feet as they flew over the centre of England. As the light gradually faded, they were treated to a panoramic view of the countryside. They saw the smoke wafting from the chimney of a thatch-roofed cottage, a car snaking its way along country lanes, sheep and cows grazing peacefully in green pastures. It was a real-life picture postcard, a world away from the stomach-churning horror that awaited them on the other side of the Channel.

By the time they reached Reading, the sky was dark and cloudless with no moon. To the Allied airmen that meant one thing: searchlights. They began their climb, reached Beachy Head on the south coast of England and flew out over the Channel. From their height the water looked calm but black and treacherous.

Soon the French coast came into view. They expected searchlights, but there were none to be seen. The Germans were not prepared to show their hand so soon. Dave and the crew flew deeper over France without any sign of enemy defences; all they could see below was the occasional car or a light at a farmhouse in defiance of the nightly blackout order.

An hour into the flight Tony, sitting in the nose, was the first to see a string of searchlights pointing north to south across the bombers' route. A lone light pointed south to north, illuminating a line that would lead the German night fighters to their prey. Dave got on the intercom to Bill and Jock and told his two gunners to be on the lookout. At 9.40 Dave, Bill and Tony saw an explosion in the darkness as a bomber was hit and went down about 60 miles ahead on their starboard side.

Dave's initial thought was, 'Poor buggers, but we're OK. Our luck's in.'

The newlywed Jock, isolated in his rear turret, called his navigator on the intercom.

'How long until we're over the target, Hoppy?' he asked.

'About an hour and a half, Jock.'

The young Scotsman cursed quietly and stared out into the night sky.

———■———

Jock never saw it coming. None of them did. Reinhard Kollak was too cunning for that. The 29-year-old Oberfeldwebel— Flight Sergeant—had been a Luftwaffe night-fighter pilot since day one. A career military man, he had transferred from the army to the air force in 1935 and received his pilot's wings in early 1940. Posted to Zerstörergeschwader (Destroyer Wing) 1, stationed in Damm, Germany, he flew a Messerschmitt Bf 110 C heavy fighter during the French Campaign and the Battle of Britain. The German aircraft, although heavily armed, proved no match for the manoeuvrability and firepower of the RAF's Hurricanes and Spitfires. In one three-day period, 53 Messerschmitts were destroyed by RAF fighters, 30 on one day alone. The Luftwaffe began the Battle of Britain on 10 July 1940 with 237 Bf 110s. By October 31, when Hitler and his air commander Hermann Göring abandoned their plan to destroy Britain's air defences, they had lost 223.

After the Battle of Britain, with Allied bombers free to cross the English Channel virtually unchecked, the Luftwaffe high command found another use for the Bf 110. In June

1940 Kollak's unit was re-formed as NJG 1, the Luftwaffe's first dedicated Nachtjagdgeschwader (NJG)—night-fighter wing—based in the Netherlands. Its insignia was a falcon with a lightning bolt in its talons, diving at its prey—England. For the first twelve months, the German night fighters had little success against the invaders, but after refining their tactics with the introduction of the box system of coordinated radar guidance, the tide turned. On 16 June 1941, Kollak and his longtime radio operator, Hans Herman, recorded their first 'kill', a Whitley twin-engine bomber from 51 Squadron RAF, shot down over Belgium. Kollak was on his way to becoming the most successful non-commissioned night-fighter pilot of the war, with 49 confirmed kills from over 250 missions. A much-reproduced photograph from September 1942 shows the quietly spoken farmer's son at the controls of his Messerschmitt. Painted on its tail are ten 'victory bars', each signifying the destruction of an aircraft and the end of up to seven young lives. Kollak was awarded the German Cross in Gold in April 1943 and, five months later, after his 30th kill, the Knight's Cross of the Iron Cross. By 24 February 1944, Kollak was with Squadron 8 of NJG 4, flying out of Juvincourt in northern France. His aircraft now displayed 32 bars on its tail.

From Juvincourt to Metz is a distance of 170 kilometres, about half an hour's flying time in Kollak's Bf 110. At 9.00 p.m., as the Allied bomber stream, led by the Pathfinders, approached his radar 'box', Kollak was perfectly positioned thanks to constant updates from radar operators on the ground. By now an ace, skilled in the tactic of *Schräge Musik*—attacking the RAF bombers from below and firing upwards with slanted cannons to avoid detection from the rear gunner—Kollak must have found the situation almost routine. He spotted his quarry and moved in for the kill.

The first aircraft in Kollak's sights that night was Lancaster JB241 from 405 Squadron RCAF, Canada's only Pathfinder squadron, piloted by Flight Officer Basil George Jackson DFC. Flying at 20,000 feet, Jackson had seen the flares dropped by other Pathfinders to indicate that a fighter was in the area. He was about to perform a slight evasive action when Kollak emptied his two 20-mm MG FF/M cannons into the belly of the Lancaster. It shuddered and the starboard inner engine and wing burst into flames. With no controls, Jackson gave the order to bail out. The aircraft climbed, stalled and began to spin. Navigator J.A. Radford opened the nose hatch and jumped, followed by bomb aimer R.H. Freiburger and Jackson. Seconds later, the aircraft exploded into the ball of flame that had been spotted by the crew of *J for Jig*. Four of the crew were killed—Canadians Douglas Eastham, 35, and Solomon Kay, 22; and the RAF's Frederick Abery, 34, and Percy Redstone, 22. The three survivors—Radford, Freiburger and Jackson—saw out the war in the infamous prisoner-of-war camp Stalag Luft III—site of the so-called Great Escape—160 kilometres south-east of Berlin.

During the Battle of Britain, one of the biggest disadvantages of the Messerschmitt Bf 110 had been its inability to perform a tight turn in a dogfight with the more manoeuvrable RAF fighters. In a night-fighter engagement against the slower, straight-flying bombers, the aircraft's turning circle was not an issue. Kollak, seeing the Canadian's fuel tanks explode, flew in a wide arc to port so that when he straightened he would be behind and below the next bombers in the formation. Some seventeen minutes after shooting down JB241, he spotted another Lancaster, *J for Jig*. He moved up behind it and prepared to perform some deadly *Schräge Musik*.

—■—

To maintain the element of surprise, the night fighters' cannons were fitted with flash reducers and did not fire tracer bullets. Instead, the Germans developed ammunition that gave off a faint glow. When Kollak fired his first burst, he missed on the starboard side, but the bullets went so close and travelled so far in front of the aircraft that Tony thought they must have come from Bill firing ahead from the upper turret. Seconds later, there was another burst. There was no question where that came from. The Lancaster shuddered as the shells thudded into it. The starboard wing erupted into flames, and the aircraft went into a dive.

'Get out, quick!' Dave called over the intercom. Then, as the aircraft righted itself, he had second thoughts. 'Wait a moment. Pete, feather the starboard inner.' As Pete shut down the engine, Tony pulled his parachute from its hold and placed it on top of the bombsight. Dave struggled to regain control of the aircraft, all the while looking at the starboard wing. The fire continued to spread, giving off so much light that he couldn't see his instruments.

'It's no use, Pete,' he decided. 'Tony, jettison the bombs.' Tony asked Dave to open the bomb-bay doors then pushed the button to let the bombs fall.

Dave got back on the intercom and gave the signal they had only ever heard during training.

'Abandon the aircraft. Go.'

Tony looked back to make sure the bombs were falling, clipping on his parachute as he moved to the emergency exit. Dave continued struggling with the controls. Pete placed a parachute on Dave's knees and headed down to the nose. As Dave undid his seat harness and clipped on the parachute, he thought he sensed Cliff Hopgood go past as well, but it could have been the shadows caused by the flames. Then over the intercom came the voice of nineteen-year-old Jock. Trapped in his turret, he was desperately calling for his best man, Fergy, to come and help him.

Back in the nose, Tony lifted the exit cover to throw it out, but the slipstream pushed it back down and it jammed. He gave one violent kick. The cover fell out and away into the darkness. Tony caught a glimpse of Pete coming down into the nose as he eased himself through the exit, just as the Lancaster went into a dive. Something hit him hard on the chest as he got out. Then he was free of the stricken aircraft, spinning over and over in the blackness.

Bill had started to move as soon as Dave gave the first order. Knowing how difficult it would be to manoeuvre his large body out of the turret, grab his parachute, clamber to the crew door, open it and get out in the frantic, crowded moments of an emergency evacuation, he had gone through this eventuality many times in his mind. It all went exactly as he'd planned. He pushed himself away from his gun position and down through the tube into the fuselage proper, grabbed his parachute, and clipped it on as he headed to the side door. All he had to do was push the door open and jump out. Then he heard Jock's voice on the intercom.

'Fergy, help me.'

There was no reply. Flight Sergeant Ronald Cedric Ferguson, 26 years old, from Bundaberg, Queensland, was already dead. He lay slumped over his radio table, killed by the burst of shells from Kollak's cannons.

By now Dave had given the second order to abandon the aircraft. Tony had got out. Pete and Hoppy should have followed. As Bill reached the door, the intercom crackled again.

'Fergy. Someone, anyone. Get me out of here.'

Bill was seconds away from safety. All he had to do was open the hatch and jump. He had visualised the situation a thousand times. Push the door, roll out head-first, open the chute, live another day. Then he heard Jock's voice. His hand dropped from the lever that would open the door. He turned away from the door and started moving further down the aircraft, towards Jock's position. Even in ideal conditions, getting to the rear turret would have been difficult for the heavy-set 32-year-old. It required turning to face the front of the aircraft, sitting on the raised and boxed-off tail spar, sliding backwards and swinging the feet round. Then it was a case of pushing, pulling and sliding the rest of the way feet first.

These were anything but ideal conditions. Bill, burdened by his heavy clothing and parachute, struggled to get to Jock while at the nose of the bomber Pete and then Hoppy pushed their way through the exit hatch. In the cockpit, Dave fought furiously in an attempt to hold the aircraft level as the others bailed out, but it was futile. The tailplane and rudders had either been shot off or badly damaged. *J for Jig* went into a spin—what Bomber Command veterans refer to as the 'death roll'—and began to break up. Bill was thrown back into the body of the heaving aircraft. Dragging himself to his feet, he stumbled towards the crew door but never had the chance to open it. As the aircraft spun and screamed in its death throes, the Perspex H2S radar dome, splintered by Kollak's guns, began to tear away from the fuselage. Bill fell and was sucked through the hole in the floor, badly gashing his forehead on the jagged edges of Perspex and metal as he fell out into the blackness.

The Lancaster turned belly up.

Dave had waited as long as he could before leaving the controls. The signal that the last man from the forward stations had made his way to the escape hatch was a tap on Dave's shoulder from either Hoppy or Fergy as he went past on his way to the nose. Dave had seen Pete head down to join Tony, and thought he had sensed Hoppy go past, so that left only Fergy. The tap never came.

As the aircraft turned upside down, Dave fell from his seat and crashed through the Perspex roof of the cockpit. A few minutes earlier he had been following the routine that he and his crewmates knew as well as their two-times tables. All had been going to plan, all was as it should be. Then the pressure of Reinhard Kollak's thumb on the firing button of his cannons had sent the lives of the seven men on *J for Jig* into mayhem. Dave's body remained caught in the falling aircraft while his head and shoulders protruded through the roof. The freezing air rushed into his face, the heat and flames from the burning engine adding to his hellish predicament.

The only thing preventing him from freeing himself was the bulk of the parachute pack. With all the strength and agility that had made him a champion on the sports fields around Wonthaggi, he gave a couple of mighty kicks to the control panel and found himself falling through the darkness.

—■—

It was only a few minutes since Tony D'Arcey had been the first out of the aircraft, but to him it felt like hours. As Tony fell through the hatch, three sensations hit him almost simultaneously. The air was knocked out of his lungs by the slipstream; because he'd removed his gloves during the flight, his hands were freezing; and, strangely, all seemed eerily silent. He turned over several times and put his hand to his chest to pull the ripcord on his parachute. It wasn't there. 'This is it,' he thought. 'I'm going to die.' He deduced that he had failed to clip on the parachute in those final frantic moments before he jumped, but then realised his harness was in place. Just then he felt something lightly brush the top of his head and remembered the heavy bump on his chest as he'd exited through the hatch. He ran his hands along the harness straps above his head—and there was the parachute pack. Finding the ripcord, he gave it a tug, and after what seemed an eternity, there was a jerk as the canopy filled with air and he began floating earthwards. As he descended, Tony watched the burning Lancaster falling further and further away in the distance, the scene made all the more surreal by the complete and continued silence he was experiencing. Realising his ears had been blocked in the fall, he put a near-frozen hand to his nose, squeezed his nostrils closed and blew. Immediately, the silence was replaced by the sound of aircraft passing overhead. He looked up at the shadowy formations of bombers continuing on their way to Germany, then back down as his own aircraft continued its dive, exploding in a ball of fire as it hit the ground. The large flames died quickly, leaving only a small glow. Tony could see the flashes of dozens of small bright lights as the ammunition exploded. He looked at his watch.

It was 10.45 p.m.

15

VILLERS-SOUS-PRÉNY

The first that the people of Villers-sous-Prény knew of the seven Allied airmen who would come to mean so much to them and their village was when Tony had pressed the button to jettison the Lancaster's bombs. The initial explosions shook the windows of the houses. At the presbytery, a group of young people were rehearsing a play under the supervision of the parish priest, Father Xénard. They ran outside to investigate the noise.

Nearby, in the centre of town, Armand Casalini, not yet four years old, and his older brother Noël, seven, were awoken and cried out in fear as their house shook. Their mother, Lucie, came into the room and lay down on the bed to comfort them. Seconds later there was another explosion, so loud and close that it shattered the windows of the Casalini house and cracked the tiles near the front door. Almost immediately there was a second, less violent explosion, and then a third as the Lancaster crashed into the ground and burst into flames. Then silence—apart from what sounded like firecrackers as the ammunition for Jock, Bill and Tony's guns ignited and exploded.

Armand Casalini was too young at the time to still remember the night the war came to the village, but as with every resident then and since, it has come to be part of his life. Those who were there that night have told the story to those who weren't. It has been passed on through generations and translated into different languages. The people of Villers-sous-Prény have never forgotten the sacrifice made by 'their airmen', and continue to recount with pride what they themselves did that night and in the days that followed.

For Armand, the crash of Lancaster *J for Jig* is more than local folklore. Yes, he has heard the stories so many times that as he retells them it is almost as if he'd been there for every moment. But he is more than a teller of tales. He is a keeper of the flame who has made it his life's work to keep the memories alive. His home is full of mementos salvaged from the wreckage, ranging from small items of equipment from the cockpit to pieces of the fuselage. He has interviewed the villagers who were first on the scene, and those who risked their lives in the days afterwards, and meticulously recorded their recollections.

As Armand relives the drama of that night—more than 70 years after he lay in his mother's arms, frightened by the noises outside—it is almost as if it was he, and not Monsieur Vermot des Roches, who led the way to the crash site.

There was an orange glow to the south-west of the village, in the direction of Vilcey-sur-Trey. In that direction was the farm of Celestin Fathe. Vermot des Roches worked on the farm and he knew the area well, so as the people came out of their houses, he led the way. The bombs had fallen in the fields, and the road to Vilcey was half covered with dirt. There were large craters, about two feet deep. The plane had crashed about one kilometre from our village. The people walked through the field and saw the wreckage. It was burning, and there were three bodies lying on the ground.

Not far from the plane, there was a parachute spread open. As the villagers came near, it appeared to lift upwards and a voice underneath it called, 'Comrade, Comrade!' M. Vermot des Roches ran over and lifted the parachute from the man, who collapsed back to the ground. He had a serious gash to his head and he was in a bad state. Again he said, 'Comrade,' and Vermot des Roches told him, 'You are in France,' and asked him his name. 'William Martin,' he said.

The villagers went to the three bodies. The men were dead. Someone thought they heard a groan, but a quick search of the area found no one else. Vermot des Roches lifted Bill Martin onto his shoulders and began carrying him back towards town.

'As he did,' Armand continues, 'the other villagers walked with him and discussed what should be done. It was strictly forbidden to help Allied airmen or escaped prisoners of war, under penalty of death.'

The village baker, Eugène Schuller, pushed his way to Vermot des Roches' side.

'Take him to my house,' he said. 'I have contacts in the Underground.'

They took Bill to the baker's house. Schuller's wife, Simone, cleared the dining table and Vermot des Roches laid him on it. Bill's Irvin jacket was removed and placed on the back of a chair. In the pockets of his RAF battledress were his identity discs and rosary beads. The kitchen was packed as the villagers watched Madame Schuller do her best to tend the wounds.

There was a deep gash across the left side of Bill's head above the forehead and a cut running upwards from his right eye. He had a wound above his right ear, and his nose and lip were split. Unbeknown to his rescuers, he had also suffered spinal injuries.

The less serious wounds could be cleaned and dressed, but nothing could stem the bleeding from the head gash. With Bill drifting in and out of consciousness, a villager was sent to fetch the doctor from the town of Pagny-sur-Moselle, about seven kilometres to the north. The doctor dressed the wound but said Bill would need surgery.

By now the mayor of Villers-sous-Prény, Ernest Sophron, had taken charge. He, Vermot des Roches and Schuller went to another room to talk. They had all acted instinctively in the heat of the moment, but things were now very serious. The other villagers could go back to their homes and, if they wished, deny to the Germans that they had even been to the crash site. Even if they admitted that they had gone to Fathe's farm and been in the Schullers' kitchen when Bill Martin had been lying there, what crime had they committed? But Vermot des Roches and the Schullers were a different matter. Vermot des Roches had physically aided and abetted an Allied airman; the Schullers had given him shelter and medical treatment. Under German military law they could be severely punished, even shot. Mayor Sophron was deemed equally liable for punishment if treason had occurred in his area of jurisdiction. Without access to adequate medical facilities, and with Bill in no condition to be moved to a safer location, it was decided there was no alternative but to hand him over to the Germans who had just arrived in the town from the military headquarters at Nancy, some 35 kilometres to the south.

A German guard was placed on the crash site, and soldiers moved through the fields and village searching for any survivors. Mayor Sophron sent word that one of the RAF airmen was at the baker's home, and within a few minutes there was a bang on the door.

'There were two or three soldiers, led by an officer and an interpreter,' Armand Casalini recalls. 'They interrogated William Martin about how he had got to the house and who had helped him. He gave them no information, and despite numerous attempts, the Germans never found out how he made his way from the crashed plane to the village.'

After the interrogation, the officer ordered Bill to be taken outside to a waiting vehicle. Two soldiers pulled him to his feet and half walked, half dragged him into the street. Then he was loaded into a truck and driven away. His leather and wool Irvin jacket was left on the chair. For the rest of her days, Madame Schuller would wear that jacket as she did her early morning deliveries of bread and groceries. It was, she said proudly, '*le manteau de mon aviateur*'—the coat of my aviator.

At daybreak, lorries carrying German soldiers arrived from Nancy and began a door-to-door search for any missing airmen. Others marched through the centre of the town and out to the crash site, followed by villagers. Arriving from another direction at the same time was a small car carrying two members of the Underground from Vilcey-sur-Trey. They had heard that Bill Martin had been saved and that there might be other survivors, but when they saw the Germans, they quickly turned around and left.

In the daylight it was easier to assess the crash site and see the bodies. Two were close by the plane—best mates Jock Dunlop, who had not been able to escape from the rear gunner's position, and Ron Ferguson, killed by the initial burst from the German fighter. Peter Mallon was a few metres away in a plough furrow. It appeared that his parachute had become entangled after he exited the aircraft. The fourth man, Cliff Hopgood, was found on the other side of the paddock. He had managed to exit the plane but he had landed badly and was lying across a fence, his neck broken.

After the Germans had inspected the bodies and confirmed that all four men were dead, the villagers placed them on the horse cart of Jacques Starck and followed him as he led the cart back to town. The bodies were carefully unloaded at Sophron's home, where they were laid out in a front room. Leaving one soldier to guard the wreckage of the Lancaster, the Germans continued their search for the two missing men, Dave and Tony. Even so, villagers managed to recover items such as a compass, Hoppy's 'bombardier' map bag and a machine gun, which they hid in a hedge and later smuggled to the Underground. Another gun was taken to Fathe's farm and hidden in the attic under sawdust.

With no sign of the missing men, Schuller and the deputy mayor, Henri Guichard, were summoned to the German commandant in Nancy for interrogation, but they were unable to give any information and were released. They returned to help organise a funeral for the four dead airmen. The villagers were determined to make this a tribute to their sacrifice and a sign of defiance to the Germans. Over the next few days, the four bodies lay in state in the front room of Mayor Sophron's home. Hundreds of people from Villers-sous-Prény and surrounding villages came to pay their respects.

Unbeknown to the Germans, a collection was taken up in shops and by volunteers going door to door, to raise money for coffins, headstones, wreaths and flowers. While the Germans were well aware that a funeral was being planned— the commandant of the POW camp in Nancy even agreed to supply a number of French colonial prisoners to form a guard of honour—they warned that the gathering should not be large and that no photographs should be taken. They might as well have ordered the Allies to halt preparations for D-Day. The Underground spread word that the funeral was an opportunity for a show of solidarity against the Germans, and thousands of mourners from the north of France poured into the tiny village. Photographs taken on the day show the streets clogged with a mass of people headed to the church where the four fallen airmen—two Australians, two Scotsmen—were to be buried, wrapped in their parachutes, side by side in one grave.

The Catholic ceremony, performed by Father Xénard, was held on 27 February 1944, three days after the crash. Armand Casalini recalled the scene:

Our small church and cemetery were too small to accommodate the flood of pilgrims. The paths were black with people. In the crowd were Germans hoping to arrest any photographers, but there were so many people that they were powerless to act.

The Gestapo did several searches to find these photographs without luck, and Mayor Sophron, Deputy Mayor Guichard and M. Schuller were held for 24 hours at the German headquarters in Nancy in hopes of making them reveal where the film was hidden. It was never found. It was hidden under a beehive in the garden of M. Schuller and later sent to England. Mayor Sophron was fined for allowing the grand funeral ceremony to take place, and the Germans threatened to take hostages if information about the night of the crash and the funeral was not forthcoming. The case dragged on, but four months later the D-Day invasion took place and the Germans were busy on other matters.

—■—

When *J for Jig* did not return to base, the wheels of military procedure, well greased by thousands of identical tragedies, began moving with all-too-practised efficiency. The first official mention of the fate of Dave's crew came in 460 Squadron's Operations report for 24 February. Marked 'Very Secret', it began: 'Night Operations. Schweinfurt was the main target, 734 aircraft being despatched to make two separate but co-ordinated attacks, following a daylight attack by the Eighth Air Force.

'The first force, due to arrive at the target at 23.05 hours, comprised 392 aircraft, namely 70 Lancasters of 1 Group, 22 of 3 Group, 66 of 5 Group, 13 of 6 Group, 87 and 64 Halifaxes respectively of 4 and 6 Groups, with 6 Mosquitoes, 44 Lancasters and 20 Halifaxes of 8 Pathfinders Group.'

The skies were cloudless, visibility good and the target was well marked by the Pathfinders, the report said. Those fortunate enough to make it back safely were almost dismissive of the resistance they had met.

'Both forces went in from the south, but on the way home the first took a northerly route and second a southerly. Fighters were active over the target and on the way in, particularly from Stuttgart to the target, but few fighters on the homeward routes have been reported. Several aircraft met very little opposition, one reporting that activity was lacking to the point of boredom.'

In what seemed almost an afterthought, the squadron's operations report ended: '33 aircraft are missing.'

On the day that Hoppy, Fergy, Jock and Pete were buried in Villers-sous-Prény, their 23-year-old commanding officer, Wing Commander Horton 'Spike' Marsh, sat down at his desk at Binbrook and began adding names and signatures to a pile of pre-typed letters.

VILLERS-SOUS-PRÉNY

27/2/1944

No. 460 Squadron RAAF

RAF Station

Binbrook

Lincoln

Dear [name written in by hand]

Before the arrival of this letter you will have received advice that your husband [son] is missing from operations carried out against Schweinfurt on the night of the 24th February 1944. I write to offer you the sincere sympathy of myself and the Squadron during the anxious time you will be passing through.

Your husband [son] was very popular in the Squadron and had carried out his duties in an extremely conscientious manner. It may be of some consolation to you to know that a number of missing airmen are eventually found to be Prisoners of War, and I hope I will have the pleasure of passing such good news to you before long.

Your husband's [son's] personal effects have been collected and placed in safe keeping with the R.A.F Central Depository, Colnbrook, Slough, Bucks.

Yours Sincerely [handwritten]

H. D. Marsh [signed]

Officer Commanding

Wing Commander Marsh's letters were written on 27 February but, sent by air mail, they reached the Australian families well after the telegrams sent the next day from the RAAF offices in Melbourne.

Personal: [Identity number, name]. Regret to inform you that your husband [son] [name] is missing as a result of air operations during night 24th February 1944. Details are he was member of crew Lancaster aircraft detailed to attack Schweinfurt Germany which failed to return to base presumably due to enemy action. The Minister for Air joins with Air Board in expressing sincere sympathy in your anxiety. When any further information is received it will be conveyed to you immediately. Air Force, Anderson Street, South Yarra.

It was, and remains, the kind of telegram that every relative of a military service member fears receiving.

Dave's younger brother Ron will never forget the moment the telegram arrived at 17 Reid Street, Wonthaggi. 'My mother was sitting in the lounge when she read it. She burst into tears. So did I.'

On 3 March, *The Powlett Express*, the local newspaper that had proudly reported that former sports star Dave Baxter had received his pilot's wings in Canada and commenced operations over Berlin, published a sadder story under the headline 'Dave Baxter "Missing" Over Germany':

It is with deep regret that we announce that Mrs Baxter of North Wonthaggi has received word that her second son, Pilot Officer Dave Baxter, has been reported 'missing' as the result of air operations over Germany. Dave is a Lancaster Pilot attached to an All-Australian Squadron. He was 21 last month. Dave has been on operational flying for a long time—he has bombed Berlin on a number of occasions.

Deepest sympathy is extended to Mrs Baxter and Family in their anxious moments. It is hoped that the time is not far off when news will come through that he is safe and well.

The families of the two Scottish boys received similar notifications from the RAF. Peter Mallon's parents put the telegram back in its envelope and placed it in a drawer, as they did with all subsequent official correspondence about their son. They told his siblings first that he was missing and then that he was confirmed dead, but they never showed them the letters or discussed their contents.

When Silvy Dunlop, Jock's wife for all of two days, was informed that he was missing in action, she caught the train to Ayrshire and moved in with his mother, Mary, and his sisters. Less than four years earlier, Mary had lost her husband. Now she faced the prospect of losing her son. Jock's sister Jenny recalled that in the days between the arrival of the telegram saying he was missing and the arrival of the one confirming his death, Mary and Silvy sat by the radio listening to BBC bulletins, hoping and praying to hear his name among the latest lists of POWs.

It was a cruel waiting game being played in Australia as well. Nine telegrams had been sent to the listed next of kin of the five RAAF crew members. All but one were sent to their home addresses; Ron Ferguson's wife, Doris, received her telegram while she was on a nursing shift at Canberra Community Hospital. To the families of the missing men, the minutes, hours and days following the receipt of those initial telegrams were filled with the rawest of emotions. To the military machine, the same hours were filled with clerical procedure and paperwork. The inclusion in the standard 'missing on operations' letter of a paragraph informing relatives of the whereabouts of their loved ones' personal effects—surely a minor concern for them at that precise time—reflected the massive and often pedantic bureaucracy that underpinned the war effort. In the ensuing days, weeks and months, the RAF in the UK and the RAAF in Melbourne would exchange cables about the possessions left behind by Dave's crew and inform their relatives of the fate not just of the men but of their shaving kits, toothbrushes and, with dogged determination, their bicycles.

Nothing was considered too trivial to be recorded and itemised. On 1 March, a week after the crash, RAAF Headquarters in London received two separate forms in relation to P/O D'Arcey A. One noted: 'Herewith 5 Canteen Orders valued at 2/- each found in the effects of the above named airman. Serial Numbers N.574931—N.574935.' The other was accompanied by '2 USA 1 Dollar Bills. 3 Canadian 1 Dollar Bills. 2 Canadian 2 Dollar Bills and 1 Canadian 5 Dollar Bill' and listed their serial numbers.

On 6 May 1944, Bill Martin's wife, Anne, received a letter from the Casualty Department of the Department of Air in Melbourne, signed on behalf of the Secretary, Melville Cecil Langslow.

Dear Madam,
With reference to the Service affairs of your husband, Flight Sergeant William James Martin, who is reported to be

missing as the result of air operations on the 24th February, 1944, I have to advise that a bicycle owned by him is held at his former unit.

In view of the difficulty experienced in storing articles of this nature, and of the fact that it is not practicable to return them to Australia, the practice is to hold them for approximately three months from the date on which the member became missing. If he is then still posted as missing, such articles are then sold and the proceeds are held on his behalf.

However, an opportunity is given to you, should you so wish, to nominate some person in the United Kingdom to take delivery of the bicycle instead of selling same.

If it is desired to make such a nomination, it is important that this Department receive advice as to the name and address of the person so nominated not later than the 27th May, 1944. If no such nomination is received by such last mentioned date, sale will be effected as abovementioned.

Anne dutifully replied to the Department, asking that the bicycle be passed on to another member of the squadron. What happened to it next is unknown, but one thing is certain: the fate of an old bicycle was the least of Bill's worries.

The Germans had put Bill Martin in the back of a truck, and with one armed guard on either side keeping him seated upright, he was taken on a painful hour-long drive to Nancy, a key German military base. With D-Day and the advance through France still some four months away, Nancy and

Metz were busy but relatively quiet outposts at the time Bill was captured.

The two cities would be taken by the US Third Army after a three-and-a-half-month operation beginning in September 1944. Nancy was the first to fall, after a ten-day battle in which the city was encircled by two tank divisions, one led by Lieutenant Colonel—later General—Creighton Abrams Jr, who would go on to command US military operations during the Vietnam War.

Bill was taken to Frontstalag 194, a large prisoner-of-war camp at Nancy. This housed mainly French colonial soldiers— those from Africa were known collectively as Senegalese for the country many came from—and Indians serving in the British army. Too badly injured to be interrogated further, Bill was taken straight to the camp's lazaret—military hospital— for treatment. He remained there for five weeks. During that time, on 16 March, the Swiss diplomat Gabriel Naville carried out an inspection of the camp. While Naville did not meet with Bill—and erroneously described him as an 'Austrian airman'—he mentioned his existence and the authorities' assurance that he was being well cared for, a claim he upheld in his report. Naville wrote:

The lazaret for prisoners of war depends administratively on Stalag 194. It is installed in very spacious buildings in the centre of the town which used to be occupied by a religious hospital and asylum for old people. It is chiefly for French prisoners and the medical attention is under the supervision of a German medical officer. It seems very well installed.

The buildings are grouped around a large courtyard with trees and flower gardens and are in good condition; the yards are spacious, very well lighted, and clean. The Indian prisoners have two large rooms of their own with accommodation for about 60 patients. They are furnished with single iron beds and the prisoners are very comfortable indeed.

Naville added that he 'was told that in another part of the lazaret three American and one Austrian airmen were lying, who had been recently shot down in the neighbourhood; however, I was not allowed to see them as they had not yet been interrogated by the German authorities. This lazaret makes an excellent impression, the prisoners had no complaints and the medical attention seems satisfactory.'

Nursing care at Stalag 194 was provided by the French nuns who had run the hospital before the war, which proved fortunate for Bill. When he arrived and was undressed and placed in a bed, a nun had found Bill's rosary beads in his battledress pocket and placed them in his hand as he lay half conscious. From then until he was sent to a Dulag Luft (air force transit camp) five weeks later for interrogation and transfer to a permanent POW camp, at least once a day, as one of the nuns checked his wounds, she would sneak him an egg hidden in the folds of her habit.

Bill then spent three days at Dulag Luft Oberursel, near Frankfurt. He gave interrogators his name and service number but stuck to his story of how he had come to be at the home of Eugène Schuller: that after his parachute landed he had wandered in a daze and knocked on the first door he came to. At one point the interrogating officer read from a sheet of paper on his desk and said matter-of-factly, 'Your comrades, Ferguson, Hopgood, Mallon and Dunlop . . . all dead . . . buried at Villers-sous-Prény.'

On 5 April, Bill was placed on a train and sent to Stalag Luft VI, near the town of Heydekrug, in a part of Lithuania annexed by Germany just before the start of the war. Germany's northernmost POW camp, it was a four-day rail trip from Frankfurt in a crowded cattle truck, with just a bucket as a toilet for all.

When Bill and his fellow POWs arrived at Heydekrug, they were marched about three kilometres to the camp. They were photographed, fingerprinted and inspected for vermin. Bill was then sent to the British compound.

Set on 35 acres, Stalag Luft VI was an NCO camp consisting of four compounds, three of which housed up to 7000 prisoners. One was allocated to British and Commonwealth prisoners, of whom about 150 were RAAF members. There were separate compounds for American and Soviet prisoners and the fourth was left vacant.

Each compound held eight single-storey wooden buildings: one each for latrine, wash house, cookhouse and administration, and four sleeping blocks, each divided into nine rooms and accommodating up to 60 men. When Bill arrived, the British and Commonwealth barracks were full to overflowing, so he was billeted in a large unlit tent, jammed in with around 240 other men. Like those in the wooden barracks, they slept on three-tier timber racks, with straw palliasses and a single blanket.

After they had found their sleeping quarters, Bill and the other newly arrived RAF personnel were visited by the prisoners' elected camp leader, Sergeant James 'Dixie' Deans, one of the most remarkable and respected POWs of World War II. He had been shot down over The Netherlands in 1940, and his natural leadership qualities and fluent German made him an obvious prisoners' representative—known as a 'man of confidence'—at every camp in which he was incarcerated. An unrelenting advocate for the rights of his men—at one camp he refused to let the Germans segregate Jewish RAF prisoners—he was equally involved in escape activities, setting up committees to plan and coordinate escape attempts, bribe guards and build radios. He would also monitor German operations by quizzing new prisoners and maintaining a network of 'friendly' guards, information he sent back to military intelligence in England via coded letters to his wife. In his orientation speech to Bill and the other new arrivals, Deans—who had earlier been interned at Stalag Luft III, famous for the Wooden Horse and later the Great Escape—explained the camp routine, outlined the entertainment and recreation facilities, and stressed the prisoners' duty to escape.

Many prisoners at Stalag Luft VI took that duty very seriously. A month before Bill's arrival, the camp's second most famous prisoner, George Grimson, had made good his escape with Deans' assistance by walking out the front gates dressed in a German uniform obtained by bribing a guard. He subsequently met up with members of the Polish Underground and set up and operated what was referred to as the 'Tally-Ho

Network' to help other shot-down airmen and escaped POWs make their way home.

Soon after Bill's arrival, all prisoners were summoned to a special roll call. After Dixie Deans called the parade to attention, a large number of German soldiers armed with machine guns took up positions surrounding the prisoners. A German major then read out a statement announcing that 50 RAF officers had been shot dead 'while resisting arrest' during an escape bid at Stalag Luft III. In fact the Allied airmen, including five Australians, had been murdered in cold blood after having been recaptured during what became known as the Great Escape. After a period of stunned shock on hearing the news, some prisoners began murmuring and then shouting at the German officer, and the troops' fingers tightened on their triggers. It was only the cool head and calming words of Dixie Deans—who had been part of the escape committee at Stalag Luft III and would have known most, if not all, of the murdered men—that prevented what could have been another massacre. The prisoners were marched back to their quarters.

Bill soon settled into the monotony of camp life. He reported for roll call twice a day, watched and took part in games on the parade ground, and used the library set up by the prisoners' entertainment committee. He was able to cope with the boredom, the close contact, inadequate latrine facilities and showering once a month. What he struggled with most was lack of food. Rations consisted of watered-down turnip soup, rye bread, sauerkraut and an occasional small piece of horse meat. While the quality was reasonable, the quantity was meagre at best. A big man when he was captured,

Bill found himself perpetually hungry. One thing he would not go without, though, was his faith. He managed to hold on to his rosary beads throughout his travels and would pray with them every day. When other Catholics in the camp approached him, he started what they called the Rosary Group. Each day at least a dozen men would come together and say the rosary, led by Bill.

Bill was incarcerated at Stalag Luft VI for almost three months before he was told in mid-July to collect his belongings for transfer to another camp. A month earlier, on 6 June, he and the other prisoners at Stalag Luft VI had heard the news broadcast by the BBC on the radios that Dixie Deans had secreted throughout the camp. The Allies had landed in Normandy and, as they and the Soviets moved towards Berlin, the Germans were getting edgy. If things deteriorated, the POWs could prove valuable as hostages, so they were moved from vulnerable areas and brought closer to Berlin. For Bill and his fellow prisoners, the move would be a painful experience endured with the knowledge that the end was in sight.

16

EVASION

Descending through the night sky Tony looked around in the desperate hope of spotting more parachutes, then down at the glow of the burning aircraft as he drifted further away from it. His mind raced with random thoughts: he ran through in his mind which of the lads he had seen coming down into the nose, and whose voices he had last heard. He was angry that they had not completed their tour and been sent home together; he thought about Madge, the WAAF corporal at the sergeants' mess, and how she would be preparing the bacon and eggs for the boys' return. He thought about the prospect of walking all the way to Spain and, momentarily, how much easier it would be if a German soldier met him as he landed and sent him off to a POW camp.

He saw a dam or lake about 5000 feet below and was glad he was wearing his Mae West, then tried to relax in his harness as they'd been trained, and waited for the ground to come up and meet him. Seconds later, he landed solidly in a field but, before he could stand up, he was dragged along the hard, frozen earth as the canopy filled with air. He tried to release the harness, but his fingers were too stiff from the cold, so he turned the release ring and rolled on his stomach, hoping the weight of his body would do the rest. After being dragged another 50 metres or so it did. He sat and watched the canopy collapse, then climbed to his feet. He was shaking so much, perhaps from the cold, perhaps from shock, that it took about five minutes to get his Mae West off. He spotted a bitumen road about 45 metres away and headed towards it.

Like all airmen, Tony had thought often about being shot down and bailing out. He had always pictured all seven of the team getting out together, floating to earth, regrouping and planning their next move. It was only as he trudged towards the road in the silence of the night, with the bombers long since passed on their way to Schweinfurt, that it struck him: he was all alone.

He reached the road and looked around. On the side he had come from were ploughed fields and grazing land. On the other side were scrub and dead trees. Seeing no sign of life, he started down the road. Eventually he came to a crossroad, and a house. He went up to the gate but froze when a dog began to bark. Quietly he retraced his steps and walked up to the signpost on the corner. He was relieved to see it was printed in French, not German. In one direction it pointed to Verdun,

72 kilometres away; in the other to Limey, four kilometres away. He was about to head to Limey when he remembered his parachute lying in the field. He went back, found it and left in the nearby woods.

As he walked back onto the road a shape emerged from the darkness, coming towards him. Tony tried to bluff it out and kept walking, hoping it was a farm worker getting an early start. No such luck. It was a German soldier.

'*Halt!*' he said.

Tony kept walking.

'*Halt!*' said the soldier and stepped into his path.

An hour or so earlier, as he had floated towards earth in his parachute harness, Tony had thought how easy it would be to give himself up and spend the rest of the war in a POW camp. Now confronted with the prospect of capture, his fight-or-flight instinct took over. Tony lashed out with his heavy boot and kicked the German as hard as he could in the crotch. As the soldier staggered forward, Tony ripped his rifle from his grasp, and the two began to wrestle. The German's field cap was knocked off as Tony slipped behind him and grabbed his arm, pulling it backwards with all his strength until he felt it snap. As both men fell, the soldier's head hit the ground and he was knocked unconscious. Tony dragged him off the road and behind some pine trees. After using his parachute harness to secure the German, Tony went back, picked up the rifle, threw it into the trees and hurried away back down the road towards Limey.

—■—

Dave landed about ten kilometres east of the crash site—some twelve kilometres north of Tony's landing point—near the town of Jaulny. He walked west through the night and hid in woods outside the town during daylight. At dusk he headed south-west and soon realised the error of choosing to wear his suede boots for the operation rather than his fleece-lined flying boots. They were not meant for walking, and within a few hours his feet were badly blistered. He had no emergency rations and took to foraging for vegetables at night in fields and gardens, but the weather was too cold for crops and he found nothing. His hunger, coupled with the pain from his feet and a deep gash in his cheek—suffered when he pushed his way through the shattered Perspex cockpit roof—made for slow progress. He passed through the World War I cemetery of Saint-Mihiel and as day broke came to the village of Broussey-en-Woëvre, almost 25 kilometres from his starting point. His plan was to make it to some woods just south of the town and hide for the day, but with his physical and mental state deteriorating, he didn't know how much longer he could continue. As he passed through the village, he was spotted by several people. He was hard to miss: limping, unshaven, his face and hands cut, and wearing an RAF battledress, white sweater and those brown suede boots. He limped up the road for a short way past the village, then dragged himself up a rise to some trees. Flopping down, he leaned back against a trunk and closed his eyes for an hour or so before continuing his journey.

He was a kilometre past the town when a middle-aged man caught up to him on a bicycle.

'RAF?' he asked.

'Yes,' Dave nodded.

The man motioned up to the woods.

'You wait,' he said in hand signals.

Dave went back into the trees and waited. He didn't know who the man was and whether he would be returning with help or German soldiers, but at that moment he was almost too sore and exhausted to care.

Three hours later he saw the man walking up the hill towards him, carrying a small basket. Inside was wine, some hard-boiled eggs and a small loaf of bread. It was one of the best meals of Dave's life. When he had finished eating, the man again told him to wait and headed back down the hill. That night he returned and led the way back down the rise, through the village and to a small farm. He took Dave out to the barn and showed him where to sleep.

'You are safe here,' he said, and headed to the farmhouse, closing the barn door behind him.

—■—

Tony arrived at Limey around 3.30 a.m, cold and hungry. He tried the door of the church, hoping it might be unlocked. No such luck. He walked to the school, where the only door he found open led to a small lavatory. He used it, then continued walking through the town. On the outskirts he saw a light and walked towards a small building. He knocked quietly on the door and, getting no response, looked through the keyhole, coming eyeball to eyeball with a calf. It was a cow stall, and someone had left the light on all night.

EVASION

Tony made his way to a small wooded area above the town. There were some old World War I trenches, so he sat in one to try to get out of the icy wind. Every half hour he got up and walked around, trying to keep warm. He ate his chocolate bar and went through his escape kit. There was a little silk map, compass, a file, some Benzedrine tablets for energy (known as 'wakey-wakey pills' by the airmen) and a small sum in francs. He took the file and cut off the tops of his flying boots so they resembled a pair of ordinary shoes, made certain that none of his uniform was visible under his Irvin jacket and, looking as French as possible, set off southwards down the road.

After four hours he came to a signpost to the town of Ménil-la-Tour, which he found on his map. 'Gee, I'm a long way from Spain,' he thought, and realised he couldn't make it to the border without assistance. He decided to go into a church and ask the priest for help. He walked until the village of Lagney came into sight, nestled on the side of a steep hill. From his position Tony could see that the church was at the highest point of the town, near some woods. He decided to circle the outskirts of the town and approach the church through the woods to avoid being seen. He walked through an orchard and followed a dirt cart track, which led to a bitumen road. He was about to make a dash across the road to the woods on the other side when he heard the sound of marching feet. A squad of 35 German soldiers, under command of a sergeant, was coming along the road on the way to the village. He stood still and watched as they passed within a few feet of him, unaware that there was an enemy close by. Tony crossed the road, rejoined the track and made his way through the woods until he was above the church. As he made his way towards it, he heard a metallic banging noise. He looked through the trees and saw a clearing where mechanics were working on a number of lorries painted with *Balkenkreuze*—German military black crosses. He edged his way around them and got to the church.

The church was open but empty. Tony went inside, sat down in the second pew from the front and began to pray. After fifteen minutes an old nun came in and knelt at the other end of the same pew. She prayed for a few minutes and got up to leave. As she did, Tony stood and approached her. His hair was unkempt, his face and hands cut and scratched, his trousers covered in dull red mud from where he had been dragged by the parachute. The old lady gave him a disarming smile and asked how she could help him.

With her speaking no English and with Tony's French rudimentary at best, it took several minutes before it became obvious that they were never going to understand each other. Finally, the nun indicated that Tony should follow her and led the way to a house connected to the school adjoining the church. She rang the bell and a middle-aged woman came to the door. Her husband stood behind her listening as the nun spoke rapidly in French. When she had finished, the couple spoke heatedly for several minutes, the man apparently trying to persuade his wife on a course of action. Eventually she seemed to agree, and the man pulled Tony inside and led him into the kitchen.

'RAF?' he asked. Tony nodded.

'Parachute?' he said, making a hand signal of a canopy fluttering earthwards. Tony nodded again.

'Hungry?' he asked, pointing to his mouth.

'*Oui*,' said Tony emphatically.

The woman brought soup and an egg, which Tony devoured in seconds. The couple explained that this was the presbytery; they were the caretaker and housekeeper, and the priest would be home at 6 p.m. The woman prepared a bed for Tony on a sofa in the next room and pulled down the blinds. He was asleep almost before they had shut the door.

The next thing Tony knew, the man was shaking him awake. He looked at his watch. It was 7 p.m. They went into the kitchen, where the table was set for four. A few minutes later the priest came in. He was young, under 30, and had a glass eye and a scar down his cheek—the result, he told Tony, of fighting in the French army against the Germans in the early days of the war. Tony asked about the Underground, but the priest said he had no contact with it. Tony asked if he could stay the night at the presbytery and leave at first light. The priest shook his head.

'Impossible,' he said. There was a German officer billeted upstairs. He had already been downstairs for his dinner and asked why the living-room door was closed.

'Just blown shut by a draft,' the priest had told him.

The priest then showed Tony where he was on a map, and advised him not to go through the town of Toul as he headed south because there were a lot of Germans stationed there. Tony thanked the couple for their help and embraced them both. The priest walked him through Lagney until they reached the road to Toul, and they said their goodbyes.

Dave awoke the next morning as the barn door opened and in came the farmer, his wife and a girl and boy. The couple introduced themselves as Pierre and Jeanne Simon and their children as Jocelyne and Christian. Pierre said he was a member of the Underground and that Dave was the second Allied airman he had assisted. He said he would help Dave escape to Switzerland, but he must be patient and not leave the barn, as the Germans were searching for him.

Dave stayed in the Simons' barn for the next two days. Twice German soldiers came to the farm, but Pierre and Jeanne made much noise in greeting them and Dave hid without being detected. On Tuesday, 29 February, Pierre took Dave by car the 32 kilometres to Toul, which was 25 kilometres west of Nancy. When they arrived in Toul, Pierre led the way into the Café Croix de Lorraine, owned by Pierre Mathy. The Cross of Lorraine, consisting of one vertical bar crossed by two horizontal bars, one long and one short, is the emblem of Lorraine, the region in which Nancy sits. To have a café with such a name in Nancy was nothing out of the ordinary, but during the war the cross had added significance: it was adopted as the symbol of the Free French Forces as their answer to the swastika.

They took a seat at a table, and Pierre Simon turned the salt and pepper shakers in a certain way—a code indicating that he had an Allied evader with him. Pierre Mathy nodded, came over to the table, and took Dave by the arm upstairs to a bedroom. He would stay with Pierre and his wife, Suzanne, for the next two weeks.

For the first two or three days Dave remained in the room, unable to go downstairs for fear of being seen by the many

Germans who visited the café, but when Pierre supplied him with civilian clothes and an identity card, he became more confident. Each night Pierre and Suzanne would take him for a walk with their children through the streets of Toul and along the country roads. He became a familiar sight, and although many of the villagers deduced that he was an Allied airman, no one alerted the military authorities. Twice German soldiers came into the café as Dave sat at a table drinking coffee, but none gave him a second glance. Occasionally for exercise he would dig in the back garden—on one occasion helping Pierre to transplant a plum tree, pausing to lean on his spade and watch the Germans as they practised their drill in the field nearby.

On the afternoon of Sunday, 5 March, Pierre told Dave that he had a surprise for him and that he should get ready to go out that night. Thinking he was going to set off on the next part of his journey to Switzerland, Dave had a spring in his step as he walked down the road with Pierre and Suzanne. But instead of heading to the railway station or a waiting car, they arrived at the town picture theatre. Pierre bought three tickets, and Dave sat through the first part of *The Count of Monte Cristo*—all in French, with no subtitles. They were back the next Sunday night for part two.

On the second Saturday that he was with Pierre and Suzanne, Dave convinced them to accompany him on a bicycle ride to the nearby airfield in the hope that he might be able to steal a plane and fly to freedom. He was disappointed to find that the only aircraft were light trainers that would not get him far.

Two days later, on Monday, 13 March, Pierre took Dave to Toul railway station, where they were met by a woman in her 30s who said she was from the French Intelligence Service, and a young girl. Pierre said goodbye and Dave and his two female companions, now looking like an ordinary French family, boarded the train for the 45-minute journey to Nancy. The train was crowded, and Dave was forced to stand shoulder to shoulder with a German soldier. When they arrived, the soldier prepared to get off but had trouble extricating his rifle from the luggage rack. Dave helped him. The soldier thanked him politely and stepped onto the platform, with Dave and his companions following behind.

—■—

Tony reached Toul on 26 February, two days after being shot down and 48 hours before Dave would be driven to the town by Pierre Simon. Tony's welcome was not quite as warm as that given to Dave at the Mathys' café. Walking through the streets near the outskirts of Toul, he turned a corner and bumped into two German soldiers. When he was a few metres past them, one shouted, '*Englander!*' and Tony bolted, running up a side street and then turning up one road after another until he had given them the slip. He went through the centre of town and came to the first of several bridges. In nine months' time, the engineers of US General George Patton's Third Army would have to rebuild the bridges of Toul after they were destroyed by the retreating Germans, but as Tony tried to make his way through the town they were still intact and heavily guarded. There was a sentry on the first bridge, and Tony watched as he let locals cross with barely a second glance. Trying his luck, Tony walked closely behind a small group of villagers and got over without difficulty. Other bridges were more vigilantly monitored, and he was forced to detour, on one occasion walking over a frozen canal. South of the town he found a deserted house, badly damaged by shellfire and missing the roof and one entire wall. As darkness was now falling, he went upstairs with the plan of staying for the night. An hour later he heard footsteps coming up the stairs. It was the two Germans who had chased him earlier. He evaded them by jumping through the destroyed wall and scrambling down the rubble alongside the building, then ran with all his strength through the darkness.

Following a railway line, he continued south until dawn began to break. Exhausted and discouraged, he toyed with the idea of giving himself up to the Germans but decided to ask for help from the next French person he encountered. He saw a signal box up ahead and had advanced to within ten metres of it when a man rode up on a bicycle and began talking to someone inside. Tony crouched down in some long grass and listened. When they ended their conversation with '*Heil Hitler*' and crisp salutes, he swerved around the box and continued on his way. At around 11 a.m., he came to a little railway hut. Opening the door, he found it was empty, but there was a fire burning and on the table were a bottle of red wine and a basket containing a loaf of bread. He put these in the pockets of his Irvin jacket and headed into some woods. After the meal, he kept walking for another three or four hours. He spotted a small railway station consisting of a two-storey building and a tin-walled shed. The sign said Ruppes. Nearby was a hill covered in long grass. Exhausted from walking and lack of sleep, he went over to it and lay down, pulling the hood of his jacket over his head. Suddenly he heard footsteps and a voice speaking quickly in French. Tony pushed back his hood and saw a young man. In his less than fluent French, Tony explained that he was 'RAF'. The young man asked if he was hungry. When Tony answered yes, the man looked around and beckoned for Tony to follow him back to the railway station.

Inside were a man and woman aged in their 40s—the stationmaster and his wife. Tony could see that from their office they had a clear view of the grassy hill where he had tried to sleep. They quizzed him and gave him some food. The younger man then led the way out to the shed, which was divided into two sections by a thin wall. The half that Tony was led into was set up as a barn, with straw on the floor. Through the wall came the sound of timber being cut. The young man put his finger to his lips as a sign to be quiet, and told Tony, '*Boche*.' (German). He signalled for Tony to lie on the straw, gave him a blanket and covered him with more straw. Tony slept for a few hours until the young man returned and woke him. By now it was dark. They went outside and the man motioned Tony to follow him. The stationmaster and his wife came to the door of their office to wave them off.

'God speed, *bonne chance* and *bon voyage*,' they said.

Dave and his two companions were met at Nancy railway station and taken to a nearby house where he was fed and kept out of sight. They later returned to the station and boarded another train for the 250-kilometre trip south to Belfort. At the station they were met by a man who walked up to Dave's female companion and spoke to her in French. She turned to Dave.

'Do you have any money?'

He reached in his pocket and pulled out some German-issued franc notes, probably worth a few pounds, that had been in his escape kit.

'Give it to him,' she said.

He did as he was told, and the man led the way to a small van. The four drove in silence for about half an hour to a small village near the town of Delle. Leaving the car at the side of the road, they walked a few kilometres to an isolated farmhouse. A man met them at the door and ushered them inside. A meal was prepared and after they had eaten, around 9 p.m., all five left and began walking through light falling snow. After 90 minutes without talking, the woman turned to Dave and said with a small smile, 'You are in Switzerland.'

They walked on for a few more kilometres and came to a farmhouse. The owner was expecting them. The women embraced Dave and the two men shook his hand, then his companions headed back out into the snow. The owner of the house told Dave to be seated and went to a telephone to call the police. After speaking for a few minutes he hung up and started putting on his coat.

'They won't come up in the snow,' he said. 'We will have to go to them. Come on.'

——■——

Back in France, Tony walked alongside the young man for a few kilometres to the village of Martigny-les-Gerbonvaux. The man knocked on the door of a small house and they were let in by a young woman. The man explained that she was his wife. They had been married for 18 months and had a four-month-old baby. The woman prepared some food, while the man gestured for Tony to take off his boots and handed him a pair of slippers. Tony told the man his story: that he was an Australian flying for the RAF, that he had been shot down and was headed to Spain. The man shook his head.

'Impossible. The snow. You cannot cross the Pyrenees for months. You should go to Switzerland. They will have you back to England in a week.'

He rummaged in an old trunk and found a map, then drew Tony a rough route to Switzerland. The woman called them for dinner in their combination kitchen–bedroom, giving Tony the major share. When he asked if he was eating her portion, she told him she was on a special diet because of the baby.

Tony slept in the living room and was woken by the man at 4.30 a.m. They had coffee and some bread in front of the fire, and the man gave Tony a beret and a silver table knife. It was still dark when they left, the man walking beside Tony for about five kilometres before they parted. The man headed back to Ruppes, while Tony continued south, his sights now firmly set on Switzerland.

He reached Attignéville around dawn and walked on through Removille and Viocourt, then skirted around Houécourt because it was a larger village and there were a lot of people headed to Sunday church. After a rest in an orchard, he came to Belmont-sur-Vair, where he tried unsuccessfully to buy a bicycle from a man working in a field for 1000 francs, all the money he had. He continued on towards Vittel, through ever-increasing snow. South of Norroy, he began climbing a slight slope. He was about halfway up when a large group of people, dressed in civilian clothes, crested the hill and walked towards him. Behind them came two German soldiers. Tony's first instinct was to run and hide, but he realised that would only raise suspicions so he decided to bluff it out. He stood and smiled and nodded as the first of the group came nearer. As they passed, he heard they were speaking English. It became clear: they were English people who had been living in France when the Germans occupied the country and were now interned. The soldiers were taking them out for exercise. Some of the English looked closely at Tony and, despite his disguise, guessed he was a member of the RAF. The Germans didn't give him a second glance; they were too focused on speaking to two pretty girls. If the Germans didn't know who Tony was, at least one of the girls worked it out. She gave him a quick wink as she walked past.

At Vittel he walked through a racetrack and golf course. He avoided German sentries with rifles and fixed bayonets outside a group of large châteaux, then came to Vittel Palace, which was surrounded by barbed wire and sentry boxes and obviously being used as a prison. He passed eight sentry boxes and took a sharp right turn to get away from the military presence, only to almost bowl over a high-ranking German officer. With a quick '*Pardon, m'sieur,*' he bowed his head and took off out of the town as fast as he could.

Tony walked west until he cleared the outskirts of Vittel, then headed south again, reaching Lignéville about 5.30 p.m. He walked to the church and knocked on the window of the house next door. A woman and a small boy came out. Tony explained who he was and gestured at the snow, saying he needed a bed for the night. The woman shook her head but told the boy to take him to another house nearby. He waited in the cowshed of that house until the woman of the home finished milking her cow. She and her husband told Tony he couldn't stay. They were too close to Vittel, where there were a great many Germans. He asked about the priest. He was away, they said, and pushed him back onto the road.

The next town Tony came to was Provenchères-lès-Darney. By now it was 7.15 p.m. and almost dark. Tony had been walking for fourteen hours. He was exhausted and becoming desperate. He walked up to the church and tried the door, hoping to stay inside until the priest came to lock up. He was too late. The door was already locked. Outside, a group of five young boys were standing in the town square, watching him. Tony had planned to walk past them, but he noticed one was wearing a Cross of Lorraine—the emblem of the region but also the symbol of the Free French. Chancing his luck, Tony walked up to the boys and, in a combination of broken French and sign language, told them who he was and that he needed help. They stood with their mouths open. They looked so astonished that Tony told them to look at each other. They burst out laughing. Tony worked out that the youngest, aged about eight, and oldest, around ten, were brothers; the others were their friends. The youngest boy seemed to grasp the situation best and, taking Tony by the arm, led him to his home. When they arrived he ran through the front door shouting in French, 'We've got an RAF pilot!'

Tony was taken into a combination living and dining room, where he met the boys' parents, a sister and an older brother. They invited him to share their meal and then showed him to a bed in an upstairs room. He was asleep almost immediately. The next thing he knew, the light was being switched on and the room seemed to be full of people. Fearing he had been betrayed, he sat up, but a woman in her early 20s sat down beside him. 'Do not be afraid,' she said. 'I am your friend.'

It turned out that she had studied English at school. One of the boys had ridden his bicycle some 20 kilometres to tell her there was an English-speaking pilot at their house and that she should come quickly. By the time she arrived, many of the neighbours had also heard the news and come to see this RAF airman. More came and peeked through the doorway as the girl spoke to Tony. After about an hour, he could stay awake no longer.

That night, Dave had been sleeping in the barn of Pierre Simon. Bill Martin was in the POW hospital in Nancy. Their four crewmates had been buried earlier that day. It was 27 February.

The next morning, Tony and the boys' father set off around 6 a.m. After about two kilometres, the older man shook Tony's hand, sent him on his way, and headed back home. Tony continued through a forest, across a big canal at Selles, then south through Vauvillers. Heading south-east, he took a wrong turn and ended up walking east instead. By now it was around 6 p.m.

and getting dark. Emboldened by his experience of the previous night, Tony walked up to a woman who was washing clothes with her daughter at the back of a house. He explained what he wanted. The woman called to her husband. They spoke for a minute or so, then said 'Non.' Tony looked dejected and pointed to the frozen ground, gesturing, 'This is where I will have to sleep.' They were unmoved, so he turned and began walking away. He was 20 metres down the road when the man caught up, put his arm around Tony's shoulder and said, 'Come inside.'

Tony went in and sat in front of the open fire. He took off his shoes and laid them on the hearth. On the woman's urging he removed his wet socks, which she took away. The girl noticed Tony's lips were badly cracked. She rummaged in her handbag and gave him a tube of salve. After dinner he slept on the lounge and woke the next morning at 5.45 a.m. The family gave him coffee and bread and the woman handed back his socks, washed and dried in front of the fire. When he put them on he felt like a new man.

Finding the route again, he walked south-east through a series of villages. Just past Saulx, he saw an old man driving a horse cart full of hay towards him. As it passed him, the cart went over a rock and out from under the hay and onto the road slipped a trussed live calf. The man was full of explanations, but Tony just shrugged, helped him get the calf back onto the cart, and continued on his way. After about six kilometres, he walked along a cart track that led abruptly onto a road. As Tony reached the road, a car sped past, then stopped and reversed back to him. It was driven by a German officer with a civilian seated beside him.

'Is this the road to Vesoul?' the officer asked in German. Tony replied in his best French that he did not understand German. The officer tried again, this time in English. Again Tony said he didn't understand.

'Fool,' said the German, and drove on.

Shaken, Tony walked on. About ten kilometres on, he saw a woman picking vegetables in her back garden. It was starting to get dark, and by now he had his routine down pat. The woman seemed to understand his story and agreed that he could stay the night. She took him into the building, in the front of which was a small café opening onto the street. He sat down in the kitchen, took off his shoes and warmed himself in front of the fire. A girl about nine years old and a man in his late 20s came in and joined them for dinner. Afterwards they played cards, then the man and Tony went out to a room above the barn, where they slept.

When Tony woke early the next morning, the man was already up. Tony dressed, but his Irvin jacket was missing. He went up behind the man, slipped his arm around his neck and placed his knee in his back.

'Where is my coat?'

The man said he did not understand. Tony applied pressure to his throat until he admitted that perhaps he might know where the jacket was after all. When Tony released him, he grudgingly retrieved the Irvin from a trunk in the wardrobe. Tony put it on and left immediately.

He walked on but soon felt exhausted. He had now been trudging along roads and through fields for over five days. He looked at his watch. It was only 9 a.m. He opened his escape kit and took one of the Benzedrine 'wakey-wakey' pills, then set off again through the falling snow with renewed energy. The map the young man had given him back at Martigny-les-Gerbonvaux did not extend as far as he had travelled, so he was back to using the silk map. He was headed for the Lomont Mountains, but the direct route became increasingly difficult in the snow. By trial and error he found an easier path through what by now were low hills. As the ground grew steeper, the snow grew deeper. Even with the help of Benzedrine, it was slow, laborious going. Skirting villages and small towns, he pressed on, sinking to his knees at times, his feet and ankles sopping wet. At one point, he saw a light bobbing up and down, coming towards him through the trees. He lay in the snow without moving as two Germans wearing snowshoes walked past a short distance away. He was now just eleven kilometres from the Swiss border. With little cloud and a half moon, visibility was good, but the going was still slow. Just before midnight on Wednesday, 1 March 1944, he came to a stone sticking up out of the snow. On the side where he stood was the letter 'F'; on the other side, 'S'. He looked around, stepped smartly onto the side marked 'S', and kept walking. After about 800 metres he saw a frontier guard.

'Where am I?' he asked.

'Switzerland,' said the guard.

Tony raised his hands above his head.

'RAF,' he said. 'I surrender.'

17

BARBED WIRE AND BOBSLEIGHS

Bill was marched to the station at Heydekrug, where he and 3000 other Allied prisoners were herded into railway horse trailers. On the sides were painted the words in French: '40 Men—10 Horses'. Each car was divided into three sections, including one originally used for the horses and one for their attendants. The prisoners were jammed into the third area, the guards having the attendants' section to themselves. There was not enough room to lie down, and only a wooden bucket for a toilet, making it a long and uncomfortable 600-kilometre journey south-west from Lithuania to the heart of Poland.

The train reached its destination, a remote station near the town of Thorn (now Toruń), on 19 July 1944. The prisoners were offloaded and, stiff and sore from days crammed together in the railway cars, marched four kilometres at rifle point through the town to the camp. As they filed through the railway yard, they saw bedraggled-looking groups of local women working as forced labour, re-laying crushed stone ballast under the tracks. It was anything but an encouraging sight, and the men's first glimpse of their new home did nothing to raise their spirits.

Built on sandy ground, Stalag 357 consisted of characterless barracks blocks surrounded by barbed-wire fencing punctuated with guard towers. On one side was an artillery range, on the other the railway track. The men were taken first to a processing area where they were held for two days, sleeping on the usual three-tier racks with damp straw bedding. From there they were taken to a compound newly built for the incoming Allied air-crew NCOs. The arrival of 3000 new mouths to feed was, understandably, not welcomed by the 7000 army POWs already being housed at Stalag 357, and the reception the air crews received was not overly friendly. The prison population's already meagre rations were halved, and all communal facilities became stretched beyond capacity. The only high point of the incarceration at Thorn was when news spread through the camp of the assassination attempt on the life of Adolf Hitler the day after Bill's arrival. The hidden radio at the camp—smuggled from Heydekrug under the direction of Dixie Deans—soon relayed the information that the attempt had been unsuccessful and the perpetrators—along with almost 5000 suspected co-conspirators—had been executed, but this further evidence of the unravelling of the Nazi regime reinforced the POWs' belief that the end was near.

Bill was at Stalag 357 for only two and a half weeks before he was instructed on 8 August to collect his few belongings and prepare to move. With each passing month the Germans had become more concerned that the Soviets descending from the north and the Americans and British pushing up from France would reach the POW camps and liberate the Germans' possible bargaining chips. The prisoners were continually moved further away from the advancing Allies. This time, Bill's destination was Fallingbostel in Germany, 60 kilometres south of Hamburg. The 700-kilometre train journey was torture, made worse by his back problems. Crammed into cattle trucks, the prisoners endured a miserable two-day trip that saw them at one stage come under fire from three US aircraft that were strafing a fuel-tanker train on the parallel line. The sight of American aircraft in the skies above Germany was further proof of how far the Allies were advancing, but it did not lead to any lessening of the Germans' grip on the prisoners. In fact, just the opposite happened. With the noose tightening around them, the Germans became edgier and more paranoid. The nine months that Bill would spend at Stalag 357 Fallingbostel— the camp number was transferred from Thorn along with the prisoners—were the worst of his time in captivity and the worst of his life.

Fallingbostel was not just one POW camp. A large area that had once contained 25 villages, it was resumed by the Nazis before the war for the construction of a sprawling complex of military training camps. The workers used to build these huge training camps were housed in temporary wooden barracks in a small village just outside Fallingbostel. When the Germans invaded Poland in September 1939, they brought Polish POWs back to Germany to serve as forced labour. One of the areas chosen to house them was Fallingbostel, and fences were erected around the former workers' barracks to create Stalag XIB. By May 1940, as the Germans moved through the Netherlands, Belgium and France, large numbers of POWs, including British servicemen, were captured and imprisoned, and 40,000 were sent to Stalag XIB. The one-time workers' camp was hopelessly inadequate. Hygiene became a major problem, and an outbreak of typhus resulted in thousands of deaths.

After the Germans invaded the Soviet Union in June 1941, huge numbers of Soviet POWs were brought back to Germany. The first influx of 12,000 alone was too great for the already overstretched facilities of Stalag XIB, so the Germans fenced off a large, flat open area a kilometre to the north-east, designated it Stalag XID and placed the Soviets there. Considered subhuman by the Germans, they were largely left to fend for themselves. In less than 12 months, more than 6000 had died from typhus.

Over the next few years, while Fallingbostel still operated as a major training centre for Panzer and infantry units, the numbers of prisoners held in camps around the area continued to swell. In September 1943, after Italy surrendered to the Allies, Italian POWs were added to the mix. One entire Italian motorised unit training at Fallingbostel was simply disarmed by their former allies and marched from their barracks, down the road and through the gates into Stalag XID. Considered traitors by the Germans, the Italians were treated almost as badly as the Soviets.

When the Germans decided to transfer Stalag 357 from Thorn to Fallingbostel, the Italian prisoners were set to work upgrading facilities at XID in preparation. But when Dixie Deans led Bill and the other prisoners from Thorn into the 'new' 357, they would have been hard pressed to notice any 'improvements'. The Commonwealth POW compound was better than the pitiful conditions endured by the Soviet and Italian prisoners, but that was not saying much. With the arrival of the prisoners from Thorn, there were upwards of 96,000 POWs in the camps and sub-camps at Fallingbostel. They were guarded by *Landesschützen*, home defence battalions, usually made up of old men or those unfit for military service, under the control of officers and NCOs who had been excused from active duty because of physical or psychological disability.

Even so, security was tight. The camps were surrounded by two high barbed-wire fences about two metres apart. If a prisoner managed to get over or through the first, he would be confronted with bales of coiled barbed wire blocking his path to the second, outer fence. The 'no man's land' was lit by arc lights at all times except during air raids, and guards with machine guns and searchlights looked down from towers spaced evenly around the perimeter. This was in addition to regular patrols by guards with dogs. The use of dogs was more prevalent at Fallingbostel than at many other camps, with guards encouraged to sool the animals on prisoners who were slow to follow orders. This did not always have the desired effect in the Soviet compound: two dogs sent into a hut to break up a disturbance were killed and eaten by the starving prisoners. Even though the huts were too far from the fences to make tunnelling a viable option for escape, the Germans regularly drove a small heavy roller around the camp in the hope of collapsing any tunnels that might be in progress.

Accommodation in Stalag 357 consisted mainly of stone barracks or wooden huts, each holding around 60 men. Bill was housed in one of the former, but neither option was remotely comfortable. All the barracks suffered from leaking roofs, broken windows and insufficient lighting. And of course there was never enough food. It became the men's obsession. As he drifted off to sleep fitfully each night, Bill wondered if he would ever again know what it was like to not feel hungry.

Tony was transported by car under police escort to the Swiss town of Porrentruy, less than a kilometre from the French border. Arriving at 1.30 a.m. on 2 March, he was taken to a hotel, where he was given some food and then led to a small bedroom. As he lay down on the bed, he heard the door being locked from the outside.

Switzerland was a neutral country during World War II, but that did not mean that all Allied troops who found their way across its borders from occupied territories were immediately free, or that a return to their home bases was a matter of simply contacting the British or American consulate and waiting for transport to arrive. Far from it. The Swiss were in an invidious position. They had remained neutral, but were always under threat of being invaded by the Germans through France or Italy and therefore had to maintain a balance, making themselves valuable to both sides.

The Germans took great advantage of the Swiss banking system, while the Allies benefited from Switzerland's being a safe haven for escaped POWs and shot-down airmen. The country also acted as an intermediary during negotiations for exchanges of Axis prisoners of war for Allied personnel being held in Switzerland.

While not a signatory of the Geneva Convention—the agreement covering the treatment of wounded and captured prisoners during warfare—Switzerland nonetheless followed its stipulations to the letter. This meant appearing to scrupulously adhere to the Geneva Convention rules for the treatment of foreign military personnel within its borders—and not playing favourites. The result was often an almost laughable game of sleight of hand, wherein the Swiss would turn a blind eye to certain indiscretions on the part of the warring parties, but could not be seen to be doing so. As an example, in April 1944 a Lancaster from 35 Squadron RAF was shot down over the southern German town of Friedrichshafen, near the borders of Switzerland and Austria. Four of the crew bailed out, but the other three ditched the aircraft and paddled an emergency dinghy to the Swiss side of the lake. They were then interned in a camp. In October, the RAF air attaché in Bern sent word to the airmen that following negotiations with the Swiss there would be no objections if they wished to attempt an escape—but that if they were caught, they would be sentenced to six months hard labour by the Swiss authorities.

The treatment meted out by the Swiss under the Geneva Convention varied according to specified categories. Most important of these as far as Allied airmen were concerned was whether they were classed as 'escapers' or 'evaders'. Simply put, escapers were those who had been in enemy hands and escaped, usually from a POW camp or while being transported to or from a prison camp, and made their way to Switzerland. Evaders, in most cases air crew, had evaded capture after being shot down in enemy territory and then managed to cross the border—or, in some cases, had crash landed in Switzerland while returning from an operation. Under the rules of the Geneva Convention, escapers were placed in military internment camps but were entitled to attempt to escape. Evaders, under a 'gentleman's agreement', were expected to stay in Switzerland in hotel accommodation until the end of the war and were therefore given more freedom within certain allotted areas. Accordingly, MI9, the British Military Intelligence unit whose job it was to encourage—but not facilitate—the escape of POWs, advised Allied air crew who made it to neutral territory to claim to be escapers rather than evaders, and to have a credible cover story ready in order to convince Swiss authorities.

At the hotel in Porrentruy, Tony put together a cover story. Whether it would be found credible was another matter. He was awakened by a Swiss Army corporal about 7 a.m. and given a breakfast of coffee and a bread roll. The manager of the hotel then asked him to sign the register. Until his status was determined, Tony's room and board would have to be paid by the Swiss government, and paperwork was required for all expenditure. After the manager had explained this, Tony asked for a shave and haircut, plus a toothbrush and some toiletries, to be provided and added to the bill. He was then taken to the police station to be fingerprinted, weighed and measured.

At 11.30 a.m., he and the corporal went to the railway station, where they had lunch at the buffet. The corporal told Tony he was taking him 100 kilometres south to Bern for interrogation. On the train the corporal played cards with some other soldiers while Tony took in the scenery. An hour into the journey, a red-headed man walked past on his way to the dining car. He gave Tony a close look, and on his return came over and asked if he was 'RAF'. When Tony replied that he was, the man introduced himself as Squadron Leader Smith, an RAF pilot who had been shot down and imprisoned in Italy but had escaped along with many other POWs after Italy capitulated to the Allies. Smith, who appeared to know his way around, asked Tony's guard if he could take him to the dining car for a cup of tea. The guard, engrossed in his card game, waved them away. Over a cuppa, the garrulous Smith told Tony that after his interrogation he would be quarantined in Bern for three weeks and would then join other Australian evaders at Arosa, a ski resort 270 kilometres to the east.

Arriving in Bern, the Swiss capital, Tony and his guard walked to an old palace that now housed government offices. Tony was sent to sit in a room that was empty except for a table and two chairs. After a few minutes he was joined by a large Swiss Army captain who aggressively told Tony to give him the facts about who he was and how he had come to be in Switzerland. Knowing that he would have to spin quite a tale in order to be accepted as an escaper rather than an evader, and so have at least a chance of getting back to England and re-entering the war, Tony let his imagination run wild.

'I was shot down over Berlin on 2 January,' he said.

I was captured by some local residents who were going to kill me, but one of them talked the others out of it and they handed me over to some soldiers. From there I was sent to Frankfurt and put in solitary confinement for a long time. They questioned me every couple of days, but I didn't tell them anything, so in the end they said they were sending me to a POW camp in Poland. I was on the train to Poland with one guard and after a while I told him I had to go to the toilet. There wasn't room for both of us, so he waited outside and I opened the window and jumped out. That's how I got these cuts on my face and hands. I then got on a goods train headed south and got off at Strasbourg. Then I started west and crossed the Rhine . . . have you got a map?

The officer opened a map on the table.
'Here,' said Tony, pointing.
'How?' the officer asked.
'How what?'
'How did you cross the river.'
'I stole a little boat and rowed across.'
The officer didn't comment, so Tony continued.
'From there I continued to Nancy and Metz,' he said, getting on to the real route that he had taken.
'Why did you go so far west?' his interrogator asked.
'My original plan was to go to Spain, but there was too much snow on the mountains, so I had to change direction and head to Switzerland. Believe me, I wouldn't have come here if I didn't have to.'

It was probably the only part of the story that rang true. If Tony had got to Spain, he had a good chance of getting straight back to London. As an evader in Switzerland, he would have to sit out the war, and not only was the Swiss officer not buying his story that he was an Allied escaper, he wasn't even convinced that he was a member of the RAF.

'I don't believe one word of that. I think you are a German deserter. I will check and send you back to Germany.'

Tony asked to see the British Consul immediately. The officer slammed his hand on the desk and told Tony he wouldn't be seeing anyone until he gave a satisfactory account of himself.

'You can have a few days in a cell to think about it.'

The officer called for Tony's escort, who took him back to the railway station, where they caught a train to Olten, about half an hour's journey due north. Tony was handed over to a Swiss Army corporal who walked him to a grim-looking two-storey building that backed onto a river. Tony asked what the building was, and the corporal told him it was a prison for political prisoners. When Tony asked how long prisoners were usually held there, the soldier said, 'We have one who has been here since the last war.'

Tony was placed in a small cell behind a thick wooden door. After a few hours, a girl brought him some soup in a dirty jug and a cup of coffee. He tried both but couldn't finish them. When a man came by to collect the dishes, Tony asked if he knew how long he would be kept there. The answer was a lot more encouraging than the one he'd received earlier.

'Just the night. Then you will be taken to the headquarters of the Swiss Air Force in Zürich for questioning.'

The man asked Tony where he was from. When Tony said Sydney, the man told him he had been there on a ship after the First World War. He said he had seen pictures of the Sydney Harbour Bridge, and asked Tony what it was like. The friendly conversation slightly eased Tony's anxiety, and he was later able to stretch out on the wooden bed and sleep under a dirty blanket.

Next morning, he was taken down to the basement of the building and given a bucket of cold water to wash with. Looking on from behind barred doors was a collection of miserable and pathetic-looking prisoners, each confined to a separate cell. Unshaven, pale and staring at him with lifeless eyes, they had obviously been imprisoned for a long time. A guard told Tony they were the country's worst political prisoners, allowed out of their cells once a week and with no hope of release. Resigned to the fact that he would not be accepted as an escaper, Tony resolved to put on a good show at the Air Force headquarters and present himself as an evader so that at least he would never have to return to that building.

The corporal from the previous day took Tony by train to Zürich, another hour's trip north. At Air Force headquarters, Tony was met by a young lieutenant who shook his hand pleasantly and asked if he had eaten lunch. When Tony said he hadn't, the officer led the way to a lounge, where he ordered food and offered Tony a drink.

When Tony refused, the officer smiled.

'You don't drink?' he asked.

'I do, just not now,' Tony replied. The officer shrugged and began asking questions. Some, like name, rank, service number and home address, Tony was happy to answer. Other information, such as Tony's squadron, what operation he had been on and other specific military information, he would not—or could not—provide. The officer told Tony that he had still not given any proof that he was an Australian in the RAF, as he claimed. Was there anyone who could vouch for him? Tony grabbed at the only straw he had and mentioned Squadron Leader Smith, whom he had met on the train.

'Smithy?' said the lieutenant. 'You know Smithy? I interrogated him when he arrived in Switzerland.'

The officer left Tony to finish his meal and returned half an hour later.

'All is good,' he said. 'You will stay in Bern for three weeks' quarantine and then be taken to Arosa for the winter with the other Australians.'

Almost before he had left the headquarters of the Swiss Air Force, news of Tony's status as an evader was being processed, and details began working their way through official channels all the way to Melbourne. On 6 March, less than a week after he turned himself in to the Swiss border guard, a cypher message was sent to Australia from RAAF overseas headquarters in London:

Information received through Intelligence branch reports F/O D'Arcey A arrived neutral country. Request inform next of kin to treat news as confidential and not release to press. Correspondence should be addressed care of Air Ministry, King Charles St, London SW1. Parcels should not be sent.

Reclassified safe neutral territory. Officer states as he was first to bail out he has no news of rest of crew.

Another young soldier took Tony back to Bern, to a hotel that would be his home for the next few weeks. The daughter of the owner checked him in to his room and led the way into the dining room. There were five young men sitting at a table. Two were English and two American. The fifth stood as he approached and put out his hand.

'G'day, mate,' he said. 'Les Simpson. RAAF.'

Flight Sergeant Leslie Robert Simpson, born in Western Australia and enlisted in Melbourne, was an old hand at life as an evader, having arrived in Switzerland all of eleven days before Tony. He took the newcomer under his wing, showed him around the hotel and explained the routine of life as a guest of a neutral country.

Unlike the escapers, many of whom had escaped from Italian POW camps and made their way to Switzerland after Italy ended its alliance with Germany in September 1943, he would be relatively free to come and go within the perimeters of the township in which he was housed. While the escapers were housed in 'military internment camps' (usually disused factories or school buildings) loosely overseen by Swiss soldiers and local police, the evaders lived in hotels and guest-houses and were able to take advantage of all amenities, such as cinemas, libraries and winter sports, unsupervised.

As the war had dragged on and more Allied personnel arrived, the Swiss had been hit with an accommodation crisis. The solution was to open up the winter sports resorts to the east of Bern and send Allied internees on a rotation basis for a month or so at a time. The idea was to make the best use of the facilities available, give the foreigners a change of scenery, and boost the local economy. With their usual clientele not coming from Europe for the ski season due to the war, the hoteliers and inn-keepers of once popular resorts such as Davos, Adelboden, Arosa and Klosters—where the US evaders were sent—were more than happy to have their rooms filled by Allied soldiers and airmen, all paid for by the Swiss government.

Accommodation was not the only thing in short supply. With the Swiss suffering from the same food shortages as other European countries during the war, the Australian evaders received a daily food ration just like the local populace. Food and all other necessities, including clothing, toiletries and entertainment, were purchased in local currency supplied in a monthly allowance by the British legation in Bern.

With 'Simmo' as his guide and companion, Tony spent three weeks in Bern. Then, at the end of March, he went to Arosa for his spell in the Alps. It was four hours on the train but a world away from Bern, let alone the North Shore of Sydney, where he had grown up accustomed to the aroma of backyard barbecues and the sound of kookaburras in the neighbours' gum trees.

The sight that greeted Tony as he arrived seemed like something from the cover of a Christmas card. With the ski season in full swing for another month or so, the whole area was covered with snow, the locals and holiday-makers could be seen skiing and tobogganing on the slopes, and the rustic

221

hotels and guesthouses that dotted the hills added to a pictur-esque setting a world away from war and Bomber Command.

At the station, Tony was directed to Edelweiss Villa, a family-owned guesthouse a short walk from the township. Located on a small lake, close to hiking trails through the forest and with stunning views of the snow-capped mountains, it was to be a friendly and warm home base for Tony and some fellow Australian evaders for the next few months. The rooms were comfortable and well appointed, and most had balconies. The villa had its own restaurant and livestock. There were trout to be caught in the lake, access to skis, toboggans and bobsleighs, and, as the weather warmed, benches for those who wished to rest and take in the views while hiking in the forest.

But impressed as Tony was by the Edelweiss, it was not thoughts of a good shower or fresh eggs that made his heart leap as he signed the registry book. It was the name that he read a few lines above his.

'David Baxter, Wonthaggi, Australia.'

—■—

Just like Tony some three weeks before him, Dave had spent his first night in Switzerland under guard at Porrentruy. When the police refused to come up the mountain to take him into custody, the Swiss farmer, at whose door the Frenchwoman left him, had taken him to the police station. (Later Dave would learn that he was the last Allied airman the woman led to freedom. She was killed by the Germans on her next journey.) Like Tony, Dave spent a night in a Porrentruy hotel before being taken by train to Bern, where he was interrogated by a

Swiss Army officer. Thanks to a lack of suitable accommodation, he stayed only two days in the Swiss capital before he was sent 80 kilometres north-east to the hamlet of Bad Lostdorf. While Dave was there, the Swiss authorities informed the RAF attaché in Bern of his whereabouts and status as an evader. Exactly a week after he had crossed the border into Switzerland, a telegram was despatched to his mother in Wonthaggi:

Mrs J. Baxter. Pleased to inform you that your son Pilot Officer David Wright Baxter previously reported missing arrived in a neutral country on 14th March 1944. Request you treat this information as strictly confidential and do not release to press. Correspondence should be addressed to your son care of Air Ministry at 1 King St London W1. Any further information will be conveyed to you immediately. Air Force, Anderson St, South Yarra.

'We both started crying again,' recalled Dave's brother Ron, 'this time because we were happy.'

So happy, in fact, that they found it impossible to keep the news to themselves. Despite the official request to 'treat this information as strictly confidential and do not release to press', it was not long before the local newspaper published the latest instalment in its coverage of the wartime exploits of Wonthaggi's schoolboy star turned war hero. Headlined 'Pilot Officer Dave Baxter Reported Safe', the story read:

Pilot Officer Dave Baxter who was reported 'missing' over Germany on February 24, is now reported alive and well.

CREW

At the end of February Dave was a Lancaster pilot attached to the RAAF. He was bombing Schweinfurt, Germany, when he was reported missing. Dave has also been over Berlin. Nearly a fortnight ago Mrs Baxter received news that her son had received his commission, the commissioned rank dated back to January 24, exactly a month before he was reported 'missing'. His many friends in Wonthaggi will be looking forward to his return in the near future.

After completing his quarantine at Bad Lostdorf on a diet of soup and potatoes, Dave was relieved to be sent to Arosa and the Edelweiss.

Seeing Dave's details in the register, Tony excitedly asked the manager where he could find Pilot Officer Baxter. The manager led him into the lounge, where Dave was sitting. It was a joyful reunion, the two men embracing and quickly bringing each other up to date on their adventures. Tony's elation at seeing Dave soon turned to sadness. As he had been the first out of the stricken aircraft, and as he knew the skipper would be the last, he had assumed that the other five were also safe.

'Are the others here?' he said, looking around the room.

Dave shook his head.

'Just me. I don't know what happened to them.'

They were silent for a moment, thinking of their crewmates, but then both agreed that if the two of them had managed to get out and make it to Switzerland in one piece, anything was possible. For all they knew, Hoppy, Fergy, Jock, Pete and Bill were already back in the mess at Binbrook, waiting for their return.

224

As Dave told Tony, the Edelweiss, and Arosa itself, was full of Australian airmen. Under the terms of their status as evaders, they were able to come and go as they pleased. The only stipulation was that they stay within the precincts of Arosa, but if they wished to leave the area to sightsee or visit fellow evaders staying at other resorts, it was a simple process to obtain a travel pass from local authorities. Once a month they would receive an allowance, in Swiss francs, and any mail, from the British Military Attaché in Bern via the Executive Officer, a high-ranked evader who had headquarters in the nearby resort of Wil. The money, deducted from their pay, which continued to be paid as usual to their accounts in the UK would be used to settle their hotel 'extras' bill, and they could spend the remainder in the local shops, restaurants, taverns and cinema. As well as receiving their pay as if they were still serving with their squadron or unit, the evaders continued to accumulate leave and remain eligible for regular promotion. (Based on time served, Dave was promoted to Flying Officer on 24 July, five days after Tony received the same promotion.)

With Arosa's winter season lasting only until mid-April, Dave and Tony did not try to learn to ski, but they enjoyed watching the locals and some fellow evaders testing themselves on the slopes. Soon they fell into a routine of exploring the town and surrounding areas and socialising with their fellow evaders. These were mainly from Australia and Canada; the British and New Zealanders stayed at Wil. It was a surreal experience for the young men, who only weeks earlier had been dropping bombs over Berlin and dodging spotlights, exploding anti-aircraft shells and night fighters in the hope of beating the less than 50-50 odds of living another day. Now here they were, in a picture-postcard world of skis, sleighs and afternoon drinks on the terrace. If they tired of outdoor activities they could get together a group for a visit to the Hotel Schweizerhof for a few hours play at the *kegelbahn*—bowling alley—and there were large group lunches and dinners at local venues, including the grandest establishment in the valley, the 110-year-old, five-star Hotel Kulm.

Wherever they went in Arosa they were welcomed and feted. The locals not only appreciated their much-needed custom but in many cases welcomed them as allies, as it was felt that without the intervention of the British, and then the Americans, it would have been only a matter of time before Germany invaded Switzerland. The evaders were invited into the homes of the locals, and to dances and parties, and close friendships were formed. One Australian, Flight Lieutenant Fred Eggleston from Melbourne, even married an Arosa girl, Heidi Tagman.

But much as the men appreciated their surroundings and their freedom, the fact remained that they were military airmen, young, fit and trained to do a job. That they were sitting around looking at the mountains or playing games while their mates were fighting and dying 1000 kilometres or so to the north ate at them. Not only did they no longer feel like military men, they didn't look like them. They wore 'civvies' instead of their uniforms and were referred to as 'Mr' rather than the air-force rank to which they had once answered with such pride. There were even instances of Allied and Nazi military personnel coming into contact with each other and acting as if the war had never happened. US Air Force navigator Arthur Foster—who was shot down on the infamous 'Black Thursday' daytime raid on Schweinfurt five months before Dave and Tony came to grief en route to the same destination—did his Bern quarantine at a hotel over-looking the city's golf course. When winter came, he and his fellow American evaders were sent to the resort of Klosters. In his memoirs, he recalled a bizarre encounter with the enemy during a day's ski trip.

> We made many skiing expeditions, including to the Davos ski facilities. The famous Kublis and Klosters ski runs from the Davos mountain peak were quite memorable. Some of us also skated, and others entered bobsled races. About a dozen of us also scaled the Silvretta Glacier in the spring of 1944, where we skied the entire next day to the consternation of certain German armed forces down below us at the border location. One day a number of Luftwaffe flyers sat near us on the funicular tram taking us all to the top of the Davos peak to begin our ski runs. They were about the same age as ourselves—20 to 22—and were supposedly there on Rest and Recuperation treatment for tuberculosis. We all laughed at that potential subterfuge and exchanged tales of the various combat missions we had experienced where all of us might have been firing at each other. Such can be the strangeness of war.

The novelty soon wore off for Dave and Tony. When the winter ended and they could no longer spend their time on the slopes, boredom set in. Arosa came to feel less like a holiday resort and more like a prison.

On 21 April, after less than a month at Arosa, Dave wrote to Sergeant Vic Pollard, a friend from 460 Squadron, bringing him up to date on life in Switzerland. Though safe from the dangers of warfare, he did not paint a picture of blissful contentment.

Dear Blue, just a few lines to let you know I am still alive and well. I am in the pink now and have only one scar on my cheek to remember the last few weeks.

I have been living up in the Alps, 6000ft above sea level. We are surrounded by mountain peaks, one of which is 10,000ft high. They look very pretty but were much nicer a couple of weeks ago when they were covered with snow. It is surprising how quickly the snow has disappeared this last week. The mountains are almost bare and the road and foot-paths are free from snow and slush at last—thank goodness. I hated walking through the slush and sometimes sinking up to my knees.

We had many visitors for Easter—the main attraction being skiing. Tony and I had the opportunity to learn but seeing the season was almost finished we didn't consider it worthwhile.

Most of the time is spent in walking. We have walked everywhere there is to walk so it is getting very monoto-nous. In the morning we have a stroll after breakfast and in the afternoon we go out for afternoon tea and come back in time for supper. We also read and play cards but it gets very boring. Last week there was an American picture showing at the cinema. I went along but it was poor. This week there was a German film so I didn't go—my knowledge of German wouldn't allow me to understand it. I can speak two words. Yes and No.

A fortnight ago I spent two days in Bern, the capital. It's a lovely place and I would have liked to stay longer. Whilst there I visited the pictures which were quite good even though I had seen them a few years ago.

I have to duck off for a while, Blue. Tony has come to drag me off for afternoon tea. Needless to say I don't need much encouragement.

After a break of four hours, he was back to finish the letter, and ask his mate for some help regarding Joyce, his sweetheart back home in Wonthaggi.

I have consumed the tea and apple pie, several beers etc. and my dinner, so please excuse any mistakes.

I would be very grateful if you could help me with the following. Joyce sent me a present for my 21st birthday and if you can grab hold of it, hang on to it. If any cakes and parcels of food etc arrive and can't be sent on to me, I'm sure you can find some use for them. Also, Tony and I would be pleased if you could keep your eye on our belongings and see that they hang on to them.

Well Blue, that's all the news at the moment so I'll close. Hoping you are well. Tony sends his kindest regards.

Cheerio and best wishes, Dave.

P.S. My regards to the boys.

Dave would have to cope with the relative monotony of Arosa for another month. In June, he and Tony were instructed to pack their few belongings and travel four and a half hours by train to Glion, a village above Montreux, overlooking Lake Geneva. The crewmates' new digs were in the Hotel Placida, another privately owned guesthouse that had also served as a refuge for Allied military men in World War I. Comfortable and friendly, its best feature as far as Dave and Tony were concerned was its close proximity to the far grander Hotel Bellevue, where the majority of the British evaders, as well as some Australians and Canadians, were housed. The Bellevue boasted an unsurpassed view of Lake Geneva from its large terrace, and its lounge-bar and restaurant became an unofficial Officers' Club for the Allied evaders.

Once again, Dave and Tony settled into a routine, exercising by walking, or swimming in Lake Geneva, and answering letters from home. They were free to travel to nearby cities and towns. Once a month they would go to Caux to pick up their pay, which was distributed by the Allied Executive Officer at the camp where escaped POWs were housed. This was located in the splendid-looking Caux Palace Hotel, said to have been used by Walt Disney artists as the model for the castle in the animated movie *Snow White and the Seven Dwarfs*. But even here, the war was never far away. On 23 July, Dave and Tony stood helplessly on the terrace of the Hotel Bellevue with their fellow evaders and watched smoke rise from the other side of Lake Geneva as the SS burned the French–Swiss border town of Saint-Gingolph in retribution for the death of two German soldiers in a skirmish with local Resistance fighters.

BARBED WIRE AND BOBSLEIGHS

Located 20 kilometres from Glion, Saint-Gingolph was a key centre for the French Resistance. The River Morge, which ran through the town, served as the border between France and Switzerland. Bridges spanning the river were well guarded by the Germans on the French side, but unbeknown to them, the Resistance was using an old stormwater drain linking the two sides to smuggle arms into France and sometimes persecuted Jews into Switzerland. On 22 July, two German soldiers and two Resistance fighters were killed in a skirmish in the town. The next day, the SS began rounding up suspected Resistance sympathisers. Eight prominent townspeople, including the local priest and the postmaster and his thirteen-year-old daughter, were taken in for questioning. More would have been arrested if not for the action of the mayor on the Swiss side of the river. Against German orders, he opened the border, allowing 300 townspeople to flee into Switzerland. The postmaster and his daughter were released, but the others were taken to the town square and shot. The Germans then torched the town.

As the war went on without them, the Allied airmen could only try to keep themselves occupied and dream of home. On 11 August, Dave wrote to Joyce:

My dearest Joyce, it is a beautiful afternoon but I have decided not to go swimming as I am suffering from the after-effects of a hard day's work yesterday. Instead I am sitting in the shade of a tree, writing. Tony is opposite me also writing. Yesterday Tony and I thought a little exercise was needed so we decided to climb to the top of 'Rochers du Naye', a 6000ft peak a few miles from here. We left just after 10 a.m. and managed the first half of the trip fairly well as we had a good road to walk on. We left the road and proceeded along a narrow track covered with loose stones. It was hard work here as we were slipping and sliding. At this stage I had removed my shirt and was losing a gallon of perspiration an hour. After two and a half hours we arrived at the top, having climbed the last few hundred feet in clouds. It had been very fine when we left so we were very disappointed to find cloud at the top. At one o'clock we ate our lunch which we had carried with us. There were some breaks in the cloud and the view was marvellous. We could see almost the whole of Lake Geneva and the rugged peaks to the north and east, however we could not see Mont Blanc which is visible on a clear day.

One of the glider clubs launches their gliders from the Roches. There were half a dozen lying about as the chaps were waiting for the clouds to disperse. It did so when we were half way home and we saw one of the gliders in the air. At 3 o'clock we decided to come home and this time we used a different route. It was much easier to walk but much longer. Nevertheless my feet were complaining all the way down. I finished up with a couple of blisters. It took us almost two and a half hours to come down. We covered about 15 miles during the day. Today my legs are a little stiff so I don't think I would enjoy swimming.

In this country August 1 is the National Day and the people had quite a celebration. In the evening they started off with a procession; many of the people wearing costumes which I had often seen in educational magazines etc. Then followed speeches and a fireworks display. After that came the dancing. I went to one café and, believe it or not, danced half a dozen times. I had a very good time and arrived home at 3.30 a.m. The following day one of the Canadian lads and I took our lunches down to the lake for the day. The water was beautiful and I thoroughly enjoyed the swimming.

This week a lot of English and Australian mail has arrived but as yet I have received none. I hope to get some in the next couple of days. Tony received some cables and airgraphs from home. That's all the news so cheerio for the present. Kindest regards to all at home. All my love, Dave xxxx.

It would be the last letter Joyce would receive from Switzerland.

Dave and Tony had never given up hope of getting back to England in time to have another crack at the enemy. While at Glion, they had applied for permission from the Swiss to make a day trip to Geneva. On 8 June, they travelled the 95 kilometres to the British Consulate in Geneva, where they were photographed and issued with a document titled Emergency Certificate, which stated they were British subjects, having been born in Australia, and that 'This certificate is valid for the journey to the United Kingdom and residence in Switzerland. The validity of this certificate expires TWO years from the date of issue and must be surrendered to the Immigration Officer at the place of Arrival.'

The two crewmates had no intention of staying in Switzerland for two years, but the prospect of 'the journey to the United Kingdom' was never far from their thoughts. All they needed was an opportunity. It was not long in coming. On 15 August 1944, US forces launched Operation Dragoon—the invasion of southern France—with amphibious landings around Saint-Tropez, less than 600 kilometres south of Montreux. The US Seventh Army then began pushing northwards. Dave and Tony decided to go and meet them. They packed their belongings, most crucially money and the emergency certificates, and walked down the front stairs of the Hotel Placida. Dave looked down the street and raised his hand.

'Taxi!'

18

HOMEWARD BOUND

The cab driver asked Dave and Tony where they wanted to go. Their first inclination was to answer, 'Australia,' but instead Dave pointed down the road towards Geneva and said, 'France.' The trip took around an hour and a half, and the driver dropped them within a mile of the border. Just as they had done some five and half months earlier, albeit in the opposite direction, they walked the rest of the way and stepped across. Having made their way back into enemy-held territory, their main objective was to find the advancing Allied forces. In Annemasse, the closest French town, they bought bus tickets to Grenoble, some 150 kilometres south.

It was a good place to start looking. Occupied by the Germans in September 1943, Grenoble had emerged as the headquarters of the French Resistance during the latter part of the war. Throughout November 1943, local residents and Resistance fighters had embarked on a series of demonstrations and attacks against the occupying forces. After workers in German-run factories went on strike and held anti-Nazi rallies on 11 November, the anniversary of Armistice Day, 400 of them were arrested. Two days later, several pieces of German artillery were destroyed by the Resistance, resulting in eleven public executions. These reprisals only led to greater resistance.

After the D-Day landings in June 1944, sabotage operations planned and carried out from Grenoble caused major problems for the Germans, who could not spare enough manpower to keep control in the area. When the Americans landed in southern France on 15 August and started moving northwards, the German high command ordered a strategic withdrawal. As the Americans reached the outskirts of Grenoble on 21 August, the German commander pulled out his troops and headed towards the Alps. By the time Dave and Tony arrived two weeks later, Task Force Butler—the motorised component of the Allied advance—had been and gone.

If the two Australians had been hoping to find a bustling scene of activity and noise punctuated by the constant arrival and departure of US transports, they were sadly disappointed. The US intelligence forces remaining in Grenoble, busy carrying out interviews with locals and investigating allegations of collaboration with the Nazis, were not in the business of helping downed RAAF officers get back to their units in England. Dave and Tony were told they should try to catch up with the main advance, which was near Lyon, another 115 kilometres to the north-west.

'How should we get there?' Tony asked, hoping to be offered a ride.

'Same way you got here,' came the answer. 'Catch a bus.'

The sight that met Dave and Tony as their bus arrived in Lyon on 5 September was far more encouraging than what they had seen in Grenoble. The Germans had pulled out only hours earlier, and the town was a hive of activity as the US 36th Division took over. The two Australians were directed to the temporary headquarters of the occupying forces and, after telling their story and showing their emergency certificates issued in Switzerland, were offered a ride in a vehicle headed back to Saint-Tropez, 420 kilometres to the south, where the Americans had landed some three weeks earlier. It was here, four days later, that they hit the jackpot. Ushered to the head-quarters of the US Sixth Army, commanded by General Jacob L. Devers, they were issued with travel orders that instructed them to 'proceed without delay from this station to Naples, Italy, reporting upon arrival to Base Operations for further instructions. Travel by military aircraft is authorised. By command of Lieutenant General Devers.'

Taking the precious document to the air base the next day, the two men hoped for a quick direct flight south-east to Italy, but General Devers' forces were moving north at a cracking pace and all available aircraft were needed to get supplies to the front line. To get onto a flight headed south, Dave and Tony would first have to go north. Early on 10 September, they were put on a USAAF Air Transport Command C-47

Skytrain heading straight back in the direction from which they had come, 420 kilometres north to a temporary airfield at Ambérieu. There they caught a flight that followed almost the same route back again and further south, to the island of Corsica. Their third and final flight of the day was to Marcianise airfield, about 30 kilometres north of Naples, which had been a base for 12th Air Force bomber units during the Italian campaign. There, the Aussies came up with a new plan. As their journey had been taking them ever further from England and closer to Australia, they decided to ignore General Devers' orders and head to Sydney rather than London. They took a train to the port of Taranto, 360 kilometres to the south, on the inner heel of the 'boot' of Italy.

The next ship due to leave Taranto was the RMMV *Capetown Castle,* a British passenger and cargo liner that had been converted into a troop ship in 1940. In mid-September 1944, it set out for Port Said, Egypt, having taken on two new passengers: Flying Officers D.W. Baxter and A. D'Arcey, RAAF. After almost a week at sea, the two crewmates disembarked at Port Said and talked their way into a ride on a military transport to Cairo. The Pyramids of Giza were only a few hours away, but Dave and Tony had another attraction at the top of their 'must-see' list—Shepheard's Hotel.

Opened in the 1840s, the opulent Shepheard's was one of the most famous hotels in the world from the 1920s until it was burned to the ground by rioters in 1952. Millionaires, maharajas, kings, queens and princes would sip their afternoon tea while sitting back in wicker chairs enjoying the view from the hotel's terrace. Over the years guests included

Lord Kitchener, T.E. Lawrence, Theodore Roosevelt, Winston Churchill and the explorer Henry Stanley. No visit to Cairo in the 1930s was considered complete without a drink at Shepheard's, and while they were still at sea Dave and Tony had agreed to make it their first port of call. As they walked through the foyer and headed to the bar, an RAAF officer fell into step with them.

'You sound like a couple of Aussies to me,' he said and offered to buy them a drink.

Handing them each a beer, he asked, 'So where are you chaps from, then?'

When they mentioned Switzerland, he almost dropped his glass.

'You wouldn't be Baxter and D'Arcey, by any chance?' he asked. When they nodded, he introduced himself as Group Captain J.E. Graham, Commanding Officer of the RAAF liaison office, Middle East.

'Half the British Army has been out looking for you two,' he said without smiling.

When Dave and Tony explained that they were on their way to Australia, Graham let them know in no uncertain terms that their travel plans had just changed. At each step along the way so far, until they had fallen off the radar at Marcianise, their progress had been reported and orders had come back: 'Get these men to Britain.' Now that he had them, Group Captain Graham was not letting them out of his sight until he had seen them safely onto a plane headed back to the UK.

Hours later, they were on an RAF transport bound for Tripolitania, a former Italian colony in northern Libya. Another

transport took them back across the Mediterranean to Capo-
dichino (today Naples International Airport), a former combat
airbase taken over by the US Air Transport Command.
Finally they had reached the destination to which General
Devers had sent them, although the trip from Saint-Tropez to
Naples, which should have taken a maximum of five hours in a
C-47 Skytrain, had turned into a 4500-kilometre, three-week
odyssey by plane, train, road and sea.

The next night RAF Transport Command flew them the
final leg of the journey, from Capodichino to RAF Lyneham, in
Wiltshire. As the aircraft touched down, it had been 223 days
since Dave had pulled back on the stick of Lancaster *J for Jig*
and he and his six crewmates had left England.

Two days later, telegrams were despatched from 'Air Force
391 Lt Collins St Melbourne' to the homes of Mrs J. Baxter and
Mr A. D'Arcey. They were marked 'Ordinary', but they were
anything but. They read: 'Pleased to inform you that your son
arrived in the United Kingdom on the 3rd October, 1944.'

For two families, at least, the nightmare was over.

It would be almost eight months before a similar telegram,
addressed to Bill Martin's wife, Anne, would arrive at 232
Doncaster Avenue, Kensington.

Like the other next of kin of the *J for Jig* crew members,
Anne Martin had been forced to maintain an uneasy relationship with military officialdom. The families were desperate
for news about their loved ones; the RAF and RAAF were
institutions that relied on following process and procedure.
In their correspondence with the RAAF, it must sometimes
have seemed that the authorities were more concerned with

the disposal of possessions than with the fate of the men, but for the families to voice their frustration would risk alienating the only source of information and help they had. Tony's father, Anthony, as an ex-serviceman and former POW, was well acquainted with the ways of the military machine, so he took it upon himself to be the eyes and ears of the *J for Jig* crew's next of kin. He gathered whatever information he could and shared it with the other Australian relatives. With the support of Anne Martin, he even petitioned RAAF HQ in Melbourne to pass on his letters to the families of Peter Mallon and John Dunlop in Scotland. The RAF no doubt found this highly irregular, but it was done. Still, Anthony was careful not to push too far. He knew that in order to keep the lines of communication open they had to be patient, polite and play the game to official rules, hard as that might be.

Concerned that information, no matter how seemingly trivial or innocuous, could fall into the wrong hands and jeopardise any possibility of escape from enemy territory, the RAAF policy was to drip-feed news to relatives selectively if and when it became available—and even then, sometimes only sparingly.

Dave's mother, Jean, had received the telegram notifying her that her son was alive and in Switzerland on 21 March 1944, and had been given the best address through which to send mail. Tony's family were also notified that he was safe—but initially, not a word was passed on to the other families. It was not until several weeks after Dave had travelled from Arosa to the Swiss capital of Bern and been interviewed by the RAAF attaché that the news of Dave's and Tony's survival was finally sent out to the remaining crew's next of kin.

On 15 April 1944, a message marked 'Secret' was sent on microfilm from RAAF Overseas Headquarters in London to the Secretary of the Department of Air in Melbourne. Headed 'Pilot Officer D.W. Baxter (Safe in neutral territory)', it read:

> The following is an extract of a secret communication transmitted from the Air Attache, Bern, to the Foreign Office, London, concerning the circumstances of the casualty of Lancaster aircraft of which Pilot Officer Baxter was captain:—
>
> P/O Baxter D.W. reports his aircraft attacked by fighters at 21.45 hours on Feb 24th 10 miles south KORITZA. Starboard inner engine caught fire. Aircraft went out of control. P/O Baxter baled out. Sgt Mallon (RAF) only seen by him to leave aircraft. Aircraft believed totally destroyed by fire.
>
> 2. Pilot Officer Baxter and Flying Officer D'Arcey have both been reported safe in neutral territory.
>
> 3. No details have as yet been received concerning the fate of Flight Sergeant Hopgood, Flight Sergeant Ferguson, Flight Sergeant Martin or the two RAF members.
>
> 4. Pilot Officer Baxter in his statement has made no reference to the possible fate of the other Australian members of the crew.
>
> (Signed) K.D. Seaman, Flying Officer for Air Vice Marshal, Air Officer Commanding.

With this information now on record in Melbourne and already given to the families of Dave and Tony, it was proving difficult to keep it secret. Dave had written to Joyce and his mates back at the squadron, and even readers of the local newspaper at Wonthaggi were by now well aware of their local boy's escape. Much as the RAAF had the best of reasons for attempting to keep a lid on things until the whereabouts of all crew members were confirmed, it was probably inevitable that the news would reach the relatives, especially with Anthony D'Arcey ensuring that any information received by one family was shared with the others.

On 25 May, after yet another letter from the RAAF regarding the bicycle left behind by her missing husband, a frustrated Anne Martin wrote back: 'It has come to my knowledge that there has been news of some members of the same crew as my husband and I am wondering, if there has been any further word, why I have not been notified of same? Would you please let me have any information available without delay. I would also like if permissible the names and addresses of the next of kin of the other members of the crew including the two RAF men.'

With little alternative, the Casualty Section at 391 Little Collins Street sent out a stock letter signed on behalf of Secretary of Air M.C. Langslow to the next of kin of the three missing Australians. Anne's was sent on 2 June:

Dear Madam,

I refer to your husband, Flight Sergeant William James Martin, who is reported missing as a result of air operations on the 24th February, 1944.

I desire to inform you that two members of your husband's crew have been reported safe, but interned in a neutral country. One of these members was the Captain of the aircraft and he has stated that the machine was attacked by enemy fighters about 10 miles South of Koritza, at approximately 9.45 p.m. on the 24th February, 1944. The aircraft went out of control and the Captain managed to bail out. He saw only one Royal Air Force member of the crew leave the aircraft, and is unable to make any statement as to the possible fate of your husband and the other members of the crew. The Captain believes the aircraft was totally destroyed.

I deeply regret that I am unable to give you any further information, and desire to add that it is requested that you treat the above report as confidential and do not discuss it outside your immediate family circle.

You may rest assured that should any further information become available it will be conveyed to you immediately by this Department. In conclusion may I extend to you the sincere sympathy of this Department in your great anxiety.

A week later, Anne replied:

Dear Sir,

I am in receipt of your letter dated 2nd Inst and thank you for the information contained therein. As you can understand I am most anxious for any information about my husband's plane. I have looked up several maps and have been unable to find Koritza on them and I wonder if you would give me the name of a fairly well known town which it is near. Thanking you for your past courtesy and trusting I am not asking too much.

While the RAAF Casualty Section did its best to locate Koritza for Anne Martin, it proved no simple task. Telegrams were still going back and forth from Melbourne to London a month later with no result. When Tony D'Arcey told a debriefing in Switzerland that he believed the aircraft might have gone down near Villers-sous-Prény, the search area was tightened, but still without luck. By 12 July the RAAF conceded defeat: 'Air Ministry unable to state exact location Koritza but assume to be near Villers Sous Prény.'

The lack of success was hardly surprising. They were looking on the wrong map. Koritza, now called Korca, is in Albania, 2100 kilometres east of Metz. Giving up on Koritza, the RAAF in Melbourne put its resources to work to find Villers-sous-Prény. That also proved difficult, so a plea went out to London: 'After extensive search unable to locate Villers-sous-Prény. Request advise country and nearest large city.'

Two days later the village was found—'Villers-sous-Prény is located France 14 miles south west (Metz?)'—but by the time that information was relayed to Anne Martin, it was irrelevant. On 8 June, RAAF headquarters in Melbourne had received from London a message marked 'Restricted and Important': 'FROM: RAAF Kingsway. Prisoners of War. Telegram from International Red Cross Geneva quoting German information gives following are Prisoners of War . . .'

There were five names. The last on the list was Flight Sergeant Martin, W.J.

On 13 June 1944, one day after she had written to the RAAF in a state of anxiety and frustration, Anne received the telegram for which she had been praying.

F/Sgt Martin, W.J Prisoner of War STOP Desire to inform you that your husband Flight Sergeant William James Martin previously missing is now a Prisoner of War STOP This advice received through Geneva.

The relatives of the four crew members who did not return from their mission to Schweinfurt would never experience the unbridled relief and joy that such a telegram would bring. Their worst fears were confirmed six months later, when the Americans moved through Villers-sous-Prény. On 21 November 1944, a memo was sent to the Casualty Division of the US 5th Infantry Division:

Subject: Location of Graves of Allied Dead.
Burial in the village church to the east with grave markers. I personally verified the names on the markers as Ferguson, Hopgood, Dunlop, Mallon. Village officials stated that a public funeral was held which caused the displeasure of the German officials but which nevertheless was attended by a large number of people. No other information could be obtained.
Signed, Clarence F. Golisch, Division Chaplain, US Army.

With all hope lost, Jock's wife, Silvy, widowed after only two days of marriage, bade a tearful farewell to his mother Mary and his sisters in Scotland and headed back to Grimsby. Five years after the war, Mary and her family emigrated to Ontario, Canada, where she worked as a housekeeper before opening a restaurant. Ron Ferguson's wife, Fae, continued to work as a nurse at Canberra Hospital before returning to North Queensland, where she eventually remarried and started a family.

---■---

By the time Dave and Tony arrived back in England, Bill Martin was almost two months into his incarceration at the newly named Stalag 357 Fallingbostel.

It had begun as no better or worse than the other camps Bill had been in. The food was edible if not plentiful. The guards ranged from vindictive and overbearing, in the case of the officers and NCOs, to some 'other ranks' who, perhaps sensing the way the war was headed, were prepared to be friendly. But as the Allies began closing in on Germany from north and south, and as winter began to bite, things became grim indeed.

Being in the air-force section of 357, Bill was better off than some. Stalag 357 was the smaller of the two camps at Fallingbostel, and its prisoners were at least slightly less cramped than those in the larger Stalag XIB close by. Even so, the conditions in the Soviet section were inhumane, with prisoners being whipped and set upon by dogs. The treatment of Allied POWs was less brutal, but as more and more prisoners were deposited in both camps, the already inadequate facilities were stretched to breaking point. The onset of winter made things intolerable. With barely enough wood for cooking, there was next to no heating, but at least the earlier arrivals had walls around them. By late 1944, as the Germans moved ever more POWs further west in a race against the Soviet advance, an estimated 90,000 prisoners from a dozen countries were jammed into the Fallingbostel area. In February 1945, when a large intake of American prisoners arrived at Stalag 357 following the last German offensives of the war at the Battle of the Bulge in Belgium and Operation Nordwind in Alsace, there was no space for them and they were housed in tents on the former sports field.

Not that the field would have been required for sports by that time. In mid-January 1945, recreational activities at Fallingbostel were banned as part of major reprisals by the camp commandant for supposed mistreatment of German POWs by the Allies in North Africa. The punishments included the removal of the prisoners' furniture, such as tables and chairs, their straw mattresses and half their bedboards. Any extra blankets were also confiscated.

Adding to the prisoners' misery was the disruption of deliveries of Red Cross packages as a result of Allied air attacks on rail services throughout occupied Europe. Around 160,000 of these packages were assembled by volunteers in Britain each week and sent to the International Red Cross in Geneva for distribution to prison camps by train. The contents of the parcels were carefully chosen to provide nutritional elements that were lacking in prison-camp diets. These included such items as tea, cocoa, chocolate, sugar, dried eggs, meat roll, jam and biscuits. Earlier in the war, the Red Cross had tried to ensure that each prisoner received one parcel per week. Now, without the packages, Bill and his fellow prisoners had to endure virtual starvation rations. They were reduced to scavenging outside the kitchens for scraps from the vegetables used to make the watery soups.

In his memoir, held at the Imperial War Museum in London, Stalag 357 survivor Flight Sergeant Richard Passmore gives a chilling insight into the daily struggle for food at Fallingbostel.

> We removed the suppurating potatoes and slimy swede peelings, cleaned them up marginally, boiled them and ate them. People who have been hungry will understand; those who haven't, won't. It was a miserable place. The grey brick walls were long and low and partially underground so that when you looked out of the windows the ground was only just below you. The winter was severe and we had so little food that we typically lost four stone in weight and four inches off the waistline.

Some men would attempt to capture, kill and eat sparrows. Other resorted to pulling up and eating any blades of grass that poked through the near-frozen dirt. There were reports that inside the Russian section, where conditions went beyond appalling, some prisoners had resorted to cannibalism.

In such desperate conditions, Dixie Deans did much to maintain the men's spirits. Such was the power of his personality that when Stalag 357 was moved to Fallingbostel from Thorn, the army POWs, who were housed in separate barracks and saw themselves as a separate group from the air force prisoners, joined with them in electing him Man of Confidence for the whole camp. Under Deans, discipline was tight and order maintained. The behind-the-scenes activities also continued. A radio—or 'canary', as it was called—was smuggled into the camp hidden in a hand-carved model car, and the coded letters addressed to Deans' wife continued to be sent out. The escape committee also stayed active.

All of Deans' steadying influence was required as the months dragged on, conditions worsened and uncertainty intensified over how the Germans would react as the Allies continued to tighten the noose. As more Allied POWs from other camps were moved into Fallingbostel, the rumour mill worked overtime. Prisoners feared they would be used as labourers, hostages or—having heard of the execution of the 50 RAF officers following the Great Escape—even killed by the SS.

The Red Cross parcels that arrived at Christmas provided only a brief respite; they were cut off immediately afterwards, as were letters and packages from home. The weather deteriorated. January and February of 1945 were the coldest months in Europe in the 20th century, with temperatures as low as –25°C. At one stage it rained on 41 days out of 50, and the roofs with their cracked tiles gave little protection. Bedding and clothing were damp, green mould grew on the walls of the barracks, and the men's spirits hit rock bottom.

As the war worsened for the Germans, in the camps the POWs weren't the only ones under increased pressure. Food supplies to the German public and troops that had come from former German territories dried up as they were liberated by the Allies. As the guards went hungry, their tempers frayed. The potential for violence intensified, especially as it became clearer that the demise of their beloved Third Reich was inevitable. Allied bombers could be seen or heard more regularly in the distance, on their way to and from raids over German cities. By mid-January the Russians had advanced into Poland, taking Warsaw within five days. Around that time, an RAF Mosquito flew over Fallingbostel with no sign of opposition. Although the conditions under which they were living worsened by the day, the prisoners of Fallingbostel knew that the end was near. What they didn't know was how it would come—by liberation or death.

The answer would not be long in coming. Since July 1944, when Bill had been moved with the rest of the RAF POWs from Heydekrug to Thorn, some 80,000 POWs from more than a dozen camps had been moved across the rapidly shrinking German territories. At first they had been transported by train and road, but as Allied air forces destroyed more rolling stock and infrastructure, and the remainder was needed for the war effort, they were forced to make the long journey from camp to camp by foot. The mass migration resulted in the deaths of an estimated 3500 prisoners.

On 6 February 1945, prisoners from Stalag Luft IV at Gross Tychow in Poland set off in a blizzard on a forced march to Fallingbostel, a distance of 800 kilometres that took them almost two months to cover. By the time the last of the survivors stumbled into Fallingbostel, the shortage of food was critical. There simply wasn't enough to go around, and with more prisoners coming into the camp almost daily, the Germans risked having a major incident on their hands—a situation that, with the Allies only weeks, perhaps days, from the gates, they were anxious to avoid. The Red Cross had informed Dixie Deans that they had stockpiled relief parcels at Lübeck, 150 kilometres to the north. Deans received permission from the commander of Stalag 357, Oberst (Colonel) Hermann Ostmann, to go to Lübeck and try to bring back some parcels. Accompanied by four guards, he and Warrant Officer Alfie Fripp left on 28 March and, after bribing the stationmaster, returned on a passenger train two days later, along with 6000 Red Cross parcels, enough for half per man. The respite would not last long. The next week, the Germans advised Deans that all POWs except those too ill to move would be evacuated, starting with RAF and USAAF prisoners on 6 April. They were to march around 200 kilometres to Schleswig-Holstein, the northernmost state of Germany.

Bill, with his bad back exacerbated by inadequate bedding and lack of nourishment, fell into the 'too weak to march' category. Other RAF and USAAF prisoners faked injuries, hid in the army huts, or simply lay down in the sick bay as the first columns of 1500 prisoners began to move out.

On 6 April, Dixie Deans led 12,000 prisoners out through the gates and headed north under an armed guard led by Oberst Ostmann. Deans had advised key men to make sure the columns proceeded as slowly as possible, the plan being that they would inevitably be overtaken by Allied motorised forces. After almost four weeks on the road—during which RAF fighters mistakenly strafed the columns, killing 60 POWs and injuring many more—Deans convinced Ostmann that the Germans' position was futile and he was allowed, under guard, to ride a bicycle to the British lines and negotiate a solution without further bloodshed. In a moment of ironic symbolism,

Deans personally accepted the surrender of Ostmann, whose former camp had already fallen to the Allies.

As the Stalag 357 prisoners were making deliberately slow progress on the first day of their painful journey, the British 11th Hussars were headquartered at Siedenburg, 70 kilometres south-west of the camp. In the first two weeks of April, the motorised regiment patrolled to the west of Fallingbostel, engaging German forces as they maintained a futile rearguard action. Casualties were low and the number of prisoners taken high as the Hussars cleared town after town and made their way ever closer to the POW camps. In April 1945, a squadron of the 11th Hussars met up with a unit of the 8th Hussars near the Weser River. Their orders were to join forces and head 40 kilometres north-east to the village of Dorfmark. In their path lay Fallingbostel.

The daily report for B Squadron 11th Hussars on 16 April 1945 notes simply: 'During the day a Stalag was liberated at Fallingbostel and one of the inmates was Trooper Walker of C Squadron who had been captured shortly after D Day.' For Bill Martin and his fellow prisoners—and the men who liberated them—the reality was somewhat more memorable.

The English painter and writer Edward Ardizzone had been an official war artist since 1940. He had followed the Allied advance through Europe after D-Day and, after spending the winter of 1944 in Italy, travelled to Germany for what would be the final months of the war. His diary, held by the Imperial War Museum in London, notes that on Monday, 16 April 1945, he was embedded with the 8th Hussars.

Up at 5.30 a.m. Very cold but fine. Breakfast in the half light by my tank of a fried egg between pieces of bread and a mug of tea. Off almost immediately afterwards to Stalag 357, in which over 15,000 of various nationalities were kept. Dawn light very beautiful, with the brew fires of the tanks seen here and there among the trees.

Travel some miles eastward, through the usual alternating forest country and open land. Halt by a clearing and am sent on ahead in a Dingo [scout car] to C Squadron, which was reaching the big POW camp.

When I arrived at the first encampment [Stalag XIB] troops had already been there some time. The scene was orderly and quiet, with troops of Airborne Division acting as NCOs. Many of them had only been prisoners for six to twelve months. It was amusing to see them marching off their warders. Paratroopers with red armlets, dull pink berets and clean battledress, gaiters, very smart.

Our arrival at the second encampment [Stalag 357] was very different. There were POWs who had been there for years and we were the first British soldiers to arrive. They were almost crazy with delight, mobbing our Dingos, asking questions about old friends and all demanding autographs, a very moving scene. It was pleasant to see little groups in the country outside the cage, but many still lined the wire as if out of long habit.

Some of the prisoners were in no physical state to venture outside the gate.

British Army Private Les Allen had been a POW for five years after being captured at Dunkirk. Like many who had taken part in the long march from Gross Tychow, he was in such bad shape that the Germans had left him behind when they began the evacuation of Fallingbostel. As he told authors John Nichol and Tony Rennell in 2001 for their book, *The Last Escape: The Untold Story of Prisoners of War in Germany 1944–45*, when the first Allied soldiers came through the gates of Stalag 357 he was unable to greet them: 'I was lying down on the ground when it happened. So were lots of others. We were so weak we couldn't get up and move. I was in such a dreadful state I had to have food brought to me.'

But regardless of the prisoners' physical condition, the feeling of finally being free was euphoric. As USAF Sergeant George Guderly told authors Nichol and Rennell: 'It was like New Year's Eve, the Fourth of July, your birthday and the wildest bacchanal you've ever been to all rolled into one.'

Guderly said the first 8th Hussars tanks smashed straight through the front gate of Stalag 357, followed by armoured cars. 'Everyone started hollering, and the soldiers were throwing out rations and cigarettes. I stood well back, just in case. I was damned if I was going to be killed by the very British tank that was setting me free.'

RAAF Sergeant Cal Younger, like Bill a member of 460 Squadron, had been shot down over France in May 1942. He spent most of his time as a POW in Stalag Luft III and after the war wrote of his experiences in an acclaimed book, *No Flight from the Cage*. Like Sergeant Guderly, he recalled the unbridled joy as the Hussars crashed through the gates:

People were in tears and yelling and screaming. Cheering prisoners surrounded the armoured cars, their arms held above their heads. Half a mile away the war went on. We could hear its sounds coming over the tank's radio. Germans were resisting in a wood nearby. A tank was sent, and then there was a message that 12 prisoners had been taken and would someone come and collect them. Another report said two cars were racing eastwards, with German senior officers in flight. They were to be headed off . . .

Basil Cotton, a pilot with 102 Squadron RAF who was shot down over Eindhoven in July 1941, was one of the first POWs to see freedom driving up the road. He recalled the moment on an online POW forum in 2005: 'A jeep from the 7th Armoured Division with a young man from the 11th Hussars turned up. Everyone gathered around the jeep, I knew it was all over and didn't go up to the jeep but went for a walk around the camp. Later an officer asked what we wanted and we said "tea, cigarettes and bread" and this was all brought to us that night.'

The evacuation of Fallingbostel took several days, as Basil Cotton explained: 'We stood in the square and an army man read out the list—those in [the camp] the longest went first. It was all very organised, they brought lorries. I left Fallingbostel on April 20th, was taken to Belgium and from there was flown to near Aylesbury.'

On 24 April 1945, RAAF Headquarters in Australia received a message from RAAF Headquarters in London headed, 'Prisoners of War': 'Following RAAF member liberated by Allied Armies Western Europe now safe this country. W/O Martin WJ. Air Ministry will reclassify. Request inform Next of Kin.'

Two days later, at 3.30 p.m., a telegram was delivered to Bill's wife, Anne. 'Flight Sergeant W.J. Martin safe STOP Pleased to inform you that your husband Flight Sergeant William James Martin has been liberated by the Allied armies and is safe in the United Kingdom STOP Anticipate your husband will communicate with you direct.'

After 426 days in captivity, Bill Martin's war was over. Like many who had suffered in POW camps, he would rarely speak of his time behind barbed wire, but the memories would haunt him and all those who had survived Fallingbostel for the rest of their lives.

As Les Allen, the young infantryman who was too weak to stand as his saviours arrived at Fallingbostel, and who would never recover from the injuries he sustained on the march across Germany, put it:

People wanted to know about my experiences as a prisoner of war, but I wouldn't tell them. Why? Because I had a feeling that they wouldn't believe it, so consequently I just bottled it up. It might also have been because of a sense of shame about being a prisoner of war—people might ask why I hadn't escaped. But it was also because I got the impression when I returned home that people believed we had, in effect, been in holiday camps, having a cushy time. That's why we didn't want to talk about it. Those who didn't know said we'd had a good time, that we were lucky to have been prisoners when so many other fellows had been killed.

———■———

The three war-weary survivors of Lancaster *J for Jig* who arrived back in England were very different to the patriotic, naive young men who had left peaceful Australia less than three years earlier.

In mid-December 1944, Dave wrote twice to his sweetheart Joyce from London, bringing her up to date with his efforts to be repatriated, replying to her news from home and hinting at the present he was buying for her upcoming 21st birthday.

'First off Sister Gillman, my congrats on passing the exams—I'm proud of you. It is a fitting reward for three years hard work. Congrats to the other girls too. I wish I could have been there when you heard the news and you could have cried on my shoulder. Don't forget to save your leave [holidays] until I come home; so keep in Matron's good books.'

Five days later he wrote again, but it was obvious something was troubling him. Rather than speaking mainly of the weather and local scenery, as he had in previous correspondence, he was concerned with a bigger picture. A casual chat with a woman on a train had brought to the surface his feelings that the British had been too decent and humane to Italian prisoners held in the UK. He had also been shocked by reports of the Nazi death camps, which were only just starting to reach the rest of the world.

A few lines to let you know how things are progressing. On Monday morning I cleared up a few things in London and after lunch caught the train to Brighton. It was quite a nice run taking just over an hour. It was my first visit to Brighton and it seems to be a nice place. My first call was to the O.C. Repatriation. He is a friend of Frank [Dave's brother]; they came on the same boat, so I started on the right foot. I have to wait a few weeks so I was given a fortnight leave.

I saw a few chaps I knew—some I hadn't seen for two years and the others were with me in Switzerland. I stayed at Brighton only one day—I was off to Scotland on the Tuesday evening. That's becoming a habit of mine—staying only one day in a camp.

I arrived in London about 8 p.m. and caught the 10.15 [train] for Edinburgh where I arrived just after 8 a.m. I slept a couple of hours in the train and spent the rest of the time 'gassing' with a woman. Have no fears—she was about fifty. We talked about the war etc. I told her what I thought of the treatment of Italian P.O.W.s in this country. It's a disgrace after the treatment they handed out to our lads in Italy. I've heard many of the stories from the lads who escaped to Switzerland and I could go on for hours but I would probably land myself in trouble. Another topic was the happenings in the liberated countries—it's a bad business. You will probably see a change in me when I come home—this past year has opened my eyes.

By that time, Tony had already returned to Australia. Both he and Dave had been debriefed at RAAF Overseas Head-quarters in London, where Dave's brother Frank was based.

The interview process, over a number of weeks, covered two main areas: the details surrounding the shooting down of *J for Jig*, and their experiences in France as evaders.

One question about their time in Switzerland, under the section 'Employment and Pay', was, 'What pay, if any, was made available to you during your internment? Give date thereof, frequency of payment and the use to which you applied it.' For the first two parts of the question, Dave answered: 'A third of normal rate of pay, plus 70 francs a month, sports allowance. Remainder from 14.3.44, weekly.'

For the third part of the question: 'Spent it!'

The officer interviewing Tony was obviously impressed, describing him as 'a good quiet type' and, under the heading 'Remarks by Air Attache' wrote by hand, 'This officer displayed commendable courage and initiative in order to escape from a German soldier who captured him.'

With both men being found fit and, in the words of their investigating officers, 'there being nothing to debar them from returning to operations in this theatre of war', they were asked for preferences as to their next duty. Tony listed a desire to be repatriated to Australia, 'with a strong desire to be given an opportunity to re-muster to pilot training'. If this was not possible, he indicated he was 'quite willing to return to operation in the South West Pacific Area'.

Dave's preferences were a 'return to operations on Lancaster aircraft in this theatre of war; posting to Transport Command, or instructional duties in the UK'.

A year or two earlier, such requests would have been eagerly granted, but by 1944 the air war in Europe was coming to a close. In the very week when Dave was receiving his final debriefing, the Americans were breaking out of the Siege of Bastogne, ending the Battle of the Bulge and Hitler's last-gasp attempt to change the course of history. With the final operation of the Battle of Berlin taking place on 31 March 1944, the thousand-bomber raids over Germany were a thing of the past. The corresponding drop in casualties meant there was no longer a desperate demand for Lancaster air crew. In mid-October, as a bomb aimer wishing to be retrained as a pilot, Tony was the first to be told his services were no longer required. The RAF made plans for him to be repatriated to Australia following two weeks accrued sick leave, which he took, as usual, staying with his friends Herbert and Agatha Perkins near Birmingham. First, though, there was still some unfinished business—the matter of his bicycle.

While it might seem trivial today, the continuing saga of Tony's bicycle gives an insight into the bureaucratic minutiae that went on behind the scenes of the Allied war machine. Historic footage and contemporary movies show men and women in uniform, guns, tanks, ships and planes, but almost as many men and women sat in offices pounding typewriters and handling carbon paper to ensure that nothing was overlooked—and recording it in triplicate. Writing from Switzerland in response to official enquiries, Tony had notified the RAAF that his bicycle was to go to the Perkinses. He arrived back in the UK around seven months later. As it happened, he managed to make his way to the Perkins home before the bicycle did. On 23 October 1944, Agatha Perkins wrote to the RAAF: 'Thank you very much for attending to the forwarding of flight officer D'Arcey's bicycle to Solihull Station. As Tony is now spending his sick leave with us, he was able on Friday last, to call at the station and examine the cycle before bringing it here. He says it is quite in order.'

Tony left the UK by ship on 10 November 1944 and, after a stop in San Francisco, arrived in Brisbane on 16 February 1945. For Dave, whose experience as a pilot might be required, depending on the progress of the war, the wait for repatriation would be longer. He completed several flights for Transport Command while his case was being considered, but on 30 January, RAAF HQ in Melbourne was advised that 'RAF Air Ministry was unable to employ Flying Office D.W. Baxter in any capacity in respect of the preferences he stated. Repatriation was therefore effected in the normal manner, with him embarking for Australia on 19th January, 1945.'

On his return to England, Bill Martin was posted to No. 11 Personnel Depot and Receiving Centre at Bournemouth, where he, like his Australian crewmates, had first been processed when he arrived in the UK almost exactly two years earlier. After treatment at Blackpool Hospital for his back complaint and malnutrition, Bill left for Australia by ship and arrived in Sydney on 24 July 1945.

The fighting was now over for Dave's crew, but the war would shape them for the rest of their days.

19

FINAL MISSION

The Powlett Express, 15 June 1945:

A very quiet, but pretty wedding was celebrated in St Joseph's Church on Saturday, in the early morning, when Joyce, eldest daughter of Mr and Mrs J. Gillman, 39 Hagelthorne Street, Wonthaggi, was united in marriage to Dave, second son of Mrs. Baxter and the late Mr. Baxter, Reid Street, Wonthaggi.

The bride, who entered the church on the arm of her father, looked very attractive in a blue and white striped suit, with black accessories. She was attended by her younger sister, Mavis, who wore a grey and white striped suit with black accessories.

Mr. Frank Baxter (brother of the bridegroom) acted as best man. After the ceremony, they enjoyed a quiet wedding breakfast, after which they left for their honeymoon by train.

Dave and Joyce had wasted no time in getting married. Two months earlier, Dave had been granted release from the RAAF to take up a position in the finance branch of the Department of Air. In requesting the release, the office of the departmental secretary had stressed the 'urgent necessity for the allotment of additional competent male staff'. The couple immediately moved to Melbourne, boarding with Dave's aunt and uncle in Coburg, where he had lived for a short period before the war. In the weeks before he received his first pay packet, Dave wore to work the only decent clothes he possessed: his RAF uniform.

When Joyce became pregnant, she and Dave realised they had to get a home of their own and began the protracted process of applying to the Housing Commission. At the final interview, the officer in charge advised them that with so many returned servicemen and-women seeking housing, the waiting list was long. 'You'd have more chance if you had children,' he said. Almost as soon as they returned from the city to Coburg that afternoon, Joyce went into labour. Michael was born fourteen hours later. Soon afterwards, they moved into their new home in West Heidelberg. Their second son, Alan, came three years later.

The Housing Commission house, which they would buy in 1957, was 2.5 kilometres from Ivanhoe railway station. Dave commuted to the city by train, either riding his pushbike or walking to and from the station. Alan recalls:

> Dad played cricket for the RSL club but eventually left the team because he thought they were boozers. He enjoyed a cold beer on a hot day but he was never a big drinker. The part of the club he liked was that it gave him the chance to help other ex-servicemen. There was a bloke who lived over the road from us named Harold Tippett who'd been a Rat of Tobruk and he and Dad got along very well. Harold was a carpenter and I always remember that he and Dad would be off somewhere helping people who needed a hand.
>
> Dad was Church of England and Mum was Catholic. Michael and I were brought up Catholics. We got along to church and went to Catholic schools and when we turned 18 Mum and Dad sat us down and said that we'd been taught right from wrong and whether we wanted to stay in the Church was up to us. That was the first time I found out that Dad wasn't Catholic. He always came to church and he helped out wherever he could in the parish. He did a lot more than a lot of people who called themselves Catholic. He was very community minded. Anyone in need he'd help out.
>
> I couldn't say whether that had anything to do with what he had gone through in the war. Obviously it affected him. He was 18 years old when he joined up. He went from being a schoolboy athlete in what was essentially a little country town to going halfway around the world and being in an environment where people you got to know would

be there one minute and gone the next. On my 21st I was down the backyard throwing up after drinking too much beer with my mates. When Dad turned 21 he was 20,000 feet over Berlin being shot at. How could that not affect you? I remember whenever a war movie came on TV he'd become very uncomfortable. He'd be very nervous in his chair.

He never talked about what he'd been through but he never hid it either. I think I just always knew that he'd been in the war and that he'd been a pilot. There were a few things around the house, like his old kit bag, and I've still got his old metal trunk with his name and service number on it. I don't remember him taking part in Anzac Day marches or anything like that, but the one thing he did go along to every year was the get-together of the Caterpillar Club. They were air crew who had bailed out of their aircraft. I think he felt comfortable around blokes who had experienced the same things he had. He wore a little caterpillar pin on his lapel.

Dave was also a member of the RAF Escaping Society in London, which helped him track down the two men and their families who had helped him evade the Germans in France: the farmer Pierre Simon and the café owner Pierre Mathy. When the Society advised Dave that they had sent a representative to speak with Jeanne Simon, Pierre's wife, and found that she had fallen on hard times after the death of her husband, Dave arranged to have some money sent to her anonymously.

Dave would never have the opportunity to go back to France, but indirectly, France came to him. In September 1956 a letter arrived at the Baxter home from Irvine, in Ayrshire, Scotland.

Dear Mr Baxter,

On receiving this letter from Scotland, you no doubt will be a bit surprised as to the identity of the writer. So from the start let me introduce myself. I am Mrs Annie Delury. Prior to getting married my maiden name was Mallon. I am a sister of Peter Mallon who was flight engineer in the Lancaster bomber which you piloted on February 24th 1944, and which was shot down by a German fighter near Metz in France.

I wrote a letter to Anthony D'Arcey but he was not at home on the letter's arrival, so his father was good enough to answer it and in doing so gave me the address of yourself and Bill Martin. I am expecting to receive a reply from Anthony D'Arcey himself shortly. I wrote to him for the same reason that I am writing to you now, in the hope that you can tell me what really happened that night 12 years ago, when Peter and the other three members of your crew lost their lives. As I realise that quite a time has passed since that fateful night, I think I had better explain something to you. When my father and mother received the news from the War Office, first that Peter was missing and then having been killed, our home was no longer the same. My parents took the news very badly and both suffered quite a bit in health, especially my mother. I was only 19 years of age at the time and my younger brother 18 and sister 14. We were never told anything other than Peter had been killed and all the correspondence that arrived in our house from the War Office, War Ministry and other sources were locked away in a drawer after having been read by my mother and father. We were never allowed to see any of the letters. This was my parents' way of trying to get over Peter's death.

The years passed by and my parents began to get over this tragedy. My brother and sister and myself are married and have homes of our own. My parents still live in our original home and are enjoying fairly good health. If my husband and I had not decided to visit Villers-sous-Prény next summer the letters would still be locked away. We want to see Peter's grave and to meet the people who were responsible for the burial of the members of the crew. I asked my mother to let me see the letters which she had locked away and after reading it all over and over again I realise she was only given certain information and that was all. In fact if Anthony D'Arcey senior had not written a letter to my father in May 1944 they would have known a lot less and I'm only sorry now that they didn't make more enquiries at the time. However they hadn't the heart to make any enquiries. I am asking you Mr Baxter if you could please cast your mind back over the 12 years passed and to try and tell me what happened from the time you left Binbrook that night until you yourself were thrown out of the plane when it turned on its back. I know Mr Baxter you will be trying to forget that trying ordeal you went through but if you could only write and tell us something to help clear up this mystery I myself will be very grateful.

As I have already stated I am no longer a teenager, I'm married and have two children and I can assure you that you need not be afraid to tell me all that you can. I fully realise that no amount of information can bring him back, but when I go to France and stand beside Peter's grave and his comrades I would like to be able to know exactly how he died. So please Mr Baxter as Peter's pilot and comrade would you reply to this letter as soon as possible. During the time Peter was stationed in Binbrook he kept company with a girl called Nora, do you think you could give me a lead as to who she might have been? Could she have been a member of the WAAF or even a local girl? I would like to get in touch with her even though she might be married. Among the correspondence lying before me is a note from Pete to Nora Dobbs but we couldn't give it to the girl as we didn't know anything about her. Do you think you could tell me anything about her.

In the letter I received from Mr D'Arcey senior he told me about your friends Madame Simon and Madame Mathy and I would very much like to visit these people when I go to France next summer. I only hope they can understand English, as neither my husband or myself speak French, however I am hoping that between now and the time we arrive in Villers-sous-Prény we will be able to get in touch with someone there who can speak English and act as our guide which would certainly help us a lot. Well Mr Baxter there is very little for me to say now except that I do hope the past 12 years have been good to you, your wife and family and I pray that you will be blessed with many more years to come. I only hope you don't find this letter too distressing and I look forward in anticipation to your reply. I will be ever so grateful to you. Must close now. Wishing you the very best for the future. I remain yours sincerely, Annie Delury.

Dave wrote back to Annie immediately, as did Tony and Bill, passing on all they knew of the crash and its aftermath, together with contact details for Peter's girlfriend, Nora. In November, two months after her first letter, Annie wrote again.

Dear Dave,

I trust you will not consider me too forward for addressing you by your Christian name. I feel I know Tony, Bill and yourself well enough now to do so. I received your letter dated September 25 safely and I wish to thank you very sincerely for the information it contained. With your account of what happened that night and with what Tony D'Arcey had already told me I feel that I know now all that happened up till the time your bomber broke in half. I received a letter from Tony about a fortnight ago in which was enclosed a copy of the letter sent to the British ambassador in Paris by Madame Schuller in 1945. This letter also contained a wealth of information mainly after your plane had hit the ground.

M. and Mme Schuller and the other brave people in and around Villers-sous-Prény will forever hold a special place in the hearts of my parents and myself for their defiance of the Germans and their persistence in giving Peter and his pals a decent burial. I'm looking forward to meeting some of these people this summer, when I hope to be able to thank them personally for all they did. Twelve years is quite a space of time and many who took part in the funeral preparations may no longer be there. However there are 260 inhabitants in Villers-sous-Prény and I'm sure there will still be people there who can fill in the missing part to this tragedy. I know now how the others died, but so far I have no explanation regarding Peter's death. I have thought of various ways in which he could have died but I am afraid the French people are the only ones who can help. I will let you know everything I find out when I return from my visit. There are a few things I would like you to tell me if you will. What means of identification did you carry with you on the bomber trips? Did you wear your ordinary RAF uniform below your flying suit, or did you get supplied with civilian clothes? Did you carry any personal belongings on you? Was your correct name on your parachute or was it on a disk worn round your wrist?

I intended answering your letter sooner but decided to delay my reply until I had contacted the RAF Escaping Society. I received a reply from Miss Craig the secretary last week. She stated that the society would be only too pleased to do all they could to help me. They would try and contact Monsieur and Madame Schuller or some member of their family and also anyone who could speak English. Everyone is being extremely nice and helpful and I thank you ever so much for giving me the address of the Escaping Society.

My parents are still keeping well and my father who is 60 is still working in the shipyard where he has been since

I could remember. I'm hoping to persuade them to accompany me to France. So far they know very little of what information I have got and I am waiting till after the New Year before I tell them. I was very pleased to read in your letter that your wife and two sons are enjoying good health, also yourself. Any luck and prosperity that has come your way has been earned during the war years. You deserve it and may good fortune continue to smile on you and your family. I nearly forgot to mention that I have some photos of Peter and his pals' funeral. I also intend writing to your friends as soon as I get further word from the Escaping Society. I must bring this letter to a close now Dave and I hope to be hearing from you again in the very near future. So for the present I will say cheerio, good luck and thanks once more for your letter. God bless you all.

Yours sincerely, Annie Delury.

Annie and her husband Jim made their pilgrimage to Villers-sous-Prény in mid-August 1957. Two months later, Jim Delury wrote to Dave. The prospect of recounting the emotional trip had been too much for Annie.

Now that Annie and I have returned from France and our visit to the grave of Peter and his three comrades, I'm taking this opportunity to write this letter to you and let you know how we got on. Annie has asked me to write giving you all the facts as they were given to us by the French people whom we met and stayed with. We left for London at 8pm August 14 and after train, boat and train, we arrived at Pagny-sur-Moselle where we were taken by a porter to the home of Madame and Monsieur Sophron, the mayor of Villers-sous-Prény and at this stage let me say that we never met two nicer people in our lives. During our three-day stay they could not do enough for us. They were without question the finest people we have ever come across. They made us welcome as soon as we entered their home and they had engaged a very fine French lady who teaches English to act as interpreter. She was with us most of the time. M. Sophron, over and above being mayor of Villers-sous-Prény, is also managing superintendent of a fairly large electrical engineering works and it was he who was responsible for the burial of Peter and his pals. The actual facts of the happenings on that night 24 February 1944 and of the days that followed were told to us by M. and Madame Sophron as I write them now but please remember Dave that the Sophrons were living in their own home in Villers-sous-Prény at that time and have only moved to their present home in Pagny about five or six years ago.

The sky above appeared to be full of planes that night, British bombers and German fighters all together high above Lorraine. Your plane was struck by German gunfire and caught fire after which it began to lose height. It started to turn in a circle away from the village and dropped its bombs on the outskirts doing no damage to property or person. The fire on the wing became larger and your bomber began to lose height more quickly and when it was 700 or 800 feet from the ground it exploded and so fierce was the explosion that the four engines were thrown two miles apart and the remainder of the plane was scattered over a very wide area. The villagers immediately rushed to the scene and discovered Bill Martin who was taken to the home of Monsieur and Madame Schuller who was the baker and grocer in the village at that time. Bill Martin was very badly injured and so he was kept in the house and given brandy to help with the pain. Back at the scene of the tragedy the German officer commanding in the area had arrived with three or four of his aides and he ordered that the bodies of Peter and his friends which had been found by Monsieur Sophron and his villagers some distance from each other were to be buried where they lay and he also demanded to know where the remainder of the crew were. He was taken to the Schullers' home where Bill Martin was handed over.

M. Sophron the mayor was ordered by the German officer to have his villagers search for yourself and Tony, this being done in such a way that the people paid no attention. M. Sophron then took the German officer and his staff to his home and in an upstairs room held a mock party to celebrate the downfall of yet another British bomber and when the Germans were dead drunk, he ordered his village friends to bring the bodies of the four British airmen to his house. This they did, placing them on the floor of the dining room downstairs and while the German officer was in a drunken stupor M. Sophron got him to sign a paper giving him permission to bury the bodies in the village churchyard of Villers-sous-Prény. Word was soon spread by the Underground that such a funeral was taking place within 48 hours. Four coffins were made and the bodies placed inside, their parachutes being used as the shrouds and the men of the village took turns of standing guard over them day and night until the time came for the burial. On the day of the funeral people from far and near were pouring into Villers-sous-Prény bringing with them wreaths and money used to pay for the four coffins, four marble stones, wreaths and Masses. In one long procession 7000 French people followed the four coffins up the hill from the village to the churchyard. They were there to pay their respects to four young men who had given their lives for them and they were there also to show the Germans they were still on the side of Britain. The village priest with his altar boys led the procession and in a small piece of vacant ground he held a short service, consecrated the ground and then the coffins were laid to rest side-by-side in the one grave.

I know Dave that what I have just written may appear to be far-fetched and hard to believe, but when M. Sophron told us these facts he also handed over to Annie and I a dozen pictures taken at the time of the actual funeral and for which the Germans searched in vain. They show the four coffins sitting outside his home, the priest giving a short service over them before starting on the journey up the hill to the churchyard, they show thousands of people following the coffins and overflowing into the courtyard and they show the priest saying his last few words before the coffins are lowered into the one comrades' grave watched by thousands of bare-headed men and women. I fully realise that it is difficult to believe that such a thing could happen in an occupied country during war times, but these are facts and the pictures taken at the time are documented proof.

Now the German commander in the area naturally heard about the funeral and the respect shown by the thousands who attended it and he was furious. M. and Mme Sophron were both arrested. Madame Sophron was only held for a few hours but her husband was held much longer, however the anger of the people was so great when they heard about the arrest that the Germans released him. He was returned to his home but was informed by the German officer that he must consider himself under open arrest until he was tried. His trial took place at Nancy and he was fined 3000 Francs and denied all privileges and this remained so until the Americans liberated their village at the end of 1944.

Well Dave, that is the story as given to us by M. Sophron and his friends and the pictures he gave us is unquestionable proof. You can realise how difficult it was for Annie and I to thank them for what they had done. We took over to France with us two wooden musical cigarette boxes, each one had a silver plate on the front with a message of thanks inscribed in it from Mr and Mrs Mallon. We gave one to M. Sophron and the other to M. Schuller, but to try and repay these people for what they had done and the risk they took is just impossible. However I'm certain that God will see to it that their actions will receive a just reward in the next world.

Having served in the Army in the last war myself and having been in France I know that many French people take snaps of the dead before burial and I told Annie this before we left, so when M. Sophron handed her two snaps kept separately from the rest she was not as surprised and shocked as she might have been, although it did not stop her from breaking down. One was a photo of Ferguson, Hopgood and Dunlop lying dead side-by-side and the other was a photo of Peter lying dead. Those pictures were taken in the dining room of M. Sophron's home. On asking what killed each of them we were told one was killed by the explosion of the plane and the other three died from their fall, their parachutes failing to open properly in time. Peter was one of these three, but all died instantaneously, this we were assured of. They do not know anything about the tail of your bomber being shot off, but they admit it could have been just before the plane exploded, however I don't believe anyone can cast their mind back to 1944 and be really sure of all that happened that night and after all it makes no difference now. I'm enclosing some snaps we took of the grave and you will find there is some writing on the back of each one and I will be sending a similar letter to Tony with some snaps enclosed.

I was down at Binbrook last weekend. I was paying a visit to Nora, the girl that Peter used to go with and to whom he left some money. I had promised her that I would go down to see her again after we had returned from France and bring her a picture of his grave. Annie intended going with me but at the last minute she found herself unable to make the journey and I took my little son aged six years with me. We had quite a nice time and while I was there

I visited Binbrook airfield. It was very interesting. It is the same today as it was in 1944 except of course the planes. They are all jets—the Lancaster bomber is a thing of the past. Well Dave I feel I have come to the end of this letter and I'm quite certain you will have found the content interesting. Annie will be writing to you very soon so you can look forward to a letter from her. For the present I will say cheerio and good luck and I hope to be hearing from you again in the very near future.

Yours sincerely, Jim Delury.

PS I forgot to mention in this letter Dave that M. Sophron received a decoration for his work and service from the French people and is highly respected by the villagers and all his friends.

Jim and Annie Delury were the first of several relatives of the four airmen buried at Villers-sous-Prény to visit their graves. They were followed by Cliff Hopgood's wife Margaret and son Robert, and Ron Ferguson's nephew, Michael McBride, the son of his sister Merle. In 2012, Dave Baxter's brother Ron travelled to Ayrshire to meet Annie Delury and also attended the commemoration of the Bomber Command Memorial by Queen Elizabeth II in London. A year later, he and his wife Barbara visited Villers-sous-Prény. While there, they were hosted by Armand Casalini, who gave them Cliff Hopgood's bombardier bag. Ron later presented the bag to Robert Hopgood in Brisbane.

By the time Ron stood at the graves of his older brother's comrades, the marble headstones erected by the villagers in

1943 had long been replaced with four of the white granite stones that are standard at all Commonwealth War Graves sites. As is customary, when the stones were being carved, the families of the deceased were asked if they wished to add a personal inscription. Three of the four families—the Dunlops were unable to be found in Canada—took up the offer.

Cliff Hopgood's stone reads: *One of Nature's Gentlemen. Heaven Should be His.*

The words above Peter Mallon are: *O Take Him to Thy Sacred Heart and Let Him Rest Therein. Rest in Peace.*

And the inscription for Ron Ferguson, the boy from the Queensland bush, is simply: *His Duty Nobly Done.*

The good luck and long life that Annie Delury had wished for Dave were not to be. In 1968, when Alan turned 20, his parents helped him buy a block of land at Ringwood, on the outskirts of Melbourne. The land contained a number of sizeable gum trees. Since these would hamper building, on weekends Dave and Alan would drive out to the block and chop them down, then cut up the trunks and branches to use as firewood. On Sunday, 19 May, they were hard at work when Dave clutched his chest and fell at his son's feet. Alan desperately tried to revive his father, but his efforts proved futile. Dave was 45 years old. Alan recalls:

When it was obvious my feeble CPR attempt wasn't working—maybe 10 minutes after Dad initially collapsed—I went to the nearest house which may have been about 50 to 100 yards away. The people there rang an ambulance. When the ambulance crew arrived it was obvious to them and me that Dad was deceased. I subsequently rang Dad's older brother Frank who lived in Mount Waverley and he came to the site. I can't remember if dad's body was still there when Frank arrived—I think it was and covered up—or if the ambulance crew had already left with him. Either way I just remember the two of us standing there, bewildered. He was a fit man who either walked or rode his bike three miles a day. He never smoked and wasn't a drinker. We couldn't believe it. No-one could.

The ambulance officers told Alan that because Dave had died in a 'public space', the State Coroner would have to perform an autopsy, so Dave's body was taken to the morgue. Not knowing when he would be able to return home and not wanting to break the news to his mother over the telephone, Alan returned to the neighbouring house and rang Father George Mather, their parish priest. 'Mum was well known to him, as she helped with the church flowers and cleaning,' Alan says. 'He collected another of the ladies, a close friend of Mum's, and they went and broke the news.'

It was mid-afternoon before Alan returned home to his shocked mother.

There were plenty of what-if's. Mum was a nurse. She was saying, 'Why didn't I see the signs?' but there were no signs. Dad was his normal self. He seemed perfectly well and healthy. Two weeks earlier they had bought a new car, an HK Holden with fold-down front seats fitted, and they were planning a driving holiday, sleeping in the car. They weren't the type for fancy motels. When the coroner's report came out he said that it had been a massive heart attack. There was nothing anyone could have done. His time was up.

Though Dave had never sought the spotlight, his name had featured often in newspaper articles. From the day of his father's death, when he was photographed waiting outside the mine shaft, through his sporting triumphs, war training, bombing raids and escape to Switzerland, reporters had always found interest in Dave Baxter. Now, under the headline 'Pilot's Death', the local paper, *The Wonthaggi Sentinel*, recorded: 'A bomber pilot who miraculously escaped death in World War II collapsed and died at Ringwood on Sunday.'

One of the many letters of condolence came from Suzanne Mathy, wife of Pierre Mathy, the café owner in Toul at whose home Dave had sheltered. It was translated into English for the family by the French teacher at the local high school.

Dear Madame,

I do not know how to express the sorrow my husband and I feel at hearing of the great loss you have had concerning your dear David. We have had the opportunity to think about him because in 1944 with my husband he transplanted a fruit tree and now in the springtime when we eat fruit we think of him. My husband wanted to take a photograph of the tree so that he could know how well it has grown. The plums are big and delicious. Be sure, dear Madame, that we have been thinking of you and your children and sharing in your great sorrow. We offer you our tender and sincere condolences.

CREW

On Wednesday, 28 May 1968, David Wright Baxter was farewelled with a service at St Pius X Catholic Church in West Heidelberg. Father Mather spoke.

It is not customary in this church to say words other than prayers when a parishioner makes his last bodily departure to his resting place—but I would be very ungrateful if I did not mark this occasion, for it is a Parish's grateful farewell to a very good man.

He did not share with us the Catholic faith but he certainly put into practice in a very wonderful way all that our faith demands in virtue, kindness, family life, manly character and family responsibility. In these things in fact, no Catholic of this parish was a truer Christian than Dave Baxter.

A very quiet man, maybe with a certain innate shyness, he was always about if I wanted his help—which he always gave so gladly, especially to the training and development of character in the youthful minds and bodies of St Pius X parish.

Above all things, he was a man of tremendous charity and after all, this is the heart of Christian virtue. This was very evidenced by his continued support of the French family who rescued and looked after him following his parachute descent into France during the grim days of World War II. Only recently he arranged and attended a mass here in this church for the eternal repose of the soul of one of his French benefactors. We now pray for him.

To his family, wife, sons, brothers, sister and relatives, I say you can raise your heads very proudly and look into the face of your Maker proudly when you hear the good name of Dave Baxter.

———■———

Bill was discharged from the RAAF at No. 2 Personnel Depot in Sydney on 28 November 1945. He returned to his wife Anne and her extended family at their home in Kensington, where he would live for the rest of his life. Anne did not recognise her husband the first time she saw him after the war. He had been a relatively large man when he enlisted but had lost about half of his body weight while imprisoned. When he arrived back in Sydney, he weighed around 50 kilograms. He was also bald. In France, the German doctors had shaved his head to treat the deep wounds he suffered as he was sucked out of the stricken plane. He would tell his family that the freezing cold and poor nutrition in the prison camps stopped his hair from growing back. He would joke that he no longer needed a comb to make himself look presentable before heading off to work each morning—a quick swipe over his head with a damp bath towel would do the job.

Unable to sustain the physical demands of the machinist's job that he had left, Bill took on a clerical role in the Taxation Department. He and Anne tried without success to have children, perhaps another effect of the deprivations he suffered in the POW camps. In late 1947, they adopted a one-month-old boy, Richard, and 18 months later, a baby girl, Christine.

Bill's mother, Anastasia, died in 1948. While his two children would not get to know their paternal grandmother, they were never lacking for relatives. Their home remained a multi-generational base for the combined Carroll and Martin clans. Richard shared a room with Anne's younger brother Matt, and Christine with her great-aunt Eileen. It might seem an odd arrangement today, but Christine remembers it as completely normal.

> We were a typical extended working class family ... My grandfather worked on the roads, Uncle Matt delivered mail, Aunty Eileen, until retrenched, was at the Fountain Tomato Sauce factory and Dad was a clerk in the Taxation Department. We lived in the time when children didn't answer back to adults and all were very respectful of one another.

Bill would never recover fully from the physical injuries he sustained when he fell heavily on French soil in 1944. He would always wear a brace to support his back and there were occasions when the pain was so bad that he would have to roll out of bed and crawl to the bathroom on all fours. His daughter Christine, who shared her parents' deep faith, entered Our Lady of the Sacred Heart Convent, Kensington, and took her vows as a nun. Now Sister Christine Martin, and working as a missionary in Tanzania, East Africa, she believes the psychological after-effects of the war were often just as painful for her father as the physical.

> Dad said very little about his wartime experiences, but as a child I remember he couldn't watch any war movies that were on TV in the late '50s and early 1960s. That night he would have nightmares and call out and be in a sweat.

I know he had a very bad time when he was a prisoner. He was very reticent about it but he did tell us that they had been forced to eat grass when there was nothing else. Because of that he was always frugal with all meals, and waste was not part of our lives. He often implored us to be grateful for what we had and to be careful with everything. Throughout my childhood I remember him being in a lot of pain, but he was grateful to the German doctors who saved his life and he knew that the French people had done the right thing in handing him over to them.

He wore his RAAF badge on his suit lapel but he didn't march on Anzac Day. It was probably because he wasn't well enough, but he was against any gambling or heavy drinking due to his dad abandoning him and his mother, so that could have been a factor as well. Was there a Mass every year on Anzac Day? I do remember something about him going somewhere, and that might have been it. I'm afraid I can't say too much because Dad was so reserved about what had happened to him. He was a very gentle and humble man to the day he died.

Bill never went back to Europe. He died in 1982, aged 70, at Concord Repatriation Hospital after a long struggle with lung cancer. His daughter's description of him as a 'gentle and humble man' is echoed by his old schoolmate and fellow Bomber Command crewman, Jim O'Riordan: 'He was a wonderful man. Very quiet and shy. After the war we both worked in the Public Service . . . so we'd get together every now and then and talk about the old days. I used to go past his old house on the 303 bus, and after he died, every time I did, I'd think about him.'

—■—

Many years later, Jim would have another opportunity to think about Bill, and all the other young men with whom he had served, when they were finally afforded the recognition they had long been denied.

Following the war, the part played by Bomber Command—in 1940 lauded by Winston Churchill as 'the means of victory'—became something of an embarrassment, as the *Daily Express* journalist Adrian Lee wrote in 2012:

> Five years later on VE Day when Churchill praised those who had contributed to victory there was one glaring omission. To his shame, the Prime Minister pointedly made no reference to Bomber Command.
>
> Already the waters were being muddied and over the years there was a gradual rewriting of history in the wake of the terrible civilian toll of the bombing raids.
>
> Arthur 'Bomber' Harris became the scapegoat and, with the benefit of hindsight, wartime pride over the role of the bomber crews was replaced by growing unease. To some officials, they became an embarrassment.
>
> Some veterans were reportedly abused in the streets, while others chose to remove their war records from CVs because they feared it would harm their job prospects. They have also been accused by historians and writers of being murderers and destroying German culture.

The men who had been part of Bomber Command were forced to wait over 65 years to be officially recognised for the sacrifices they had made in the struggle for peace.

Thanks in no small part to the efforts of Robin Gibb, of the Bee Gees, who publicised what he called the 'repugnant' way the Bomber Command veterans had been treated, a public fund raised the necessary $18 million and, on 28 June 2012, Queen Elizabeth II officially opened the RAF Bomber Command Memorial in Green Park, London.

The roof of the limestone pavilion contains sheets made of aluminium taken from a Halifax bomber that was shot down over Belgium in May 1944 and found in a swamp 53 years later with three of the crew still at their stations.

On the eastern wall, above an eternal flame, are the words: 'This memorial is dedicated to the 55,573 airmen from the United Kingdom, British Commonwealth & allied nations who served in RAF Bomber Command & lost their lives over the course of the Second World War.'

On another wall is an inscription saying the memorial 'also commemorates those of all nations who lost their lives in the bombing of 1939–1945'. But its most striking feature is the 2.75-metre-high bronze sculpture of a seven-man Bomber Command air crew in full flying gear. Sculptor Philip Jackson said he felt it was important to show them returning, rather than embarking on a mission: 'I chose the moment when they get off the aircraft and they've dumped all their heavy kit on to the ground and they are looking back. Looking for their comrades.'

The memorial's opening ceremony ended with a fly-over by the last remaining serviceable Lancaster from World War II, serial number PA474, which dropped thousands of poppies over Green Park in remembrance of the Bomber Command airmen who had been lost in action. Piloting the aircraft, Squadron Leader Russ Russell radioed through to air traffic control the transmission: 'Ten POB [People on Board] with 55,573 souls.'

Robin Gibb, whose uncle was a Royal Canadian Air Force rear gunner with Bomber Command, never got to the opening of the memorial that he did so much to bring about—he died just over a month earlier—but Jim O'Riordan was there, aged 88.

There were 31 of us from Australia who went, 10 from NSW. There had been a lot of dishonour after the war. Churchill and Roosevelt had been happy to take the victory all right, but they walked away from Bomber Command because they didn't want to be associated with the civilian deaths. Well, sorry about that. Before we took off every night we were given a military target. Things might not have always worked out as they were planned and a lot of German people were killed, but it wasn't an exact science. It was dark, people were shooting at us, our mates were getting killed. It was war.

I was 40 yards away from the Queen when she pulled the cord and I remember thinking that she had just balanced out history. She restored honour to all those boys who had never got back to their families. To all of us.

—▬—

On his return to Australia, Tony D'Arcey moved in with his parents at Dee Why, on Sydney's northern beaches. Like so many others coming home after the war, he initially found it hard to reconnect with civilian life. His wife, Maureen, says:

> I felt he had never had the chance to be a young person. He had a great sense of humour, but there was always a hint of seriousness about him. He'd been through that experience in the war where he'd get close to people and then they wouldn't come back. I also think he had a feeling of guilt that he had killed ordinary citizens during the bombing and that weighed very heavily on him. When he first came back he probably didn't know what to do, but he just had this feeling that he had to help people.

As Tony's younger brother Peter put it, 'He went away as a boy and came back a man.'

Without much idea of what direction to take, Tony took the Public Service exam, trained as a patrol officer, and in 1946 was posted to New Guinea. Until it was granted independence in 1975, the Territory of Papua and New Guinea was administered by Australia, with Australian patrol officers serving as the government's representatives in the field. Based in Rabaul, a town on the island of New Britain that had been a major Japanese base during the war, Tony would be away for weeks at a time, patrolling large distances on foot with the assistance of indigenous police. His role was to maintain law and governance, observe local customs and languages, and compile maps and census reports.

After Tony had been a patrol officer for two years, a teammate in a social cricket team at Rabaul offered him a job managing a plantation at Kokopo, in East New Britain, where he remained for another two years. Away from civilisation and without English-speaking company for long periods, Tony took the opportunity to write a journal tracing his experiences from the morning of the crew's final operation to the time he arrived in Switzerland. It was more than an itemised record of dates, places and events. He also dug deep to recall his feelings and thoughts during the most traumatic experiences of his life—such as the minutes during which he swung from a parachute above occupied France, knowing neither his ultimate fate nor that of his comrades.

So I had gone for a Burton. They wouldn't know at the squadron yet—how could they? They would wait a while and then Squadron Leader Intelligence, that chap with the horrible Oxford accent, would go down to the briefing room and say to Groupie, 'WO Baxter's crew is missing, sir.' And Groupie would tell the Adjutant to send out the telegrams. Gosh, they are going to send one to Dad. What time is it at home now? Oh, I'm too tired to think and I can't do anything about it anyway. I wonder how many of the boys got out? I wonder if Pete got out? I don't think he would. Certainly Dave, Hoppy and Fergie couldn't have gotten out. Jock couldn't get out because he could never open his turret doors. I wonder if he did this time? He'd have to be pretty quick though.

I wonder what happened to Bill? I didn't hear him speak. Poor chap was probably killed by the cannon shells. I guess I must be the only one out. No. They must've all gotten out. It wasn't turning over. I wonder if Robbie and Dick from the squadron went like this? I suppose not. Each one is different, but Death gets more than her fair share. Damn Jerry. Damn war. Damn Hitler. Damn the whole bloody lot of everything.

I would like to remind you that at this stage I knew absolutely nothing about anyone's fate but my own. Bill, Hoppy and Fergie didn't say a word after the first shot was fired at us. Talking it over afterwards, Dave and I both felt that Hoppy and Fergie were killed by the bullets and knew nothing of the whole affair. I still don't know how Bill got out. Jock, our young Scotsman, who was still almost a bridegroom, must've had a terrible death. Firstly, he could see the burning tracer coming at him, and the fire and then Dave's order to abandon and he knew he was locked in his turret and couldn't get out. He called to Fergie three times that I remember, to come and let him out, but Fergie's voice was dead.

As well as using his time in near seclusion at Kokopo to set down his memories and his thoughts about the past, Tony thought about his future. During this period, his brother Peter expressed an interest in going to sea as a radio operator, and Tony lent him the money to undertake a course at the Marconi Wireless School in Sydney.

'I went to sea on a fleet of passenger ships,' Peter recalled. 'When Tony came back from New Guinea he looked at what I was doing and thought, this looks good, and followed me for the first time in our lives. He did the same course that I had and did a couple of trips on cargo ships. Then before I knew it he was borrowing my uniform and working for the same passenger line as me.'

One of the liners on which Tony worked was the MV *Westralian*. Along with the SS *Zealandia* and the MS *Wanganella*, it was one of three vessels operated by Huddart Parker Ltd that had been requisitioned as troop and cargo transports during the war. *Zealandia* had been sunk in a Japanese air raid on Darwin in February 1942. *Westralian* had been refitted as a landing craft and used by the US Marine Corps in the Pacific. After the war, she was operated by the merchant navy until 1951, when she was finally returned to her owners and restored to her original role as a passenger liner. It was on a cruise around Australia on the *Westralian* that Tony, then 35, met Maureen, a passenger from Brisbane who was seven years his junior. They were married in May 1959.

The changes marriage brought to Tony's life would be profound. During his time at sea he had put down no roots. While he would make a point of always catching up with Dave Baxter whenever his ship docked in Melbourne, he spent any extended shore leave staying with his brother Peter and Peter's wife Margaret at their home at Clontarf in Sydney. After he and Maureen were married, he gave up his life at sea and they built a home at Collaroy, on Sydney's northern beaches, where they lived for a year before moving to the Brisbane suburb of Morningside. Maureen recalls:

We both knew that the life Tony had been living on the ships was not the life for a married man so he started on the bottom rung of the Post Master General's Department. He was very keen to start a family straight away. When we moved to Brisbane for Tony's work we started going out to an orphanage at Nudgee. Tony was always keen to go there and play with the children and we would take them out on little trips during the holidays. There was one little boy that Tony really took a shine to. He was nearly two, and we adopted him. That was our first son, Mark.

Maureen gave birth to Paul in 1962. They adopted Anna in 1965, then Geraldine was born in 1967 and Gabrielle two years later. As Tony rose through the ranks within the PMG, the family moved around the country. In 1968 he was transferred to Darwin as a radio inspector, responsible for all of the Northern Territory, an area of 1.4 million square kilometres. After four years, they moved to Melbourne where they would remain, living at Glen Waverley, for the next seven years. As he had, wherever they had lived, Tony became very involved with their children's schools and volunteered with the St Vincent de Paul Society.

As Maureen says: 'He would always do whatever he could to help people. It was all part of that guilt complex that he had from the war.'

After years of 'giving back', Tony had the opportunity to 'go back'. As the telecommunications industry advanced, so did Tony's standing within the PMG. During his time in Melbourne he was often chosen to represent the organisation at conferences. In 1974, one of these was to be held in Geneva, Switzerland, not far from where he and Dave had been interned. While Tony was interested to return and have a look at the city in peacetime, it was the proximity to France that excited him more. Early in the year, through the head of his department, he wrote to the director-general of the PMG.

Enclosed is an application for leave for a period of two or three days to be taken in France during July 1974. I am aware of public service regulations concerning overseas visits, however I feel that the exceptional circumstances in this instance are such that leave could be granted. Briefly the events may be summarised as follows: on 24th February 1944 my Lancaster bomber was shot down by a German fighter over occupied France. Four of the crew were killed, one wounded and captured by Germans, another crew member was hidden by a French Underground organisation while I made my way south. During a walk of some 300 kilometres extending from the location of the crash to Switzerland over a period of six days I was assisted by a number of French people. I deliberately did not ask these people their names so I would be unable to expose them either willingly or unwillingly in the event of my capture by the Germans. I successfully reached Switzerland on 1st March 1944 and so avoided becoming a prisoner of war. Whilst this episode was successfully concluded, subsequent events took me to Egypt, England and the United States before returning to Australia in February 1945. I was thus unable to determine the names of my helpers.

If I am an Australian delegate to the World Administrative Radio Conference Maritime Mobile Telecommunications to be held in Geneva from 22nd April to 7th June, 1974, I feel I would be morally remiss not to make an attempt to discover who my helpers were and, if they are still alive, to meet them, as the events of 1944 occurred relatively close to Geneva. I have corresponded with the RAF Escaping Society of which I am a member, and the secretary is arranging for enquiries to be made in France and England. The application for leave is submitted for your consideration please.

Although it was against departmental regulations, the director-general granted the leave, and Tony was able to make an emotional pilgrimage back to Europe. With the help of his journal, the RAF Escaping Society was able to track down the priest in Lagney village who had helped Tony, and arranged for them to meet. First, though, Tony had an appointment he had been waiting 30 years to keep: at Villers-sous-Prény. Again the Escaping Society paved the way, and when Tony drove into the town nearly every resident was waiting. He was taken out to the site of the crash, where an indentation was still visible in the ground, and then made a solemn visit to the church on the hill for some time at the grave site of his fallen comrades. A mayoral reception followed.

'The gratitude of the people overwhelmed him,' says Maureen.

Another thing that astonished Tony was the accuracy of his journal. As he drove along the route he had recorded, it all came flooding back, just as he had written it—each painful step.

When Tony returned from his trip, Maureen sensed a change in him: 'I think it was some closure but I felt he suffered—if that's the word—from having been associated with the bombing of civilians over Germany. It had to have happened, even if not intentionally. He played his cards close to his chest on those matters, as did so many of that era.'

Tony wasn't the only member of his family to make the pilgrimage to France. Some 26 years later, his son Paul followed him.

I always knew Dad had flown in Lancasters and been shot down. In my teens I found out he had the story written down, but he didn't want to talk about it. They were not good memories and he didn't want to relive them. I think he put it into the back of his mind. He went to the Caterpillar Club meetings in Melbourne a couple of times. That was for people who had used parachutes to get out of planes so I suppose he felt more comfortable with them. He would never go to Anzac Day. It annoyed him. He felt that there were a lot of people at those events who had never seen action and they thought of their time during the war as glory days. Dad never felt like that, he didn't want to glorify it and he didn't want any of us to go through it either. When I graduated from high school I thought I might go into the air force or army and all Dad would say was 'don't do it'.

As my life went on I ended up travelling to Europe a lot. By then I had Dad's diary and some things written down, so it seemed a natural thing to try to follow his footsteps. The first time was in 2000. I found where the base had been in England but it was just empty land. I saw the town and found the pubs Dad had mentioned. Then I got to France and hired a little car and tried to trace his route as best I could but it was hard. I did find the village where his mates were buried. There was a public phone-box on the road coming into town and I rang Dad. It was night-time in Australia but we had a long conversation. Mum told me later that he was up all night. He couldn't get back to sleep, but he was happy I'd been there. I was happy too.

I went again in 2011. The first time, I had tried to trace his tracks as best I could but the map I had was not good. This time I had GPS and I found everything. Because of the time I was there I could do it on exactly the same dates that he did. I started at the village near where the plane had crashed on February 24, and drove a couple of hours each day. I remember thinking that in 2000 I had a map and I still couldn't find my way. I thought about how hard it must have been for him when he had little idea of where he was going and he couldn't ask directions. It was pretty emotional for me. What struck me was how young those guys were and where they had come from. The first time I was over there in 2000 I was planning to go to Berlin and meet up with some German friends, and here I was travelling through these countries that were very much the same as how they had been during both the wars. It was a strange feeling, but then again, all the Germans I met were really nice people. In 2003 I lived in Germany for six months. Dad was glad I had

German friends. He was happy that there was no animosity. He felt we shouldn't hate each other.

Tony's last posting, in 1978, was as State manager for the NSW Department of Communications, as the PMG had been renamed. He and Maureen found a home for sale at Terrigal, on the Central Coast, a 90-minute commute north of Sydney. Falling in love with the area and feeling it would be a good place for retirement, they bought the house and Tony commuted to Sydney for work each day before taking early retirement in 1983. After 20 years at Terrigal, they moved ten kilometres west to Erina.

As he approached his 80s, Tony settled into a comfortable routine. Every morning he would get up first and make Maureen a cup of coffee. As the water boiled, he would sit at the table, open his morning newspaper and go straight to the crossword, then take Maureen her coffee and return to the puzzle while he waited for her to join him. On the morning of 12 April 2004, Tony got out of bed, went into the kitchen and didn't return. Maureen says:

> I was lying there waiting for my cuppa but nothing happened. I thought he must be letting me sleep in. After a while I thought I should get up and find out what was happening. Usually when I went out to join him he would hear me coming and say, 'I hear movement at the station . . .' but this morning there was nothing. I went into our sitting room, and there he was in his chair, pen in hand, with the crossword in front of him, and his chin on his chest. I didn't

know what to do, so I rang our parish priest and while I was waiting for him to come I sat there with Tony. Of course it was a terrible shock, but as I was sitting there with him and it was so peaceful, I couldn't help thinking, after all he'd been through in the war, what a wonderful way to go. I thought, 'You lucky duck.'

———■———

A year after Dave's death, Joyce Baxter moved back to Wonthaggi and started working in a grocery business with her cousin Jack. She eventually sold the home in Melbourne and built a house near the beach at Cape Paterson, eight kilometres south of Wonthaggi. After three years, she stopped working at the shop and retrained as a nurse. But before starting at Wonthaggi Hospital—where she would remain until she retired, aged 65, in 1988—there was something she had to do.

With the help of the RAF Escaping Society, Dave had been able to reconnect with the Simon and Mathy families, who had taken such risks to hide him from the Germans. He had corresponded with them and helped them financially when he could. After his death, Joyce had remained in contact, particularly with Jeanne Simon, through a regular exchange of letters, cards and photographs. Having saved a little money after working seven days a week in the shop, she decided to fulfil a dream that Dave had spoken about but never had the money or the time to achieve. She went to France to meet Madame Simon. Once again the Escaping Society came to the fore. On 2 May 1972 she received a letter from its office in London.

Many thanks indeed for your letter of April 22, concerning your forthcoming visit to England. We note that when in London you will be at the Majestic Hotel in Brompton Road. This is about three quarters of a mile from our offices and should you be able to visit us we will be delighted to welcome you.

Re: Madame Simon's visit to Paris, unless you have any alternative suggestions we will arrange for her to meet you at the Bedford Hotel, 17 Rue de L'Arcade, Paris 8 on Thursday, July 20 at 10:30 AM. So she has no problems we will arrange to pay her fare and accommodation for her in Paris at our expense overnight. You should not have too much problem with the language as most of the hotel staff will speak some English.

In honour of Dave, Joyce wore his Caterpillar Club lapel pin on her coat during the trip. In London, she caught a black cab to her hotel. The driver noticed the pin. Perhaps an old RAF man—maybe even a wartime parachute survivor—he refused to take any money for her fare.

The meeting with Jeanne Simon in Paris was the beginning of a close bond between the two women that would continue for the rest of their lives. In 1995, when Jeanne suffered a stroke and could no longer write to 'Madame Joyce' or read the letters and cards that regularly arrived from Australia, her daughter Jocelyne took over the duty. On 2 January 1996 she wrote wishing Joyce a happy New Year. 'My mother is always wearing your bracelet, your present to her of long ago when you visited her in Paris. She is thinking of you frequently and often looks to the photo of your wedding with David. This is for her the way to remember him.'

After Jeanne died, the friendship between Joyce and Jocelyne continued. When Jocelyne wrote that her son Jean-Christophe, whom Jeanne had taken to that first meeting in Paris when he was two years old, was to be married, Joyce sent a wedding present that was not overly expensive but rich with significance, as she explained.

> Your Bon Ami card brought the happy news of your son's wedding. Congratulations. A little gift from Australia for the happy couple. I chose salt and pepper shakers because they reminded me of David's time in your family home. Two weeks after his arrival the Germans visited, so Pierre decided to take him to Pierre Mathy—a loyal member of the Underground. Salt and pepper shakers on the table were moved around—a code to tell Mr Mathy your dad had an evader from the RAAF with him. One week later David was taken into the safe country of Switzerland. The courage of these men was never forgotten by David. Maybe you were too young to recall the story. The animals on the shakers are kangaroo, lizard, two cockatoo, crocodile, platypus, green tree frog, turtle, koala, kookaburra and echidna.

In 2011, Joyce moved into Rose Lodge Retirement Home, next to the hospital at Wonthaggi. It was where her mother, and also her cousin Jack, had spent their last days. Other residents were people she had gone to school with and worked with. She felt comfortable there.

Joyce Baxter died at Rose Lodge on 10 October 2013, aged 85.

As they sorted through their mother's belongings, Alan and Michael found a small florist's card with a handwritten note. It had been attached to a delivery of flowers sent in sympathy after Dave Baxter's death 45 years earlier.

The note was addressed to Joyce, but it could have been written to any of the families of the crew of Lancaster *J for Jig*.

It read: 'He left wonderful Memories. Be Proud. Tony and Maureen D'Arcey.'

EPILOGUE
CLIFF'S TREE

A living, breathing, memorial to the men of *J for Jig* and thousands like them stands proudly in a park in the Brisbane suburb of St Johns Wood. It is a kauri pine tree, across the road from the site of Glen Arran, the house Cliff Hopgood and his young bride Margaret had built two years before he went to war. In front of the tree is a large boulder on which is fastened a small silver plaque. It reads: 'To the memory of Flt Sgt Clifford Berger Hopgood, killed in air operations over occupied France 24th Feb 1944. This tree was planted by his friends of St Johns Wood.'

As with the other relatives of the crew of *J for Jig*, it was four days after the aircraft's final mission before Margaret received notification of her husband's presumed fate in the form of the telegram from RAAF headquarters in Melbourne. A copy of the telegram, its edges torn and frayed, is held in the National Archives. It was followed on 6 April by the form letter from Wing Commander 'Spike' Marsh, ending with the words: 'It may be of some consolation to you to know that a number of missing airmen are eventually found to be Prisoners of War, and I hope I will have the pleasure of passing such good news to you before long.'

No such good news arrived. Not for Margaret Hopgood, anyway.

On 17 June 1944, she received a second telegram from RAAF headquarters, Melbourne: 'Information received from International Red Cross that one Australian member of your husband's crew Warrant Officer W. J. Martin is a Prisoner of War. Regret no news of your husband or remainder of crew.'

Four months later, Margaret was informed by a letter from the Secretary of the Department of Air that Dave Baxter and Tony D'Arcey had escaped through occupied France and made their way back to England. Tony had reported getting out with Cliff at 15,000 feet but had 'no further knowledge' of him or the rest of the crew.

The Secretary did not answer personal correspondence, but the RAAF officers who signed letters on his behalf would be Margaret's contacts at HQ and her source of early hope and ultimate sadness.

In November 1944 Margaret wrote to the RAAF's casualty section in Little Collins Street, Melbourne. Her neat, hand-written letter stated: 'It is with regret I inform you that I have had no news from my husband since he was reported missing.'

Then on 15 February 1945, almost a year after Cliff's fatal flight, Margaret Hopgood received a letter from the Secretary's office: 'It is with deep regret that I have to inform you that the death of your husband has now been presumed for official purposes to have occurred on the 24th February, 1944. The Minister for Air and members of the Air Board desire me to extend to you their profound sympathy in your great loss.'

Margaret was sent a list of the personal effects of 'the late 414565 F/Sgt Hopgood C. B.' Among such items as 18 handkerchiefs, 24 socks and a leather tobacco pouch was 'one wrist watch on leather strap, engraved "To Cliff from Margaret"'.

It was not until after the war that Margaret learned about Cliff's final moments. In September 1945, she was advised that Bill Martin, recently repatriated from Fallingbostel, 'was told by a German interrogation officer that your husband was found lying in a recumbent position in a field without any sign of external injuries. Further examination showed that his neck had been broken, apparently in landing as his parachute was open.' Eight months later came the last correspondence Margaret would receive from the Secretary's office. It explained that the Department had received a letter sent by Madame Schuller of Villers-Sous-Prény to the British Ambassador in Paris.

'As it is thought that the information may be of some comfort to you in your sorrow, a copy of the letter is enclosed,' it said. Written on 21 October 1945, and translated by the office of the British Ambassador, Simone Schuller's letter described what had happened when the Lancasters passed over Villers-sous-Prény. It was 10.25 p.m. and 'unfortunately the Luftwaffe were very active and hit your bomber in full flight'. Madame Schuller told of the crash and the part she and her husband Eugène had played in rescuing Bill Martin before reluctantly handing him over to the Germans, but it was the second part of the letter that was of heart-stopping importance to Margaret.

> The following four airmen are buried in our little cemetery. Hopgood, Dunlop, Mallon and Ferguson. My husband identified them by the names on their parachutes. I tell you straight away that they were killed instantaneously. Tell their mothers that although there is only one grave, each man had his own coffin. They lie in our little village and their grave is decorated with flowers and wreaths and always has been, in spite of the Germans. Tell their mothers also that the French fully realise what this loss must mean to them . . . I also had a son, who now lies side by side with his comrades.

By the time that Margaret received the copy of Madame Schuller's letter, the war had been over for almost a year. Now she was forced to face the reality of life for her and her five-year-old son Robert without Cliff. For three years she rented out Glen Arran and lived with relatives. Then she decided to return home.

Eight men had left St Johns Wood to serve in World War II. Clifford Berger Hopgood was the only one who didn't come home. By the time Margaret and young Robert returned in 1948, the tree was already there. Their neighbour George

Colville, a local community leader and returned serviceman, had asked the local council for permission to plant it, and they had supplied the sapling. A white timber and chain fence was constructed around it and the plaque affixed to a post. As soon as he was old enough, Robert would clear the long grass around the memorial, first with a reaping hook and then with a mower. Years later, when the fence was damaged by a council tractor, another neighbour, Ron Rees, petitioned council and a giant granite boulder was brought down from Mount Coot-tha and the plaque attached. For Robert, who always referred to it as 'Dad's tree', the healthy kauri was a constant reminder of what he was missing.

Robert, who graduated with a degree in architecture from the University of Queensland in 1963 and founded a successful building, earth-moving and furniture manufacturing company, retired to Macleay Island, 30 kilometres from Brisbane, in 1997 with Alison, his wife of over 50 years.

In 2011, reminiscing about his formative years, he lays out the few mementos he has of his father: his parents' wedding photo; the framed picture of Cliff in his Air Force uniform that stood on Margaret's bedside table until the day she died; and the 'wrist watch on leather strap, engraved "To Cliff from Margaret"'—his mother's engagement gift to his father, the watch he had worn on every operation except his last.

One of Robert's earliest memories is the day his mother took him—aged five or six—on the tram to South Brisbane railway station. They sat silently waiting on the platform as a train pulled in. 'Two servicemen in uniform got off and came up to us,' he says. 'One of them gave me a little wooden toy.

It was a penguin on wheels, with a couple of bits of leather that made a noise when you pushed it along. Then they gave something to Mum. I remember pushing this little toy and wanting Mum to look, and then I saw she was crying. It was the watch. They'd given her Dad's watch.'

When Robert turned thirteen, Margaret gave him the watch. He wore it until it stopped working a decade later. 'I've never worn a watch since,' he says.

> The way that Mum and her generation dealt with grief was that there was no counselling. You just got on with your life and tried to lock out anything that hurt you. I learnt that at a very early age. If I'd said, 'Why don't I have a dad?'—or something like that—I'd have been told to eat my dinner. It was 'we don't talk about that'. The pain was completely washed out of me. I was like, 'Yeah, I had a father, he was killed in the war, so what?' It didn't mean a thing.
>
> At the same time the influence of Mum on my life, things like loyalty and work ethic, was quite unreal. It was hard for Mum. She became very independent, she needed to be, but at a very hard time in terms of social convention. She liked to take me away on holiday, but a woman sitting alone on a beach in those days was just not done.'

Margaret returned to work at the paper-bag factory and remained there until she retired in 1971. She also became a stalwart of the War Widows Guild of Australia, representing the organisation at Anzac Day ceremonies. For young Robert, they weren't enjoyable experiences. 'I went to as many Anzac Day services as anyone,' he says.

I approached them with trepidation. As a war widow, Mum was expected to go back to the RSL club after the service. There would be all these drunk blokes and this young woman and it was very uncomfortable. I remember being upset and Mum saying to me, 'Robert, Anzac Day is that day of the year when those who've returned from the war remember those who didn't . . . but we remember them every day.'

In 1975, Margaret accompanied a group of 27 war widows on a tour of France. She had made arrangements to slip away on her own to visit Cliff's grave in Villers-sous-Prény, but when her companions heard of her plans, many of them went with her. When their bus pulled into the village, they found the footpaths lined with people. A banner across the road proclaimed: 'In Memory of Your Dear Deceased. Australian Friends, You Are Welcome in Our Village.' A public holiday had been proclaimed in their honour and a civic reception held in the town hall following a march from the site of the plane crash. As Margaret stepped from the bus, there to meet her were Monsieur Sophron, the mayor who had been fined for authorising the funeral of the four crewmates, the doctor who had attended Bill Martin, and Madame Schuller.

A year after Margaret's death in 2008, her daughter-in-law Alison persuaded Robert to also make the pilgrimage to Villers-sous-Prény.

From the day Robert had first brought Alison home to meet his mother in 1958, she and Margaret had been the closest of friends. An accomplished choral singer, Alison performed with the Brisbane Eisteddfod Choir and Margaret was her number one supporter, attending all her concerts. 'I wasn't all that keen to go to France, but Alison talked me into it,' Robert says. She adds, 'I told him, if you don't come, I'll go by myself.' The Villers-sous-Prény Robert and Alison walked into in 2009 was very different to the one that had welcomed Margaret 34 years earlier. The streets were deserted, the shops closed. 'There's no work around,' Robert says. 'The whole place was empty.' They found the church and Robert stood before his father's grave.

'Basically I was just standing there and thinking, "This is him. I really do have a dad." For the first time, I felt like I had a father.' He placed some of his mother's ashes on the grave, then he and Alison tried without success to gain entry to the church.

'It was locked up, but just by chance I saw an old woman in a garden nearby,' Robert remembers. 'I somehow managed to explain what we wanted and she went to another house and a woman came out with a big old key and unlocked the front door for us. It was a lovely little church, beautifully looked after.' As Robert sat in a back pew, Alison stood at the front of the church and sang Margaret's favourite song, 'These Are The Lovely Things'.

In her latter years Margaret Hopgood would sit quietly for hours on the veranda of the home she and her husband had built, looking across to the park at Cliff's tree, whose roots spread all the way to France. 'I'm not going to die,' she'd say, 'until it's the tallest tree in the park.'

Margaret passed away, aged 96, on 25 July 2008, with Robert and Alison at her bedside and their children Catherine,

Clifford and David close by. A modern bungalow now stands on the former site of Glen Arran. Two ageing corner fence posts are the only reminder of the house Clifford Berger Hopgood left to go to war.

But the kauri pine grows strong in St Johns Wood. It is the tallest tree in the park.

ACKNOWLEDGEMENTS

It is 1997 when I first notice the tree. With two restless youngsters in the back seat and some time to kill, I turn off Waterworks Rd at Ashgrove in Brisbane's inner north-west and cross the bridge that leads to St Johns Wood. A left turn into Royal Parade and I find what I am looking for: a playground.

As my daughters entertain themselves on the equipment, I step away and spot a large rock in front of a giant kauri pine. On the rock is a small silver plaque held in place by four chrome-plated plugs . . .

So starts 'Tree of Life', published in *QWeekend*, the colour magazine of *The Courier-Mail* newspaper, in April 2011. The article, which tells the story behind the tree planted in memory of Cliff Hopgood, won the Walkley Award for best magazine feature of the year. More importantly, it was read by Gabrielle D'Arcey whose father Tony survived the crash of *J for Jig* and wrote a journal of his experiences from the time he exited the aircraft through his escape across France to Switzerland. When Gabrielle contacted me to ask if I would be interested in reading Tony's memoir it set in progress a six-year voyage of discovery across three continents, the result of which you are reading now.

In tracing the life stories of the seven young men who came together to form the crew of *J for Jig*, I was helped by their families, friends and colleagues. It goes without saying that without their assistance and encouragement this book could not have been written. Like all historical studies, the research process for *Crew* was like following a dimly lit path through the woods. At times it seemed I had come to a dead end but just when I thought I was stumped they would put me back on the right track.

I would like to sincerely thank the following people for their invaluable contributions:

Robert and Alison Hopgood; Joyce, Alan and Ron Baxter; Maureen, Gabrielle, Paul and Peter D'Arcey; Sister Christine Martin; Gordon and Diane Ellem; Robert Norman; Jim Delury; Sandy Bell; Armand Casalini; Jim O'Riordan; Andrew Panton and Laurie Woods.

I could not come to the end of my journey without highlighting the efforts of Alan Baxter. When Maureen D'Arcey put me in touch with Joyce Baxter, who suggested her son

ACKNOWLEDGEMENTS

Alan was the one I should be talking to, I could not have imagined the wealth of information and positive support he would provide. Like his father Dave, Alan proved a good man to have on side when things got tough.

I must also make special mention of Jim Blackley from Troon, Scotland, who answered a plea for help that I had placed in the Ayrshire Historical Society newsletter after seemingly exhausting all avenues in my search for information about Jock Dunlop. Jim, who had no personal connection with the Dunlop family, took up the challenge on my behalf and succeeded in tracking down Jock's niece Sandy Bell in Canada.

Thanks also to the team at Allen & Unwin for their support, understanding and patience, notably Stuart Neal; who commissioned *Crew* for take-off; Foong Ling Kong, who took over the controls; and Tom Gilliatt, Genevieve Buzo, Liz Keenan and Sarah Baker, who brought it in for landing.

And finally to my wonderful wife Linda, who amongst her many talents is an exceptional proofreader. Her involvement in this book and just about everything else I've ever written cannot be overestimated.

In telling the stories of the seven men who flew in *J for Jig* I have been well aware of the faith placed in me by their family members, many of whom I have never met face to face.

I hope I have done them justice.

Mike Colman, October 2017

BIBLIOGRAPHY

Bowman, M. 2016, *Nachtjagd Defenders of the Reich 1940–1943*, Barnsley, UK: Pen and Sword

Bowyer, C. 1985, *Tales From The Bombers*, London: William Kimber and Co

Mayhill, R. 1991, *Bombs on Target: A compelling eye-witness account of Bomber Command operations*, Somerset, UK: Patrick Stephens Limited

Middlebrook, M. 1988, *The Berlin Raids: The bomber battle, winter 1943–1944*, London: Viking

Nichol, J. and Rennell, T. 2003, *The Last Escape: The untold story of Allied prisoners of war in Europe*, 1944–45, London: Penguin Books

Nichol, J. and Rennell, T. 2005, *Tail-End Charlies: The last battles of the bomber war, 1944–1945*, London: Penguin Books

Rees, P. 2013, *Lancaster Men: The Aussie heroes of Bomber Command*, Sydney: Allen & Unwin

INDEX

INDEX